An Introduction to the UK Economy

Fourth Edition

To Margaret

An Introduction to the UK Economy

Fourth Edition

Colin Harbury and Richard G. Lipsey

BLACKWELL
Oxford UK & Cambridge USA

Fourth edition first published in 1993 by Blackwell Publishers
Reprinted 1994, 1996

Blackwell Publishers Ltd
108 Cowley Road
Oxford OX4 1JF
UK

Blackwell Publishers Inc.
238 Main Street
Cambridge, Massachusetts 02142
USA

British Library Cataloguing in Publication Data
A CIP catalogue record for this book is available from the British Library.

Library of Congress Cataloging-in-Publication Data
Harbury, C. D.
    An introduction to the UK economy/Colin Harbury and Richard G. Lipsey. – 4th ed.
        p. cm.
    Includes bibliographical references and index.
    ISBN 0–631–18777–4 (hbk.: alk. paper). – ISBN 0–631–18778–2 (pbk.:
alk. paper)
        1. Great Britain – Economic conditions – 1945–   I. Lipsey, Richard
G., 1928– .   II. Title.
HC256.6H345 1993
330.941'08–dc20   92–46906
                                                                CIP

Typeset in 11 on 13 pt Plantin by TecSet Ltd, Wallington, Surrey
Printed in Great Britain by T.J. Press (Padstow) Ltd, Padstow, Cornwall

This book is printed on acid-free paper

Contents

housing, education and health · privatisation · regulating
natural monopolies. Questions and exercises · Appendix.

List of Figures

Data Sources

At the end of each chapter in this book are sets of questions and exercises. We encourage you to attempt as many of them as possible. This will give you valuable experience in collecting, presenting and interpreting data from readily available sources. Many of the exercises are designed to make you think about relationships between relevant facts on the UK economy and elements of economic theory. Incidentally, collecting data for the questions and exercises helps keep the book up to date.

Statistical and other material is needed for many of the exercises. Sources are suggested for these and a certain amount of data is available in appendices to the various chapters in the book. Full details of sources are given below. They are referred to by abbreviations in the end of chapter questions themselves.

It is worth pointing out that the geographical coverage of published statistics varies in some cases. Officially, the United Kingdom consists of the territories of Great Britain and Northern Ireland, while Great Britain refers to the three countries of England, Scotland and Wales. The term 'Britain' is used here loosely and for convenience, usually to avoid constant repetition of UK. Note, too, that, because of rounding, tables of statistics do not always add up precisely to make the printed totals.

Some questions call for the construction of graphs, usually of kinds found in the book itself. If you feel the need to brush up on techniques of drawing graphs, several economics textbooks have helpful material.[1] More exercises are in Colin Harbury's *Workbook in Introductory Economics*, 4th edn (Oxford: Pergamon, 1987).

---

1 There is a short appendix on Graphs in Economics in Lipsey & Harbury, *First Principles of Economics*, 2nd edn, henceforward referred to as Lipsey–Harbury, FP2.

1 Official Sources

Key   *Publication*

AS   *Annual Abstract of Statistics.* Probably the most valuable single source, a wide-ranging annual with many series which cover 10-year periods.

MDS   *Monthly Digest of Statistics.* Supplements *AS* for recent and short-term (monthly) trends.

ET   *Economic Trends.* Monthly publication (overlapping *MDS*) with some charts and articles. There is an annual supplement with longer series.

ST   *Social Trends.* Annual, similar to *ET* supplement, with social and economic coverage, e.g. income distribution.

RT   *Regional Trends.* Annual similar to *ST* and *ET* with regional breakdowns of many important series. A useful selection of such data is available on disk.[2]

UKNA   *UK National Accounts* (also known as the 'Blue Book'). Annual national income data with many series covering 20 years.

EG   *Employment Gazette.* A very useful magazine published monthly by the Department of Employment. It contains extensive statistical data relating to labour, prices, etc. (including some comparative data on overseas countries) and special articles on important topics.

KD   *Key Data.* Convenient shorter and cheaper annual, comparable to *AS* but with limited coverage of economic and social statistics.

EB   *Economic Briefing.* Occasional (one to two times a year) Treasury commentary on current economic events and institutions, with regular special issues on the Budget (obtainable free from Central Office of Information).

---

2 An extremely useful recent addition to conventional sources are disks of datasets for use with personal computers. Disks containing statistics from *Regional Trends* and *Eurostat* sources together with a data handling programme, SECOS, can be ordered from Statistics for Education, 5 Bridge St, Bishops Stortford, Herts, CM23 2JU.

2 Other Sources

Key	Publication
NIER	*National Institute Economic Review*. The Appendix to this quarterly journal of the National Institute of Economic and Social Research contains several comparative series covering major industrial countries.
IFS	*International Financial Statistics* (International Monetary Fund). Extensive world coverage of economic data for most countries, monthly with annual supplement.
ES	*Eurostat* is the EC organisation which collects and publishes data of member states, e.g. its *Regional Statistical Yearbook*. Many useful statistics on population, national income, trade, employment, etc., are available on disk for use on personal computers from 'Statistics for Education' (see n.2, page xv).
BER	*Barclays Economic Review*. Appendix to this quarterly journal (free to customers of Barclays Bank) contains useful financial data on developed and developing countries.
NWB	*Economic and Financial Outlook*. Statistical appendix to this monthly publication by the economics department of the NatWest Bank contains useful international financial statistics.
WA	*Whitaker's Almanac* is a handy source for data not easily available elsewhere.
FT *T* *IOS*	*Financial Times, The Times* and the *Independent on Sunday* are among the most useful newspapers carrying financial data.

All material taken from the following sources is crown copyright and reproduced with permission of the Central Statistical Office

Annual Abstract of Statistics
Regional Trends
Economic Trends
Financial Statistics
Monthly Digest of Statistics
United Kingdom National Accounts

Preface

Economic theory is only useful if it is understood in the context of the real world. We wrote this book as a companion to any introductory text with a theory bias, such as our own *First Principles of Economics* (to which this volume cross-refers).[1] We hope that the new, fourth edition of this book will continue, as have its predecessors, to be useful to a wide range of students beginning economics – at A-level, first-year degree courses, and to those preparing for professional examinations for accountancy, actuarial work, banking, company secretaryship, chartered surveying, etc.

The book offers an outline view of the structure of the UK economy, its principal functions, institutions and events. The figures are designed to help readers retain these features visually. We have gone out of our way to avoid cluttering pages with endless tables of statistical data, and diagrams calculated to decimal-place accuracy (though tables of statistics are provided in appendices). To help memory retention we have used a variety of diagrammatic styles and types – straightforward graphs, pie charts, histograms, bar charts, scatter diagrams, in two and three dimensions. The idea is always to aid appreciation of the economic forest without having to bother with the detailed structure of individual trees.

1   Richard G. Lipsey and Colin Harbury, *First Principles of Economics*, 2nd edn (London: Weidenfeld & Nicolson, 1992).

Each chapter ends with a set of questions and exercises, designed to familiarise students with collecting, presenting and interpreting data. They serve the additional purpose of keeping the book up to date.

The Fourth Edition

The UK economy does not stand still, hence a new edition of this book is needed four years on from the last. We have, as usual, not simply extended the timescale of the text, charts and tables, but have substantially rewritten in a great many places to take account of developments since 1988, e.g. outstandingly, the onset of prolonged recession and the impact of events in the European Community. The latter has major implications for the UK economy, with the advent of the 'single market' on 1 January 1993, and the proposals of the Maastricht Treaty of 1992. As we hand the typescript over to our (welcome new) publishers, it is not clear how far the Maastricht provisions will go ahead. We have tried to cover various possibilities, as we see them, in all the relevant places, but we should warn you that the present time is particularly critical for the EC. Finally, we should mention that we have followed the new tradition in modern textbook writing of providing 'boxes' to illustrate the relevance of material in the book to current events.

Colin Harbury
Richard G. Lipsey
January 1993

1
The Economy in Outline

The UK economy is complex, and this book covers a lot of ground. The purpose of this introductory chapter is to give a quick overview, outlining its most distinctive features within a reasonably long-term context. Details of individual topics and recent trends will receive greater attention in later chapters.[1]

The features we focus on here are:

- **Resources** – land, labour and capital
- **Production** – primary, secondary and tertiary
- **Foreign trade** – exports and imports of goods and services
- **Economic growth** and living standards
- **Employment and unemployment**
- **Money and banking** – financial institutions and the general price level
- **Government** – the economic role of the state

Resources

The physical resources of an economy are conventionally termed the **factors of production** – land, labour and capital. Land includes the free gifts of nature, such as the earth itself, forests and

1 For an introductory text concentrating on theory, see Lipsey–Harbury, FP2.

minerals. Labour is the term used to describe the human resources, men and women, who can and do produce goods and services. Capital is the name given to man-made aids to further production, such as tools, machinery and factories.

Land

The quantity of land in existence, from an economic point of view, needs to be seen relative to the quantity of other resources. In contrast to countries such as the United States and Australia, for example, land in the UK is scarce relative to the size of the population. Figure 1.1 shows the allocation of the total area of 24 million hectares among different purposes. The majority of land is, of course, agricultural rather than rural, and 18 million hectares, representing about three-quarters of the total, lies in what we would call rural areas. Not all could be described as good agricultural land. Only about two-thirds of the total is used for tillage crops and grasses, much of the remainder being at or below the margin of cultivation – classified as 'rough grazing' and woodland. The remainder is available for houses, factories and other urban uses, such as golf courses.

A breakdown of the acreage devoted to tillage crops is shown in Figure 1.2. Nearly three-quarters is devoted to cereal production, for both human and livestock consumption. Barley replaced oats as the foremost grain crop around 1960, though the area used for wheat has been greater than that for barley since the mid-1980s. The remaining land is used for rape, fodder crops, horticulture and sugar beet, the principal 'other' category being potatoes.

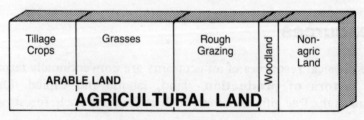

Figure 1.1 Land use, 1991
Source: *Annual Abstract of Statistics*

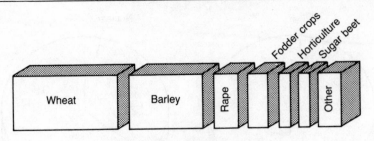

Figure 1.2 Land under tillage crops, 1991
Source: *Monthly Digest of Statistics*

The shortage of good land suitable for arable cultivation makes the livestock population of the country a vital part of its agriculture, for, by and large, livestock can thrive on poorer soils than those used for growing crops like cereals and vegetables. In 1991 there were about 120 million chickens, 30 million sheep, 12 million head of cattle and just under 8 million pigs on farms in the country.

The term land, as used by economists, conventionally includes those free gifts of nature commonly called natural resources, such as minerals and other raw materials lying above or below the land itself. Britain is not well endowed with high-grade mineral deposits. Until 1980 about a fifth of UK consumption of iron ore for the steel industry came from domestic sources, but the proportion is now well under 1 per cent.

The principal natural resource in Britain at the present time is energy. For a very long time the main source of energy was coal. Discoveries of North Sea gas and oil in the 1970s led to the displacement of coal from its dominant position as supplier of energy consumed in the UK. By 1991, as Figure 1.3 shows, less than a third of energy consumed in the UK came from coal. It seems likely that the trend will continue. At the time of writing (January 1993), the government has made a highly controversial decision to close over half the working mines in the country, though it has subsequently backed down from so large and immediate a cut.

Britain has been self-sufficient in energy supplies since 1980. Estimates of the unexploited reserves of oil and natural gas are understandably imprecise and vary with new discoveries. Coal

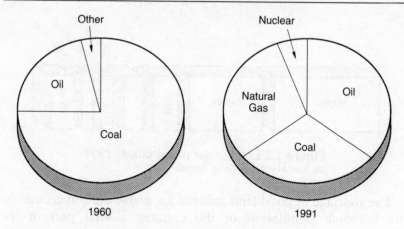

Figure 1.3 Inland energy consumption, 1960 and 1991
Source: *Monthly Digest of Statistics*

reserves are, however, substantial and the coal industry would be capable of resuming a primary role if or when North Sea reserves run out.

Labour

The supply of human resources is referred to by economists as labour – another factor of production. The amount that is available is called the labour force and depends, in the first instance, on the size of the population.

In 1801, when the first census was taken, the total population of Britain was roughly 12 million. Thereafter it grew at an astonishing rate. As Figure 1.4 shows, it doubled in 60 years, and by 1861 there were over 24 million people. It had doubled again by 1951, when the population topped 50 million. In the second half of the twentieth century the numbers continued to increase, but at a slower pace. The population reached $57\frac{1}{2}$ million by 1991, and is expected to attain 60 million early in the twenty-first century.

The population of Britain is by no means evenly spread over the whole country. It is clear from Figure 1.4 that England, Wales, Scotland and Northern Ireland have very unequal shares of the

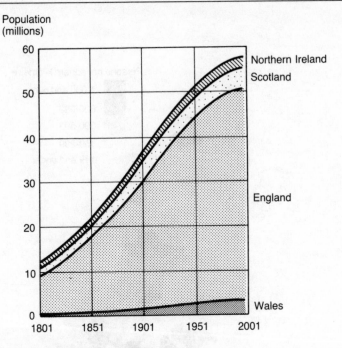

Figure 1.4 Population since 1801
Source: *Annual Abstract of Statistics* and *Monthly Digest of Statistics*

total. If the population of each of these countries is related to its size, however, the inequality is even greater, since England has over four-fifths of the people and only just over half the land, whilst Scotland has a third of the land but only about a tenth of the people. Wales has a tenth of the land but only a twentieth of the people and Northern Ireland has a twentieth of the land but a mere 3 per cent of the population. We can express these facts in another way by saying that in England there are about 900 people per square mile, in Wales about 350, in Northern Ireland less than 300 and in Scotland only about 175.

The reasons for these very unequal densities of population are to be found partly in differences in climatic conditions, but the overwhelming causes are economic. For all but a very select few of the population, where to live is decided by the whereabouts of the farms, factories, shops or offices at which people work to earn their living. When Britain was an agricultural country the population was fairly evenly spread over the good farming land. With the growth of industry the siting of factories became the predominant

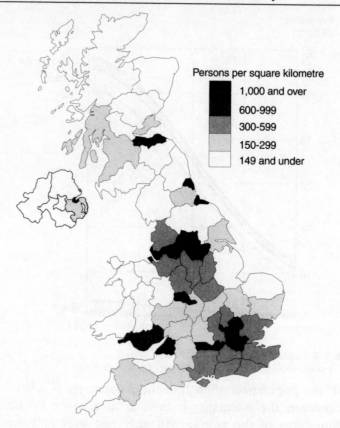

Figure 1.5 Density of population, 1990
Source: *Regional Trends*

influence. We shall examine further aspects of the regional distribution of industry in Chapter 3.

The map (Figure 1.5) reveals the main features of the geographical distribution of the population and shows the concentrations around the principal cities. At present something like four-fifths of the entire population live in urban areas and only one-fifth in the country. Even a good many of the latter work in towns. To emphasise the extent of urbanisation, note that in 1988 there were 20 cities in the UK with more than a quarter of a million inhabitants, and seven conurbations – Greater London, West Midlands (around Birmingham), West Yorkshire, South East Lancashire (around Manchester), Merseyside, Tyneside

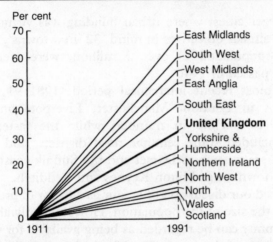

Figure 1.6 Regional population changes, 1911–1991 (percentage increase in population)
Source: *Annual Abstract of Statistics*

(around Newcastle) and Central Clydeside (around Glasgow). These conurbations together occupied less than 3 per cent of all urban land, but housed nearly 30 per cent of the people.

The regional distribution of the population is continually changing. Rural depopulation and the growth of cities began with the industrial revolution, but not all urban areas have grown at the same rate. Figure 1.6 shows the changes in the geographical distribution of the population that have taken place since the census of 1911. This period witnessed the greatest increases in population in the Midlands, South West, East Anglia and South East England, while Scotland, Wales, Northern and North West England experienced relative declines. These changes are the result of internal migration of workers and their families, attracted by employment opportunities in the areas involved, and natural increases of the populations themselves.

A more recent tendency, not observable from Figure 1.6, has been for people to choose to live in outlying suburbs rather than in the centres of large cities. In the interwar years this led to the sprawling conurbations mentioned previously. In order to prevent further erosion of the countryside, the government introduced a policy of designating 'green belts', usually several kilometres wide,

around larger cities, where urban building was virtually prohibited. With similar objectives in mind, 32 'new towns', now with a
combined population of over 2 million, were created under
legislation passed in 1946.

In the most recent intercensal period, 1981–91, inner city
populations in London, Manchester, Liverpool and the like
continued to decline in number, while the fastest growing
districts included some remoter rural districts, and resort and
retirement areas, such as Dorset and the Suffolk coast, as well as
some new towns, e.g. Milton Keynes and Redditch.

We started our discussion of labour as a factor of production by
looking at the size of the population. However, only about half of
the community can be regarded as being available for work in the
ordinary sense of the word. The labour force numbers about 28
million. This figure includes those unemployed for the time
being – a number that varies considerably over the years and
depends on the economic state of the economy. In 1992, the
economy was in deep recession and the total was approaching 3
million, representing about 10 per cent of the labour force. But

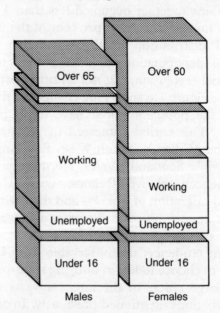

Figure 1.7 The working and non-working population, 1991
Source: *Annual Abstract of Statistics*

why are the other 30 million not part of the labour force? Figure 1.7 helps answer this question.

First, about half are growing up; the law prohibits the full-time employment of some 12 million school pupils under the age of 16, and they are, therefore, excluded from the labour force. At the other end of the scale there is a similar, though smaller, group of women over 60 and men over 65 (the ages of entitlement to retirement pensions). The remainder includes housewives, students, the infirm, convicts, people taking early retirement, and others. Most of these are not counted as part of the working population, not because they do not work, but because they are not paid a wage for doing so. Some married women are given 'housekeeping allowances' by their spouses, for example, but by no stretch of the imagination can any be thought of as being employed by them!

Capital

The third factor of production, capital, consists of man-made aids to further production, such as factory buildings, machinery, plant and equipment, which are not consumed for their own sake but are used to make other goods and services.

The size of the nation's capital stock is very large, valued at nearly £2,000 billion. It is difficult to appreciate the significance of such a magnitude. One way of putting it into perspective is to consider that it represents something like the total output of the entire economy for about three years.

Figure 1.8 shows the breakdown of the national capital wealth of the community, with buildings as the largest item. Note also that dwellings account for over 40 per cent of the total. These, it is true, are not capital goods of the kind we described. However, they are long-lasting and are for certain purposes regarded as part of the nation's capital resources.

The national wealth does not consist solely of tangible items. There is an important class of *intangible* assets which should be regarded as part of national wealth. Such assets are 'locked up' in the skills acquired by education and training, and are known as

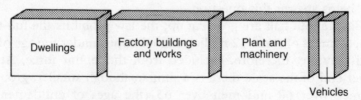

Figure 1.8 Gross capital stock, 1991
Source: *UK National Accounts*

'human capital'. They are hard to evaluate in money terms and are excluded from Figure 1.8.

The total capital of the UK includes a substantial quantity of assets held overseas. In the past, these provided a substantial

---

Box 1.1

More Than 60% Stay in Education After 16

Record numbers of young people are staying in education as youth unemployment rates rise, careers officers reported yesterday.... The trend is expected to continue with the youth labour market remaining sluggish and opportunities expanding in further and higher education. John Patten, the education secretary, has made further growth in staying on rates a priority.... Sexual stereotypes continue to dominate career choice.

Young women tend to go into hairdressing, retailing and clerical work, while the forces, construction industry and mechanical engineering remain male preserves.... Pupils from ethnic minorities were more likely than their white counterparts to stay in education. Whites were twice as likely as black 16-year-olds to take jobs or training places.

The Times, 22 June 1992

This news item is based on a report on *School Leavers' Destinations* (Association of County Councils). It shows the complexity of factors determining the size of the labour force. There is an important lesson to be drawn here when interpreting data showing trends in the *rate* of unemployment – the numbers unemployed expressed as a percentage of the total workforce. See below, Chapter 4.

component of national capital, but they are now approximately balanced by UK overseas liabilities – UK assets belonging to non-residents.

Production

We have looked at the available resources. We continue our overview of the British economy by looking at how these resources are used in the production of goods and services.

We use, first, a well-established distinction categorising production into three types, known as primary, secondary and tertiary production. Figure 1.9 shows the relative importance of the three types of production in present-day Britain, according to the number of workers employed.

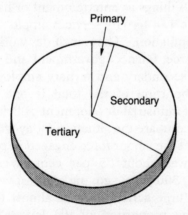

Figure 1.9 Types of industrial activity 1992; percentage of total labour force engaged in primary, secondary and tertiary production
Source: *Monthly Digest of Statistics*

Primary production

This consists of all economic activity which is a first step in the productive process, i.e. the harvesting of natural resources, especially agricultural crops and minerals and sources of energy – oil, coal and natural gas. These provide the foodstuffs, basic raw materials and power upon which other production depends. At the present time less than 5 per cent of the labour force works in agriculture, mining and energy production.

Secondary production

This is concerned with later stages in the production of finished goods. It therefore comprises all of what is called manufacturing industry and building (construction), though today that is only just over a fifth of the total.

Tertiary production

This involves the provision of services which either help other producers to do their jobs, e.g. transport, or satisfy consumer demands for such things as entertainment or hairdressing. As can be seen in Figure 1.9, tertiary services employ over two-thirds of the working population. They include workers in transport, retailing, commerce, finance, government and the professions.

The fact that secondary and tertiary employment account for such a high proportion of the total is one indication of the advanced state of industrial development of Britain. This is clearly illustrated if we compare the situation today with that of the past. The proportion of the labour force engaged in primary production 100 years ago was about 25 per cent. Were reliable figures available for, say, 300 years ago, the contrast would be even more striking. At that time agriculture was almost the only important industry, and the proportion of the labour force engaged in primary production was correspondingly high. Manufacturing business was still rare and, in those days before railways and cars, transport was difficult and the numbers in government service and the professions much fewer.

Employment in secondary production was the first to increase with the industrial revolution. As technical advances raised productivity in industrial production, resources were released for the tertiary sector, while the output of manufactured goods was maintained and even raised. Then the relative importance of the services sector increased, gaining ground from secondary production.

Employment in manufacturing peaked at around 9 million in 1960, declining by a million by the end of that decade, and by another million ten or so years later. By 1992, manufacturing employment had dropped to less than 5 million. This process of 'deindustrialisation' has come about as a result of complex changes, including the rapid advance of technology in the manufacturing sector. It has not been confined to the UK, though its implications for this country have been of considerable concern to some people, because of the traditional role that manufacturing has played in exports. The full impact of deindustrialisation on UK exports was sheltered, temporarily, in the early 1980s, by the development of North Sea oil.

Box 1.2

What a Way to Make a Living

Does making things matter? There was a widespread feeling in Britain during the 1980s that it did not. Pundits pointed to the shifting nature of the economy ... – from heavy dependence on manufacturing to greater reliance on services. The boom in financial and information services was going to usher in a post-industrial world.

That future has been indefinitely postponed. That warning went out even before Big Bang encouraged the City's new stockbroking conglomerates to entice 24-year-old bond salesmen with Porsches. As far as exports were concerned, a committee of the House of Lords reported in 1985 that there was nothing in the cupboard to compensate for any further decline in manufacturing.

The Economist, 24 October 1992

The commentary quoted above focuses on deindustrialisation as one of the major changes in the structure of the UK economy in recent decades. At this stage in the book, you would not expect to appreciate as many implications as you will when you have read later about some of the things mentioned here, such as bonds, conglomerates and stockbrokers. You might do well to be cautious before entirely accepting *The Economist*'s conclusion. On the other side of the coin is the argument that what has happened to the structure of the economy in recent years is more due to the working of market forces than at any previous period since the end of the Second World War. There is, as so often, a balance to be struck.

The Pattern of Production

Figure 1.10 shows further details of the relative importance of different industries and brings out the dominance of the major service sectors. The retail and wholesale (distributive) trades employ over 4 million persons, while over $2\frac{1}{2}$ million people are in the financial sector, which includes accountancy, banking, insurance, etc.

Fewer than one in ten employees work directly for central and local government. However, many others are indirectly involved in jobs financed by the state, e.g. in the capacity of teachers, nurses, doctors in the public sector provision of education and health, and in nationalised industries, such as the Post Office. There has, of course, been a very substantial reduction in the level of employment in the nationalised industries as a result of the privatisation programme of the Conservative governments that have held office since 1979 (see pages 59–62 and 222–3).

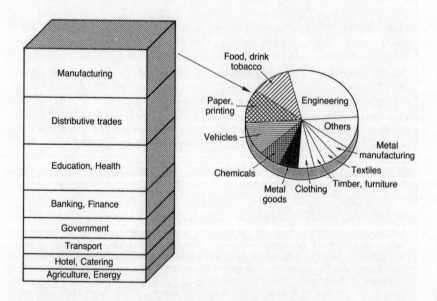

Figure 1.10 Employment in the main industrial sectors, 1992
Source: *Monthly Digest of Statistics*

Manufacturing industry accounts for the employment of just over 20 per cent of all those at work. The pie diagram in Figure 1.10 has been included to show the relative importance of individual manufacturing industries. The dominant position of the engineering industry is at once apparent, since it employs one in every four factory workers. Food, drink and tobacco, paper and printing, and vehicles (including shipbuilding) are the next largest groups. Together with engineering, these industries account for the employment of well over half the manufacturing workforce. Among others, chemicals, metal goods (a miscellaneous category including tools, cutlery and metal containers), clothing, timber and furniture, textiles and metal manufacture (mainly iron and steel) are sufficiently important to be separately distinguished.

Foreign Trade

The UK is far from being an isolated self-sufficient country; instead it engages in a substantial amount of trade with the rest of the world.

In the last century Britain held a dominant position in world trade, especially in the export of manufactured products. A hundred years ago the UK supplied almost 40 per cent of such exports. Britain's share fell to less than 7 per cent towards the end of the 1980s, but picked up marginally in 1991. The UK is now but the fifth most important nation in world trade in terms of total exports and imports – following the USA, Germany, Japan and France. More relevant in some ways, however, is the role imports play in the UK economy. About a quarter of all goods and services consumed in Britain are made up, directly or indirectly, of imports. This underlines the key place of foreign trade in the economic life of the country and may be contrasted with the situation in the USA or Japan, for example, where imported goods comprise notably lower proportions of the national income. (There are, of course, countries where the proportion of imports to national income is higher than in the UK, e.g. Belgium and Ireland – see page 144).

Commodity Composition

The traditional picture of Britain in the world economy in the past was characterised by great dependence upon foreign sources of supply for essential raw materials and foodstuffs, paid for by the export of manufactured products. This is no longer the case. The importance of primary products in the import bill has greatly diminished as a result of many factors, including the development of synthetics and the decline of some raw-material-using industries, such as textiles.

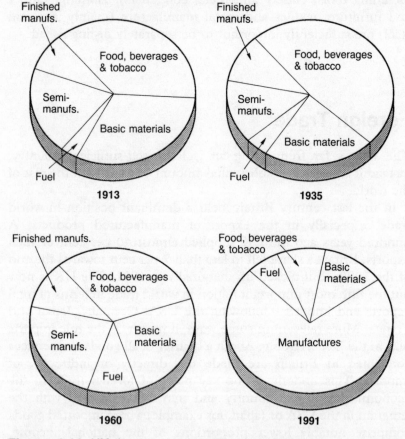

Figure 1.11 UK imports commodity composition in selected years, 1913–1991

Sources: *The British Economy: Key Statistics 1900–1970*, London and Cambridge Economic Service, *Annual Abstract of Statistics* and *Monthly Digest of Statistics*

Figures 1.11 and 1.12 show the major changes that have taken place in the composition of British foreign trade during the twentieth century. It can be seen that food, beverages and basic materials accounted for about three-quarters of total imports before the First World War, but for barely more than 15 per cent by 1991. The only material to have increased significantly has been fuel; though, thanks largely to North Sea oil, the UK had become a net fuel exporter by the 1980s. The corollary of the decline in imports of primary products, also seen in Figure 1.11, is the great rise in the importance of manufactures and semi-

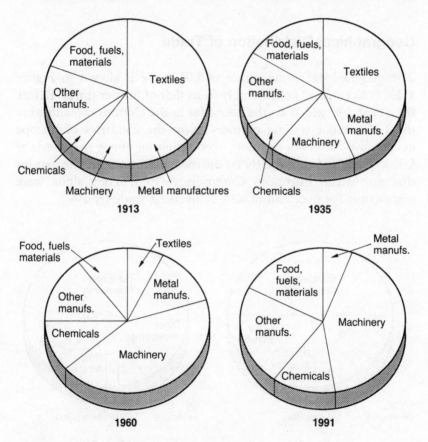

Figure 1.12 UK exports commodity composition in selected years 1913–1991

Sources: *The British Economy, Key Statistics 1900–1970*, London and Cambridge Economic Service, *Annual Abstract of Statistics*

manufactures, which nowadays account for over two-thirds of total imports. Since UK exports have remained mainly of manufactured goods (see Figure 1.12), British overseas trade is best characterised as consisting predominantly of the exchange of manufactured goods with other countries. There have, however, been substantial changes in the relative importance of different kinds of manufactured goods which are exported. To a substantial extent these reflect shifts in the structure of industrial production.

Geographical Distribution of Trade

The geographical composition of UK trade is shown in Figure 1.13. It has shifted considerably from that of former times. Before the Second World War, the countries in the Commonwealth were the UK's major trading partners. Now the countries of Europe occupy the dominant position, accounting for about two-thirds of UK imports and exports. By far the most important are the nations that are in the European Community (EC). They alone were responsible for over half of all UK overseas trade by 1991.

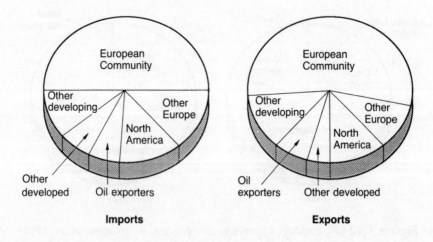

Figure 1.13 Geographical distribution of UK foreign trade 1991
Source: *Annual Abstract of Statistics*

The countries of the EC comprise an original 'six' (Belgium, France, [West] Germany, Italy, Luxembourg and the Netherlands), to which were later added Denmark, Ireland, the UK, Greece, Spain and Portugal, to make up 'twelve' (see pages 157–63). The Community is of far greater importance to Britain than simply as a trading partner. Its activities extend to many economic and political matters discussed later in this book. Among the principal economic influences in the early years were those induced by the removal of tariff barriers to trade among member nations. There is now an expectation of increased integration as a result of the Single European Act. This came into force in January 1993 and should result in the removal of remaining trade barriers and the harmonisation of many national rules and regulations affecting taxes, social policies, etc., to create a 'single European market'. Far-reaching developments for the EC are envisaged in the Maastricht Treaty of 1992, which is intended to lead to full economic union (see below pages 30–1 and Chapters 8 and 9).

The Balance of Payments

Imports and exports of tangible goods are not the only transactions that the UK engages in with other countries. There is also a considerable trade in services. Such trade is known as 'invisible', in contrast with the 'visible' trade in physical commodities. Invisible earnings arise as returns on overseas investments, from the services of financial institutions, from tourism and from other sources. Their importance for this country's balance of payments arises from the fact that the UK has a deficit on visible trade, partly (sometimes wholly) financed by a surplus on invisible items.

The net result of both visible and invisible balances is known as the 'current account' balance of payments. There is also a capital account, which records international capital transactions – lending and borrowing both short-term and long-term. As far back as the nineteenth century, Britain was a major supplier of capital for other countries. At the present time capital flows are two-way, but very substantial.

Economic Growth

Economic growth has been a dominant force among industrial nations for more than 200 years. It has raised living standards to levels where goods and services, such as cars and foreign travel, have come within the reach of the mass of the population in countries such as Britain.

Figure 1.14 shows how real output has grown in the UK during the present century. It can be seen that progress has not been steady. In some years growth rates have been high – up to 8 per cent. In others, the rate has been low, occasionally even negative, In 1991, for example, the UK growth rate was $-2\frac{1}{2}$ per cent. However, the long-term trend has been unequivocally upwards. During the second half of the present century the rate of economic growth has averaged $+2\frac{1}{2}$ per cent per annum. This figure is lower than the long-term growth rate of some other countries, especially Japan and (West) Germany and France, though their growth rates dropped substantially in the 1980s. Moreover, the UK's growth rate since the Second World War has been substantially higher than the average rate in the UK during the first half of the

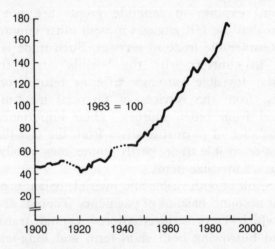

Figure 1.14 Real output, 1900–1991
Sources: *The British Economy, Key Statistics 1900–1970*, London and Cambridge Economic Service, *Annual Abstract of Statistics*

century – about 1 per cent before the First World War and 2 per cent in the interwar period. Note the cumulative workings of compound interest which can lead to rather startling results; a growth rate of 2 per cent per year, if continued for a century, will lead to more than a sevenfold increase in real national income. Thus Britain's rate of $2\frac{1}{2}$ per cent caused output to double within a generation, as can be seen by inspection of the levels of output in 1960 and 1990 in Figure 1.14. Material living standards rose by almost the same extent. Only 'almost' because the population, among whom output needs to be divided, rose by about 10 per cent, so that income *per head* rose by rather less than total output.

Employment and Unemployment

The account of economic growth in the previous section has been of achieved output, not potential (maximum) output. We know that the latter has been considerably greater than the former in some years because not all the country's productive capacity has been fully utilised. In so far as all workers are not fully employed, output is less than that which is technically possible.

Figure 1.15 traces the history of unemployment during the present century, as depicted by the percentage of the labour force

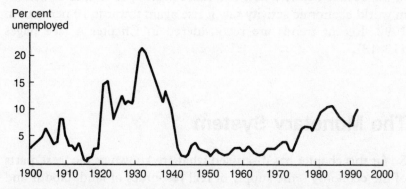

Figure 1.15 Percentage unemployment, 1900–1991 (figures for 1900–1926 relate to the unionised labour force; for 1926–1981 to the numbers registering as unemployed; and, after 1981, to those claiming social security benefits)

Source: *The British Economy, Key Statistics 1900–1970*, London and Cambridge Economic Service, *Annual Abstract of Statistics* and *Monthly Digest of Statistics*

out of work.[2] In the nineteenthth century there was a reasonably regular trade cycle of booms and slumps lasting 8–10 years. The level of unemployment varied continuously; there were no prolonged periods either of full employment or of heavy unemployment.

The period between the two world wars presents a dismal picture of heavy unemployment. The unemployment of the 1920s was an isolated British phenomenon associated with the long-term decline in some of Britain's staple export industries. The high British unemployment rate was not matched elsewhere in the world in that decade; in the United States, for example, the mid-1920s was a period of boom. The 1930s, however, saw heavy unemployment throughout the world. At the worst point in the 'Great Depression' of the 1930s one person in four was unemployed in the UK. A similar situation ruled in America and in most industrialised countries.

During the Second World War unemployment fell to an extremely low level. After the war unemployment still fluctuated, but from 1945 until the early 1970s the fluctuations were over a much narrower range than in the nineteenth century.

In 1974 the world entered the worst recession since the Great Depression of the 1930s. Unemployment in the UK began a steady upward climb that took it from $2\frac{1}{2}$ per cent in 1974 to 11 per cent in 1986. Thereafter the rate declined to $5\frac{1}{2}$ per cent at the end of the decade before a new and more prolonged deeper downturn in world economic activity saw it rise again towards 10 per cent in 1992. Recent trends are reconsidered in Chapter 4 (see pages 113–18).

The Monetary System

So far this chapter has discussed what are known as the 'real' parts of the economy – the supply of real resources of land, labour and

---

2   Changes in the way in which the official percentage unemployment rate is calculated suggest that detailed comparisons, especially involving the 1980s, should be treated with caution.

capital and the production of real goods and services. However, the economy has another side to it, a *monetary* one. reflecting the fact that resources and goods are measured in terms of their prices, or monetary values.

Money is defined as anything that is generally accepted in exchange for goods and services. It includes notes and coins, but the most important means of making payments today is through banks. Bank deposits, the sums standing to the credit of customers, are the prime constituent of what is regarded as money in the UK, though there are several alternative definitions of the money supply which will be discussed in Chapter 8 (pages 265–7).

The business of banking is mainly in the hands of four domestic banks – Barclays, Lloyds, Midland and National Westminister – though there are several foreign banks operating in London. Against their liabilities to depositors, banks hold a variety of financial assets. These are of differing degrees of liquidity, reflecting the ease and speed with which they may be used to make payments. The most liquid assets are notes and coins, the least liquid are the loans and advances made to customers, often by granting overdraft facilities. It is the last of these which are of major importance in determining the quantity of money in existence.

The monetary sector of the economy includes a great many financial institutions as well as banks, for example discount houses, building societies, insurance companies and merchant banks. They will all be considered in Chapter 8. All deal in monetary assets of one form or another. Their activities may affect key economic variables, especially the general levels of prices, output and employment. Since the banks and other financial institutions may play important roles in these matters, the government often tries to influence them in pursuit of its policy objectives. The state has many ways of doing so. One important one, monetary policy, is carried out for the government by the central bank – in the UK, the Bank of England.

The Bank of England may exert influence on the supply of money by pressuring banks to alter their lending policies. It has methods of controlling the size of the banks' cash reserves, and otherwise affecting their liquidity. The Bank can also, within limits, set the level of interest rates, i.e. the prices paid by borrowers or received by lenders of money. Businesses and consumers pay regard to interest rates when deciding on how much to spend on investment or on goods and services. The general level of prices, output and employment may then change when interest rates alter.

Inflation

Changes in the general level of prices affect real output. The strength and duration of this effect are controversial, but governments throughout the world have been worried by persistent inflation, which hardly needs describing to anyone alive today.

Figure 1.16 shows the course of the average level of retail prices in the UK since 1900. It demonstrates that, apart from a very few years after the First World War and in the early 1930s, the general trend has been decidedly upwards. Indeed, by 1992 prices were

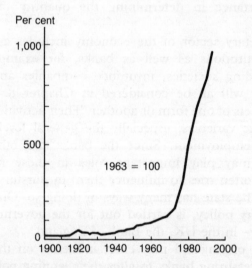

Figure 1.16 Index of retail prices, 1900–1992

Sources: *The British Economy, Key Statistics 1900–1970*, London & Cambridge Economic Service and *Annual Abstract of Statistics*

approximately ten times their level of 20 years before, or over 50 times those in 1900. Put another way, a 1992 pound had very roughly the same purchasing power as 10 pence of a 1960 pound or as 2 pence at the beginning of the century.

The first 20 years after the Second World War were those of a fairly steady, if slow, rate of increase in the level of prices – 2 to 3 per cent per annum on average. At the end of the 1960s inflation started to accelerate and first reached 10 per cent in the early 1970s – so-called 'double digit' inflation. In 1975 the rate peaked when prices rose by more than 25 per cent in 12 months. It subsequently fell, and the rate of inflation since 1982 has stayed around 4–6 per cent apart from a couple of years at the end of the decade. We discuss recent inflation in more detail in Chapter 9.

Government

The UK is a mixed economy. A great many decisions are taken by private individuals in markets where the forces of supply and demand work relatively free from government interference. However, there are important sectors where the state enters directly or indirectly into decision-making on the allocation of resources.

Figure 1.17 shows the long-term trends in the size of government activity as measured by the proportion of public expenditure to total national income since 1900 (government expenditure here excludes expenditure by the nationalised industries). This is only one of a number of indicators that can be used for the same purpose; indeed, the precise percentages obtained are sensitive to which indicator is chosen. However, there is no danger in drawing the general conclusion that the trend has been of substantial growth in government expenditure until the 1970s. While not much more than 10 per cent of the national income passed through the government's hands at the beginning of the century, by 1970 the proportion had risen to well over 40 per cent, at which it more or less settled for the next quarter of a century. Similar trends have been experienced by other countries.

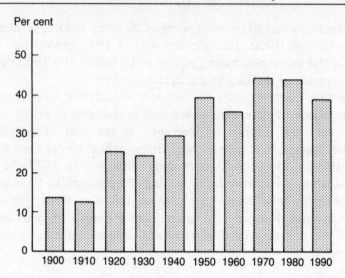

Figure 1.17 Government expenditure as a percentage of GNP
Sources: *The Growth of Public Expenditure in the UK*, A T Peacock and Wiseman (Allen & Unwin. 1967) and *UK National Accounts*

There are many explanations for the growth of public expenditure which, of course, carried with it growing government income from taxation. They include major changes in the public's attitude to the role of the state in the provision of social services (the 'welfare state') and decisions to take certain important industries into public ownership (nationalisation), especially in the early years after the Second World War.

There is also a technical reason why the public sector tends to grow relative to the rest of the economy. It is that productivity growth in government services tends to lag behind that in manufacturing industry because of the small scope for mechanisation and, therefore, for economies of large-scale production. The prices of government services tend to rise in consequence relative to those of the rest of the economy. Since the output of the public and private sectors is valued at their prices (or costs), the size of the former has a natural tendency to increase relative to that of the latter.

There is not, of course, an iron law of increasing public expenditure. Governments can try to limit disbursements from the public purse, though this may be difficult to achieve in practice. Four Conservative administrations since 1979 have been committed to reducing the size of the public sector. Various measures were set in train, including the transfer of several major activities into private hands, as part of the 'privatisation programme' (see pages 59–62). However, the size of the public sector has remained stubbornly high relative to total national income. This is partly because it takes time for government departments to adjust expenditure plans downwards in the face of stated commitments, and partly because the national income fails to keep pace with the level of social security outgoings during recessions.

Economic Policy

Economic policy in the UK, referred to in this book, should be considered within the framework provided by economic theory.[3] There are two distinct sets of policies that the government operates:

- **Microeconomic policies**. These relate to the allocation of resources, from the viewpoints of:

  Efficiency
  Equity

- **Macroeconomic policies**. These relate to the economy as a whole and concern one or more of the following:

  General level of unemployment
  General level of prices
  Rate of economic growth
  Balance of payments

3 For exposition of the theoretical framework, see Lipsey–Harbury, FP2, Chapter 1, pp. 22–3, and Chapters 21, 28 and 34.

The instruments of economic policy used by the UK government are many and varied and are discussed in the chapters which follow. It may, however, be useful to mention some of the major policy areas here, in order to relate them to the theoretical categories mentioned above.

Measures related to efficiency

Many of the policies in this category are directed to the private sector of the economy, where the state engages in interventionist actions to help certain industries and to regulate others. For example, there are subsidies for industries in need of special assistance (e.g. agriculture); loans, grants and subsidised consultancy services for small businesses; taxes to control pollution and discourage the smoking of cigarettes, measures to influence the regional location of industry; agencies for the investigation of monopolies, mergers and restrictive business practices which diminish industrial competitiveness. There are also specialised agencies, e.g. for regulating financial services; maintaining quality standards – especially in the case of dangerous products.

A major policy for economic efficiency is where the state itself engages in the provision of certain goods and services because, for one reason or another, private sector production is considered to be inappropriate. Examples under this head include the provision of armies, navies and air forces for national defence, of the police and law courts for the administration of justice, and extensive parts of health and education services. These are, in the main, non-commercial activities financed by the state out of general revenues and provided free to the community.

However, there is another group, known as the nationalised industries, which are owned and operated by the state and which levy charges for their services. In the UK, nationalised industries, which possess some characteristics of commercial enterprises, have been run by specialised agencies called public corporations. They enjoy a considerable degree of independence in the conduct of their day-to-day affairs, though they are subject to ultimate ministerial control.

The first nationalised industries appeared well before the Second World War, but the major period of extension of public ownership of industry in Britain occurred between 1945 and 1951. This was the first time that the Labour Party had held a majority of seats in the House of Commons, and coal, electricity, gas, the railways and steel were taken into public ownership.

Nationalisation was, of course, a matter with strong political implications. It was, nevertheless, accepted by both Conservative and Labour governments from 1945 until the 1970s. Thenceforward, a dramatic shift in emphasis took place. Three Conservative governments under the premiership of Margaret Thatcher and a fourth under John Major began to place much greater reliance on the working of market forces. They set off a major policy reversal with a programme for returning many of the nationalised industries to private ownership.

Such *de*nationalisation formed part of the policy better known as privatisation. The largest transfers have been of telecommunications (British Telecom), gas, airlines (British Airways), steel, water and electricity, with railways and coal on the agenda for the present decade. Several of the privatised industries retained elements of natural monopoly and their transfer to private ownership was accompanied by the establishment of entirely new agencies to oversee their activities in the public interest, especially with regard to the prices of their products. Quantitatively, the effects of the policy can be illustrated by the fact that employment in the nationalised industries fell from a figure representing 8 per cent of the labour force to less than 3 per cent during the decade 1980–1990.

Measures related to equity

The government tries to make the allocation of resources among individuals fairer, i.e. more equitable. Two types of instrument are available. One is directed to redistributing income, leaving people free to decide how to spend it in their own best interests. The other provides certain goods and services free, or at less than cost, to all who want them, regardless of income. Two ways of redistributing are of prime importance:

- the levying of taxes, especially on income earned and capital owned by individuals. Redistribution is enhanced if taxes are progressive – taking higher proportions of income of the rich than of the poor.

- providing so-called transfer benefits to persons in cash – e.g. retirement pensions, unemployment benefit, and in kind – e.g. education and health. Some benefits aim to redistribute resources in the direction of greater equality by being targeted at the poor, though this necessarily requires them to be 'means-tested'.

Control of the economy as a whole

Since the Second World War, governments have usually taken on responsibility for influencing the rate of inflation, the level of unemployment, the rate of economic growth of the national economy and the balance of payments between the UK and the rest of the world. Instruments available to these ends include (a) **fiscal policy**, which seeks to influence total spending through the government's own budget – changing its taxes and/or expenditure as required; and (b) **monetary policy**, operated by the Bank of England, which tries to influence spending through interest rates and the supply of money.

Economic Policy and the European Community

The integration of the UK into the European Community has important implications for the freedom for national governments to choose their own policy options. There are agreements for specific policy harmonisation, e.g. on hours of work and tax rates, but of immense importance is the programme for monetary union and the eventual introduction of a single currency for all EC member countries to replace sterling, francs, marks, etc. The timetable for this programme was agreed in the Maastricht Treaty in the spring of 1992, and extends over virtually the whole of the remainder of the century. However, a question mark hangs over the extent to which the EC will adopt the programme in practice, following two referenda in 1992, which saw the rejection of the Treaty by Denmark, and its acceptance by only a narrow majority in France (see below especially pages 157–63 and 327–32).

Questions and exercises

(For key to abbreviations identifying sources, see pages xv–xvi)

1 Figure 1.6 shows the long-term changes in the regional distribution of the population. Prepare a diagram on the lines of Figure 1.6 but based on changes in the last 10 years. Compare the two diagrams, and offer explanations for such differences as you find. (*AS*)

2 Calculate (i) the percentage of the area of agricultural land used to grow cereals, (ii) the percentage of the value of agricultural output contributed by cereals. Why are they unlikely to be the same?

3 Prepare a table showing (i) gross national product, (ii) gross capital stock, (iii) the current account balance of payments, for each of the past 10 years. How closely have the series followed each other? Which gives the best indication of the course of living standards?

4 Obtain a catalogue of a mail order company or a store like *Argos* or *Index* and estimate the proportion of the number of listed items that are imported from abroad in the sections Cameras, Watches and Electrical Goods. Check your proportions with the national statistics (*AS*)

5 Alan was born in 1920, his daughter Barbara in 1945, his granddaughter Claire in 1970 and his great grandson Desmond in 1993. How much would Alan need to set aside for each of his descendants to give them all the same purchasing power as £10 when he was born? (Use the Appendix in the quarterly *BER*.)

6 Put each of the following economic series into one of three groups according to whether the number has risen, fallen or stayed the same compared with a year ago: (i) coal output, (ii) total employment, (iii) total unemployment, (iv) the rate of inflation, (v) gross domestic product, (vi) the top rate of income tax. Suppose you were asked to describe changes in economic well-being between the two years. Which three of the above series would help you most? Which three additional series would you like to have to help answer the question?

Appendix 1

Table A1.1 Geographical distribution of population and land area the UK (selected years)*

Standard regions	Area (thousand sq. km)	Population (thousands)				
		1911	1931	1961	1981	1990
North	15.4	2,815	3,038	3,250	3,104	3,075
Yorkshire and Humberside	15.4	3,877	4,285	4,635	4,860	4,952
East Midlands	15.6	2,263	2,531	3,100	3,819	4,019
East Anglia	12.6	1,192	1,232	1,470	1,872	2,059
South East	27.2	11,744	13,539	16,271	16,796	17,458
South West	23.9	2,687	2,794	3,411	4,349	4,666
West Midlands	13.0	3,277	3,743	4,758	5,148	5,219
North West	7.3	5,796	6,197	6,567	6,414	6,389
Wales	20.8	2,421	2,593	2,644	2,792	2,881
Scotland	78.8	4,760	4,843	5,179	5,131	5,102
N. Ireland	14.0	1,251	1,280	1,425	1,562	1,589
United Kingdom	244.1	42,082	46,075	52,709	55,847	57,410

*All selected years were those when a census was taken, except for 1990, as the 1991 census was regarded as unreliable because of 'missing' persons, thought to be poll tax evaders (see page 186)

Source: *Annual Abstract of Statistics*

Table A1.2 Projected population of the UK to the year 2031
(thousands)

Age group	1990	2001	2011	2021	2031
Total	57,411	59,174	60,033	60,743	61,068
0–4	3,841	3,927	3,605	3,783	3,732
5–9	3,650	4,020	3,712	3,679	3,803
10–14	3,429	3,888	3,938	3,617	3,789
15–19	3,918	3,703	4,056	3,748	3,699
20–24	4,555	3,547	3,944	3,995	3,667
25–29	4,719	3,711	3,693	4,045	3,756
30–34	4,087	4,414	3,467	3,863	3,923
35–39	3,767	4,666	3,646	3,629	3,981
40–44	4,123	4,150	4,358	3,422	3,817
45–49	3,387	3,706	4,579	3,584	3,574
50–54	3,113	4,016	4,028	4,239	3,338
55–59	2,938	3,363	3,536	4,378	3,435
60–64	2,896	2,838	3,706	3,732	3,939
65–69	2,841	2,531	2,944	3,107	3,866
70–74	2,167	2,279	2,292	3,014	3,062
75–79	1,871	1,925	1,821	2,152	2,287
80–84	1,243	1,319	1,372	1,407	1,864
85 and over	866	1,171	1,337	1,351	1,538

Source: *Annual Abstract of Statistics*

Table A1.3 Employees by industry 1992 (Great Britain)

Agriculture, forestry and fishing	294	Other transport equipment	202	Wholesale distribution and repairs	1,200
Energy and water supply	396	Metal goods n.e.s.	284	Retail distribution	2,119
Metal manufacturing	123	Food, drink and tobacco	496	Hotels and catering	1,135
Chemicals and man-made fibres	300	Textiles, leather, footwear and clothing	429	Transport	925
Mechanical engineering	647	Timber and wooden furniture	202	Banking, finance, insurance	2,615
Electrical engineering	491	Paper products, printing and publishing	468	Public administration, etc	1,923
Office machinery and data processing equipment	68	Other manufacturing	271	Education	1,766
				Medical health and veterinary services	1,494
Motor vehicles and parts	223	Construction	843	Other services	1,658

Source: *Employment Gazette*, September 1992

Table A1.4 Gross capital stock, UK, 1981 and 1991 (£ billion)

	1981	*1991*
Road vehicles	45.9	54.6
Railway rolling stock, ships and aircraft	25.8	11.6
Plant and machinery	389.9	518.8
Dwellings	459.7	572.5
Other buildings and works	482.3	620.1
Total gross capital stock	1,403.6	1,777.6

Source: *UK National Accounts*

2
Organisation of Business Activity

A major area of economic theory tries to explain how business decisions are made.[1] Such decisions are affected by the institutional arrangements within which they are taken. This and the following chapter deal with these matters and describe the structure of industry in the UK. Mostly this concerns the private sector of the economy. At the end of the chapter we look also at public sector businesses, including those which changed hands as part of the privatisation programme since 1980.

Private Sector Business Organisation

We start with an explanation of the organisational features of modern firms. There are four main forms of private business organisation in the UK:

- Single proprietorships
- Partnerships
- Co-operatives
- Joint stock companies (called corporations in North America)

1 This chapter deals with material relevant to the theories discussed in Lipsey–Harbury, FP2, Chapter 12.

The Single Proprietorship

The simplest, and oldest, form of business organisation is sole ownership. The distinguishing feature of this type of enterprise is not that all the work is necessarily done by one person, though this may be the case, but that the business is owned by one individual. Such businesses are easy to set up and their owners can readily maintain control of them. However, the size of the firm is limited by the amount of capital that owners can raise for themselves. Moreover, owners are personally responsible in law for all debts that are incurred by the firm. In Britain, four out of every ten businesses consist of sole proprietorships, but because of their small size they account for a mere 3 per cent of the value of turnover. Sectors where firms run by a single proprietor particularly flourish are the building trades and retail shopkeeping.

Partnerships

Whenever a sole operator feels that the burden of the business is too great, the alternative of teaming up with one or more other people may be attractive. About a quarter of all businesses are partnerships.

Partners may have complementary contributions to make. For example, an inventor may go into partnership with an accountant. However, a major reason for seeking business partners is often that the capital needed for operations is more than a single owner can provide. In such circumstances, a partnership with others who contribute shares of the capital and take out proportionate shares of any profits may be a suitable arrangement.

Partnerships suffer as do single proprietorships in that each partner is legally liable for all the debts of the firm, including those incurred by the activity of another partner. There is no limit to this liability, which extends to the whole of a firm's debts, regardless of the amount of capital which the individual partners have originally contributed. For example, consider a two-person partnership where one partner supplied £100,000 of the capital and the other only £10,000. If the partnership incurs net debts to the extent of

£25,000 and the first partner is unable to meet any of them, the partner who put up only £10,000 in the first place may have to pay the creditors the entire £25,000, even if he or she is forced to sell his/her house and other property in order to do so.

The risk of entering into partnership with people who prove to be unreliable, unscrupulous or merely inefficient is consequently great. Partnerships persist, therefore, where mutual confidence is strong, often among families. Areas popular with single proprietorships, e.g shopkeeping and the building trades, are also commonly organised as partnerships, as are catering and farming. They are traditional also in certain professions, such as accountancy and the law. Some financial protection for individuals is provided in what are called 'limited partnerships'. In these, specified partners enjoy liability only to the extent to which they have invested money in the firm, provided they take no part in the running of the business.

Co-operatives

The third form of organisation, co-operatives, applies to businesses which are controlled either by their workers or by the consumers of their products.

Consumer co-operatives operate mainly in the retail trade. The origins of consumer co-operation are found in the political movement associated with the name of Robert Owen. The first successful experiment was in Rochdale in 1844, with co-operation in retailing expanding greatly after that. Today there are only about 200 retail societies, and their number has been falling steadily, partly as a result of amalgamation.

The distinctive feature of co-operative societies is that they are, in a sense, 'owned' by those of their customers who choose to pay a minimum deposit giving them effectively a share in the business. There are local 'co-ops' in many districts, run by elected management committees which appoint the staff. The principle on which co-operative societies grew up was one whereby goods were sold at normal retail prices, with profits distributed among members as 'dividends', proportional to purchases. The practice persists in some societies today.

Consumer co-operatives have suffered from intense competition from other types of organisation and have been on the decline for many years. They were responsible for about an eighth of total retail turnover in 1950, but by the beginning of the 1990s, their share had dropped to a twentieth – milk distribution being one area still significant. Modernisation has taken place, with the help of the Co-operative Wholesale Society (CWS), which is a large manufacturer and importer and operates its own banking and insurance business.

The second type of co-operative organisation involves employees among whom profits are shared. Producer co-operatives also flourished a hundred or more years ago and went into decline in the present century. Recently, they have enjoyed something of a revival when workers have acted to continue operations when management has decided to close down.

Joint Stock Companies

The fourth and last type of business organisation is so important that we shall discuss it at much greater length. Its full title – 'joint stock company' – is commonly abbreviated to 'company' or, especially in North America, to 'corporation'.

The prime characteristic of a joint stock company is that the liability of every individual owner (known as a 'shareholder' – see below) of the business is limited to the the amount of capital each has contributed, or promised to contribute. Such companies must include the word 'Limited' (or 'Ltd') in their names, to warn outsiders of the fact.

Public prejudice against the joint stock form of organisation in the eighteenth and nineteenth centuries was strongly influenced by the abuses of company promoters at the time of the South Sea Bubble, and it was not until 1855 that the privilege of **limited liability** was made generally available. Limited liability arises from the fact that companies are regarded in law as entities separate from the individuals who own them. A company can enter into contracts; it can sue and be sued; it can own property; it can contract debts; and its obligations are not those of its owners. Companies have a continuity of life unaffected by changes in ownership, and they have become the most important type of business enterprise in the UK. The advantages of the company form of organisation are substantial; two, in particular, are outstanding.

Large amounts of capital become much easier to raise. This follows from the relatively small risk to individual investors, who know the maximum amount of money they can lose, should the worst come to the worst. They will not be as afraid of entering business with other people whose names they may not even know as they would be in a partnership. In many large companies there are hundreds of thousands, even millions, of shareholders, the vast majority of whom contribute only a minute proportion of the total capital of the business.

Transfer of ownership can take place with a minimum of formality. Limited liability removes the need for shareholders to know each other personally. They can sell shares to anyone. Hence, there is a distinct advantage, absent from a partnership, in that shares can be sold quickly if there is an urgent need for cash. The great importance of transferability of shares has given rise to the appearance of a specialised market place where shares are bought and sold. It is called the **Stock Exchange** (see pages 48–51).

The advantages which limited liability bestows on a company are matched, to an extent, by increased risk to others, especially to companies and those others who do business with it, and to minority shareholders whose interests may be lost sight of in large companies. There is also a risk that unscrupulous company promoters may fraudulently use company funds to their personal advantage. To protect the community from such risks, a number of Companies Acts have been passed, mainly requiring publication of information about the state of the firm and its management.

There are two principal types of company, **public** and **private**. The latter is distinguished principally by the fact that it is not permitted to offer shares for sale to the general public. For this reason private companies are not obliged to publish as many details about their affairs as are public companies, which, by EC law, must describe themselves as public limited companies (plcs).

There are approximately half a million companies in Britain, but only about 3 per cent are public companies, which started life as private companies. (See Box 2.1 for an unusual case.) However, plcs dominate in terms of the value of output and the vast majority of large corporations are public. An indication of the importance of giant companies is given by the fact that the 100 largest business enterprises in manufacturing produce over 40 per cent of total output. (See pages 83–97 for a discussion of business concentration.)

Box 2.1

Sugar Heading Towards Bitter Exit From City

There was drama last week when Mr Sugar (Britain's best known former market trader and the founder of Amstrad, the consumer electronics group) revealed that he was considering taking the company private with a proposed £110 million offer for the 65 per cent that he does not own.

The past few years have been tough for Amstrad because of the sharp downturn in consumer spending which has ... led to a slump in the company's stock market worth from 220p a share to 27p last week. The decline has caused deep bitterness among shareholders, and they have now been further annoyed by what they believe is an attempt by Mr Sugar to buy the company on the cheap at the bottom of the recession.

Independent on Sunday,
27 September 1992

This news item illustrates a rather exceptional case where a single individual owns more than 50 per cent of the ordinary shares in a public company. It is unusual, too, because it tells of a move to turn a public company back into a private one, the reverse of the normal procedure. Incidentally, the report quotes a City comment: 'The buy-out price is very low and will be viewed in the City as a final insult.' An independent, cynical, observer might wonder whether for hard-headed investors in shares any relevance attaches to 'insults'!

Business accounts

Companies publish financial details in two documents: the balance sheet and the profit and loss account. The following discussion of the main items that appear in these two accounts is illustrated in the specimen balance sheet below, which lists them in simplified form for a typical company.

Balance sheet   as at 31 December 199x

	£	£		£	£
Capital and liabilities			*Assets*		
Issued capital			Fixed assets		
Ordinary shares	x		Land, buildings	x	
Preference shares	x	x	Machinery, equipment	x	
Loan from XYZ Bank Ltd		x	Goodwill	x	x
Current liabilities			Current assets		
Sundry creditors		x	Stocks of raw materials	x	
			Stocks of finished		
			products	x	
			Current debtors	x	
			Cash at bank	x	x
		£x			£x

Profit and loss account   for year 1 January to 31 December 199x

	£	£		£
Expenditure			*Income*	
Fixed costs			Revenue from sales	x
Rent	x			
Research & development	x			
Managerial salaries	x			
Interest on bank loan	x			
Depreciation allowance	x	x		
Variable costs				
Wages	x			
Fuel used	x			
Raw materials used	x	x		
(Net profit for year		x)	(Net loss for year	x)
		£x		£x

The balance sheet consists of a statement of the value of the business's assets together with its liabilities. There are two kinds of assets:

- **fixed assets**, such as land, buildings, machinery and equipment
- **current assets**, including stocks of raw materials and finished products, debts due to the company from customers, and cash

There is also a special kind of asset called 'goodwill', which is an estimate of the benefit deriving from a firm's reputation.

The liabilities of the company are financial claims on its assets. Since all assets must be owned by someone, they must be equal to total liabilities. There are two classes of liabilities:

- liabilities to the owners of the business, i.e. the shareholders
- liabilities to other creditors, including customers and those who have made loans to the company

Note, balance sheet valuations are not necessarily as precise as they appear. All assets are not continually being revalued by being put up for sale. Assessments of their value may, therefore, be somewhat arbitrary. Financial comparisons, e.g. of profit rates, both among companies and over time within the same company, may then be difficult to make.

A balance sheet portrays the financial state of a business at a single point in time – when it was drawn up. To appreciate a company's prospects, however, it is necessary to compare balance sheets over a run of years, and to observe the progress that occurs in the growth or depletion of assets. A more complete picture calls for study of the profit and loss account as well as the balance sheet. Whereas the latter describes the financial position at a particular *point in time*, the profit and loss account is a record of a company's operations over a *period of time*, such as a year. It lists all revenues, including sales, and all expenditures, including costs, deriving the company's residual profit or loss in the period as the difference between revenues and expenditures.

A typical profit and loss account distinguishes (as does the economic theory of the firm) between fixed (or overhead) costs and variable (prime, or direct) costs.[2] Only the latter change as output changes, though the longer the period of time under consideration the more costs tend to be variable rather than fixed.

An important deduction from the gross profit of a business is that for the **depreciation** of its assets, which are subject to wear and tear and to obsolescence. Depreciation allowances represent the value of capital 'used up' in the process of production. They must be subtracted from the market value of current production in order to discover whether or not production is profitable. Note that depreciation allowances are only estimates made in the face of uncertainty, especially about the future rate of inflation and hence about the value of capital equipment.

Financing the firm

Firms obtain finance for their operations in the following ways:

- by selling (issuing) **shares** in the business to buyers, who become owners
- by borrowing through the sale of **bonds** to purchasers, who become creditors of the business
- by **borrowing from banks** and other financial institutions
- by **reinvesting** profits
- by **taking over** or merging with other firms

Share issues

There are two main groups of shares: **preference shares** and **ordinary shares**, also known as 'equities'.

Preference shares, as their name implies, entitle their holders to shares in the firm's profits before other shareholders. Payments to shareholders are called dividends, which are normally a fixed percentage of the capital invested. Courtaulds plc, for example, issued a 7 per cent preference share which yields £7.50 for every £100 of shares held. So long as the company makes sufficient profit to meet the dividends of preference shareholders, all receive their dividends in full. Should the company make no profit at all, no

2 See Lipsey–Harbury, FP2, Chapter 14.

dividends are paid (the dividend is then said to be 'passed'), but even if the company has a phenomenally profitable year, preference shareholders get no more than their fixed rate of dividend.

Unless stated to the contrary, preference shares are cumulative, i.e. when a dividend is passed, shareholders have the deficiency made good in a later year if profits recover. Often this right is evidenced by the inclusion of the word 'cumulative' in the name of the shares, e.g. those of Courtaulds plc. There may also be more than one class of preference share. Occasionally, participating preference shares are issued which allow holders a share in profits over and above the stipulated figure. Preference shareholders may or may not be allowed a vote at company meetings, but they rarely have much power.

Holders of ordinary shares usually have voting rights and a residual claim on company profits. Their dividend is not guaranteed, but is decided annually (or bi-annually) when the profit position is known. The rate of dividend is declared as a percentage of the nominal value of the shares. It does not represent the profit rate for all shareholders – this depends upon the price paid for the shares. For example, in 1991–92 Dalgety plc (the makers of 'Golden Wonder' snacks and other food/agriproducts) paid a dividend of 19.5p to holders of each ordinary share. Thus, a person owning 100 shares received £19.50. The dividend yield on the share for any shareholder depends on the price paid for them. In 1992, the price of one of these shares was around £4.00. So anyone buying at that time would receive a yield of close to 5 per cent (£19.50 as a percentage of £400).

The income received by holders of equities is liable to fluctuate over time. Consequently, holdings of ordinary shares tend to be relatively risky investments. For an individual shareholder, however, a portfolio consisting of a range of shares in several different companies reduces the risk. Someone wanting to speculate, however, in the hope of a high return can choose to invest in companies in risky lines of business, e.g. mine exploration (see page 136 for examples).

The risk of holding ordinary shares depends, too, on something called the 'gearing ratio' – the relative importance of equity to other capital carrying a fixed rate of interest (see pages 46–47).

New issues

Companies wishing to raise new capital by share issues have a choice of four methods:

- They may opt for a **public issue** (to the general public). This is often done in co-operation with specialist financial institutions such as a merchant bank or an issuing house. Such issues are commonly guaranteed by 'underwriters' who, for a consideration, agree to buy any unsold shares at a price fixed in advance.
- A second method is an **offer for sale**, where the new shares are sold to an issuing house which then disposes of them to the public.
- Another alternative is a **placing**, whereby particularly small issues of shares are sold privately, by arrangement, to investors.
- Lastly, shares may be offered to the company's existing shareholders in what is called a **rights issue**. This method may help to reduce the administrative costs of the issue, but shares are normally offered on favourable terms.

Bond issues

Part of a company's capital may be in the form of bonds (known also as loan stock, or debentures). Bondholders are sometimes confused with preference shareholders, with whom they have some common features, but a debenture is essentially different from a share of any kind. It is a kind of IOU, acknowledging the debt by a company to purchasers of bonds, who are creditors of the company and who are also paid interest on the loan. The rate of interest on debentures is fixed. An example is the United Biscuit Company's 8 per cent debentures, holders of which have the prior right to receive interest before dividends are paid to any preference or ordinary shareholders. Note that raising capital in the form of bonds carries the obligation to pay interest even if there are no profits. Many a firm has been forced out of business because it could not meet its obligations in the form of fixed interest payments.

The distinction between bonds and shares should now be clear. However, hybrids exist, known as convertibles. These are bonds which carry an option to convert into shares. For example

Storehouse plc issued $4\frac{1}{2}$ per cent convertible bonds in 1987 which could be exchanged into equities at any time up to 2001 at a fixed price of £3.46 per ordinary share.

If a company makes such heavy losses that it is forced out of business, its assets may have to be sold. Creditors of the company have prior claims over shareholders to all the company's assets. Debenture holders (together with other trade creditors) have claims to the return of their capital; their holdings may even be secured by pledges attached to specified company assets.

Borrowing from banks

Businesses often borrow from banks to finance operations. This form of finance is similar to that of issuing bonds. Loans are at a rate of interest that must be paid regardless of whether the firm is, or is not, making a profit.

Gearing

The risk attaching to any holding of ordinary shares is liable to be affected by the structure of the firm's capital – in particular to the 'gearing ratio', defined as the ratio of equities to total capital. The gearing ratio is said to be high if the proportion of bonds and other fixed interest debt to equities is large (and vice versa).

Table 2.1 shows (part of) the balance sheets of two (imaginary) companies HI plc and LO plc to illustrate the meaning and implications of gearing. Both firms have the same profits available for distribution in each of two years and both have the same total issued capital. However, they have different gearing ratios. HI plc is highly geared, with 80 per cent of its capital in the form of 5 per cent debentures. When profits double in a good year from £5,000 to £10,000 it would be possible to raise the dividend on ordinary shares sixfold from 5 to 30 per cent, after meeting the obligations to debenture holders. LO plc, on the other hand, is low geared, with only 20 per cent of its capital in 5 per cent debentures. The same doubling of profits would permit a rise from 5 to only $11\frac{1}{4}$ per cent in the dividend for ordinary shareholders.

Table 2.1 Gearing of two companies

	HI plc		LO plc	
Company capital		£		£
5 per cent Debentures		80,000		20,000
Ordinary shares		20,000		80,000
Total		100,000		100,000
Profit allocation	Year 1	Year 2	Year 1	Year 2
Debentures	4,000	4,000	1,000	1,000
Ordinary shares	1,000	6,000	4,000	9,000
Total	5,000	10,000	5,000	10,000
Rates of return	Year 1	Year 2	Year 1	Year 2
Debenture interest	5	5	5	5
Ordinary dividends	5	30	5	11¼

Reinvested profits

We stated earlier that a major source of capital for new investment comes from the ploughing back of profits. This can be one of the easiest ways for the controllers of a firm to raise money. It implies holding back dividend payments in the short term, but it can lead to larger earnings for shareholders later. It is also relatively important, quantitatively speaking. Figure 2.1 shows that about a third of company profits were not distributed in 1991– a year, moreover, when profits were depressed. In more prosperous years almost half of the total profits have been retained in businesses.

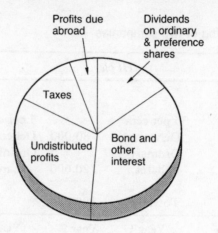

Figure 2.1 Allocation of company income 1991
Source: *UK National Accounts*

Take-overs of other firms

The final method of obtaining finance, especially important for businesses seeking expansion, is by the acquisition of one firm by another. Merger activity has been strong since the 1960s, though mergers tend to come in waves. Note, too, that the provision of finance is only one among several motives for amalgamation, which we discuss again in this chapter.

The Stock Exchange

One of the advantages of the limited liability company form of organisation mentioned earlier is that shares can be bought and sold with relative ease. The existence of specialised market places, called stock exchanges, helps greatly in this respect.

In the UK, the principal such market is the London Stock Exchange (which now chooses to call itself the International Stock Exchange). The main business of this institution is not with the raising of *new* capital for companies, but with purchases and sales of *existing* shares. Trading of shares has a long history and can be traced back to the informal meetings of traders in the eighteenth century at Jonathan's Coffee House in Exchange Alley. The modern stock exchange developed during the nineteenth century, stimulated by the Companies Acts and the institution of limited liability, mentioned earlier.

Prior to 1986, dealing in shares was conducted on the floor of the Stock Exchange by members of the Stock Exchange who, curiously enough, were not themselves permitted to enjoy limited liability but were, for the most part, organised as partnerships. Two classes of member were recognised – brokers and jobbers. Brokers acted as agents for the public, for whom they bought or sold shares or bonds, charging a commission for the service. Jobbers were 'middlemen', who were not allowed to deal direct with the public, but with brokers (or with each other). The jobbers' profit (or loss) depended on the difference in price received for shares and the price paid for them.

The system was not well suited to the nature and volume of business in modern times, and a number of major changes were introduced in the 'Big Bang' of October 1986. Three important changes were:

- the abolition of the distinction between jobbers and brokers
- the admission of corporate members (i.e. limited companies)
- the cessation of fixed, agreed, minimum commission rates charged by dealers. This had been challenged under the government's restrictive practices legislation (see pages 209–210)

The consequences of Big Bang were considerable. Large financial corporations moved into the stock market. Several were internationally based, and over half of London's brokers became foreign-owned. Some of the strongest became 'market makers', performing the role previously done by jobbers. Computer screens in city offices replaced the floor of the Stock Exchange building for business and deals are now agreed on the telephone at SEAQ (Stock Exchange Automated Quotations) prices displayed on VDUs. A new computerised settlement system, TAURUS, is to be introduced in 1993. Commission rates on large deals fell drastically, to the benefit of large institutional rather than small personal shareholders. The entire set-up became more competitive, forcing some less efficient and less well-capitalised entrants to withdraw – especially after the stock market crash on 'Black Monday' (16 October 1987) when share prices underwent a dramatic fall.

Securities traded on the Stock Exchange include shares and bonds of public companies and securities issued by our own and foreign governments. (Those of the UK government are known as 'gilt-edged' because the likelihood of bankruptcy is virtually nil.) Not every public company's shares are dealt in on the Stock Exchange. To earn the right to a full Stock Exchange quotation, companies must comply with certain rules, including the offer of a minimum proportion of shares to the general public. More than 5,000 securities are quoted on the Stock Exchange. However, to attract smaller, mainly new, companies, an Unlisted Securities Market has operated, with limited success, since 1980. 'Unlisted' is somewhat of a misnomer, but the few hundred listed companies in that market have less exacting requirements to meet for disclosure and frequency of reporting.

Investors wishing to minimise risk can buy shares in investment trust companies, which carry a range of shares. Alternatively they can buy units in a **unit trust**. This is an organisation which holds a portfolio of securities, so that the purchaser of a unit participates in the benefits and risks attaching to all the shares in the portfolio. These units are attractive to small savers and can be bought and sold in small denominations and with a minimum of formality without necessarily going through the Stock Exchange. There is, however, no way of entirely avoiding the risk that attaches to shareholding, which can bring both profit and loss. A common

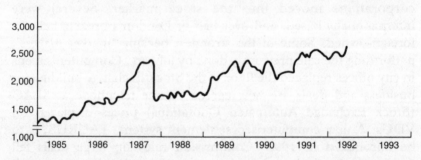

Figure 2.2 Prices of ordinary shares 1985–1992, *Financial Times* 100 index
Source: *Lloyds Bank Economic Bulletin,* June 1992

measuring rod of average price movements in the market is calculated and published by the *Financial Times* in its 'FT 100' share index, based on the price movements of the largest hundred UK registered companies (measured by the market value of their share capital) – nicknamed 'Footsie'. The course of the FT 100 since 1984 is charted in Figure 2.2. The general trend of the FT 100 index can be seen as upwards. However, there have been downward movements, occasionally sharp ones, such as on 'Black Monday' in October 1987. Thus, a lot of money can be lost (and made) by people who do not hold their shares for long, but buy and sell speedily.

Short-term investors, or 'speculators', are known as **'bulls'**, **'bears'** and **'stags'**. Bulls expect price rises; they buy shares now, hoping for prices to increase later. Bears expect price falls; they agree on a price now at which they are to sell shares in the future. Note, they do not own the shares at this point, but hope to buy them at a lower price before the contract to deliver becomes due. Stags apply for issues of *new* shares, when they expect the market price will turn out to be higher when trading begins than the price at which they are initially offered for sale. Thus, they contract to buy forthcoming issues of shares at a fixed price, hoping to sell later at a profit.

The control of joint stock companies

The standard economic theory of the firm is based on the assumption that businesses seek to maximise their profits. The proposition has some intuitive appeal in the case of small firms, where the owners run their businesses, but a major criticism of the theory centres on the question of who actually controls the firm.

Companies are owned by their shareholders, with whom ultimate control therefore lies. However, this is something of an oversimplification. In order to discover where effective control lies, we must consider three important issues:

- the power of personal and institutional investors
- the role of company managers
- the size distribution of share ownership

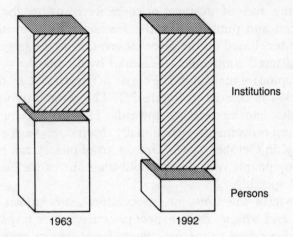

Institutions

Persons

1963   1992

Figure 2.3 The ownership of shares in companies, 1963 and 1992
Source: *Economic Trends*, April 1992

The power of personal and institutional investors

The capitalist system grew up on the basis of the ownership of shares by private individuals. However, as the economy developed, joint stock companies began to appear in the financial as well as the industrial sectors. These were large financial institutions, such as merchant banks, insurance companies and pension funds in the business of managing the funds accumulated to provide pensions for employees on retirement. These institutions came to hold increasing quantities of ordinary shares in British industry, pushing personal investors into a position of much diminished importance.

As Figure 2.3 shows, in 1963 individuals owned over half of the total value of ordinary shares; by 1992, their holdings had dropped to a fifth. The dominant position of financial institutions does not, of course, preclude private individuals from benefiting from the profitability of UK companies. Many benefit *in*directly rather than directly.

Despite the continuing decline in the market share of personal shareholdings measured by *value*, there has been a substantial rise in the *number* of persons owning shares in British companies since

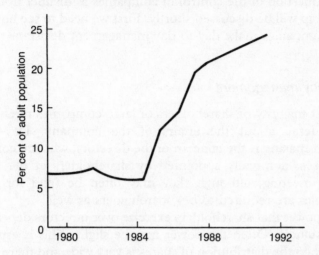

Figure 2.4 Persons holding shares in Britain since 1979
Source: *Economic Briefing 1991*

1980. Around 25 per cent of the adult population were shareholders in 1992 compared to 7 per cent in 1979 (see Figure 2.4). Part of the explanation for this may be the introduction of new tax incentives, but by far the most important influence was the government's privatisation programme. Shares in many of these were made on specially favourable terms for reasons discussed below (see pages 59–62).

Note that institutional shareholders are often large, and although individually they may not own very substantial proportions of the shares in a company, they may have a greater power than this would suggest because all may act collectively. Indeed the greater the number of small shareholders, the greater the influence that a few large institutions may have. For example, in 1992, the eight largest shareholders in Greene King plc owned nearly 38 per cent of the issued capital of the company. Of these, the largest, Britannic Assurance, owned $6\frac{1}{2}$ per cent, and together with five others, who were insurance companies or pension funds, they owned well over a quarter of the total – a figure that might be compared with the $3\frac{1}{2}$ per cent owned by all the directors of the company.

The question of the control of companies as distinct from their ownership will be discussed shortly. First we need to see how joint stock companies make day-to-day management decisions.

Company management

The vast majority of shareholders of large companies rarely know much detail about the affairs of the company. Day-to-day decision-making is the concern of the directors, who are company employees, nominally appointed by shareholders at the annual general meeting, although they may often be (and for public companies are required to be) shareholders as well.

The power that shareholders exercise over directors depends on circumstances. Often the power may be slight. This is especially likely when the distribution of shares is very wide and there are no really large shareholders. It also follows from small attendance at company meetings. Absentee shareholders have the right to appoint 'proxies' to act as agents and cast their votes at meetings. However, directors are well placed to secure proxies. Hence, they may be armed with an overwhelming number of votes and able to control meetings.

Meetings of the directors occur at a 'board', presided over by a chairman and titular head of the company, and another (sometimes the same person) who is chief executive, or managing director. Middle managers, such as the works manager, sales manager and other heads of department, are responsible to the board. Part-time, non-executive, directors are commonly appointed. They are often on the boards of several companies, and it is hoped that they are able to take a detached view of the efficiency of each.

Share ownership and control

Effective control of a company lies in the ownership of the voting shares. 'Industrial democracy' is defined as one vote for every voting share held. Any one shareholder, or group of shareholders, who can raise a majority of votes at company meetings can, therefore, control them.

There is no general rule concerning the minimum percentage of total voting shares which command a controlling interest. It is rare, except in small companies, that as much as 51 per cent is necessary. If ownership is widely diffused, and the majority of small shareholders are absent from a company meeting, the proportion of votes needed for effective control might be as low as 10 per cent. Interestingly, the substantial increase in the *number* of personal shareholders since 1979 (see Figure 2.4) must have increased directors' power, which is, therefore, strong in some of the privatised corporations. Moreover, control of large companies is less often in the hands of a single individual than in those of a group of shareholders acting collectively, related perhaps by family, or by common interest, as in the case of institutional shareholders.

In companies where directors control a large number of voting shares, they may, to an extent, be able to ignore the wishes of outside shareholders. For example, they may concentrate on growth (or maintaining the size) of the company at the expense of profits, in order to protect their jobs and remuneration. Performance-related (i.e. profit-linked) directors' pay reduces that incentive, though it sometimes leads to adverse publicity when directors enjoy very large salary increases.

Note that even when directors can control meetings, they cannot necessarily and persistently ignore the wishes of other shareholders, especially with regard to the level of profits. It might be the case for a company where a single firm or institution holds more than 50 per cent of the voting shares, but it is rare with large public companies.

Boardroom battles can take place, indicating that even the directors are not all of the same mind regarding policy. Ultimately, if the directors fail to operate a company effectively, they have to face the risk that outside interests (individuals, institutions or other companies) may acquire sufficient shares for a controlling interest, enabling them to unseat the existing directors.

Take-over bids

The threat of hostile take-over bids (defined as those not agreed by the current board of directors) may be effective in keeping

Box 2.2

Midland Ready to Fight off Lloyds

Midland Bank has put itself on a war footing for a hostile bid from Lloyds Bank which may be announced in a few days, banking sources revealed last week.

The threat of a bid loomed larger as the Lloyds board met on Friday to discuss an offer, amid continuing City scepticism over the £3.1 bn offer announced a month ago by Hongkong and Shanghai Banking Corporation. A majority of the Lloyds board is thought to have favoured a bid.

As part of its defence plans, Midland has taken legal advice from Clifford Chance, the City's largest law firm, about a possible referral to the Monopolies and Mergers Commission ... S. G. Warburg, which specialises in defending bid targets and is already advising Midland on the HSBC offer, was last week preparing to stave off a Lloyds offer.

Midland has been forced to strengthen its defences against Lloyds after a round of meetings with its leading shareholders last week failed to convince many institutions of the HSBC offer.

The Independent on Sunday, 26 April 1992

The battle between two predators for one of the four large UK banks received plenty of media coverage while the shots were being fired. Readers might like to be reminded that HSBC were the winners, despite the fact that Lloyds had made a 'friendly' approach before hostilities began.

Note the influence of the financial institutions, the threat of reference to the official Monopolies and Mergers Commission (see Chapter 6), and the mention of the merchant bankers S. G.Warburg – few large mergers are entered into without the advice of merchant banks (see Chapter 8).

managers on their toes. From time to time more than one outsider may contest for take-over. When the companies are household names the fight hits the headlines in the press – as it did in 1992 in the case of the Midland Bank where Lloyds Bank and the Hongkong and Shanghai Banking Corporation made competing offers for Midland's shares (see Box 2.2).

Sudden purchases of large quantities of shares can be disruptive and cause great volatility in share prices. This can, in turn, enable large profits to be made in the space of a few days by anyone in a privileged position with inside knowledge of what is going on (e.g.

an employee). Rules have been laid down to try to ensure that the 'game is played on a level playing field', to use the current jargon. This means, for example, that Stock Exchange dealings in shares may be suspended during a period of intense negotiations; and that purchasers are required to offer to buy all the shares in a company as soon as their holdings reach 30 per cent. Regulations aimed at insider trading have also been introduced, though few believe that they could ever be completely effective, and the City has been embarrassed by some large dealings by insiders that have come to light in recent years. The question of take-over bids is discussed again in Chapter 3, in the context of mergers and industrial concentration (see pages 92–3).

Public Sector Business Organisation

The state engages in a range of economic activities, some performed directly by departments of the central and local governments, which we discuss in Chapter 6. Additionally, there are certain industries which have traditionally attracted government intervention. Sometimes this has been because of safety, related to product quality, or to strategic importance. However, a prime reason is that certain markets are not large enough to ensure effective competition, but come to be dominated by natural monopolies. Examples are in power supplies, transport and communication.

Two approaches are possible for such cases. One is to leave the industries in private hands while regulating their activities. This option is discussed in Chapter 6. The second is nationalisation, i.e. for the state itself to own and run the industries.

Nationalised Industries

Nationalisation became a major policy of the UK government between 1945 and 1950, when the Labour Party first came to enjoy a parliamentary majority. Coal, gas, electricity, rail and some road transport industries were added to the public sector, which already included civil airlines, postal and telephonic communications and the BBC. Until 1980, the nationalised industries employed some 2 million workers, representing about 8 per cent of the workforce.

Four Conservative governments, commencing with that led by Margaret Thatcher in 1979, set about a privatisation programme including denationalisation, with the effect that, by 1992, employment in the nationalised sector had fallen to three-quarters of a million, or 3 per cent of the labour force.

Organisation of the nationalised industries

State-owned nationalised industries in the UK have been run by what are known as 'public corporations', closely resembling joint stock companies but without shareholders. They have enjoyed a degree of independence – free from day-to-day interference in the management of their affairs – though responsible to the appropriate minister, and subject to investigation and control by official bodies including the Monopolies and Mergers Commission (see page 207 below).

Unlike many other government activities, the nationalised industries were never intended to be financed from taxation, but to cover all, or the bulk, of their costs by charges. However, capital requirements over and above those generated internally have been supplied by the central government, which can usually borrow on favourable terms. In a few cases nationalised industries have been required to fulfil certain social obligations, e.g. to provide postal services and rail transport to rural areas at less than cost.

Pricing and investment in nationalised industries

Originally, the nationalised industries received little guidance on financial matters, other than to break even over a run of years. This changed after the publication of two White Papers in 1961 and 1967. As a result, prices were recommended to be set to reflect long-run marginal costs, target rates of return were set for individual industries, and a 'test discount rate' was introduced to enable comparisons to be made of the cost of capital between the public and private sectors.

The application of marginal cost pricing follows conclusions drawn from economic theory on optimal resource allocation. Marginal cost pricing is a system whereby consumers of each product pay for the cost of providing it. This avoids any cross-subsidisation, so that profits made in one line of activity are not used to allow another to be carried on at a loss.

Marginal cost pricing was widely adopted, sometimes with unpopular results, e.g. in the gas industry, where it resulted in the earning of substantial short-run profits, justifiable in terms of the need to conserve an energy source, expected to be in long-term short supply. The pricing policy, however, was not always strictly applied, but allowed to lapse when it seriously interfered with other policy goals, especially the control of inflation.

A final development in the provision of financial guidelines for the nationalised industries followed the publication of a third White Paper, in 1978, which endorsed the general commercial approach of its predecessors and recommended the setting of financial targets for 3–5 years ahead and the adoption of a 'required rate of return' (RRR) in real terms (i.e. allowing for inflation). It also introduced a new control, the 'external financing limit' (EFL), to limit the sums raised externally.

Privatisation

As explained earlier, most of the nationalised industries have been transferred to private ownership as part of the privatisation programme of Conservative governments since 1979. Other privatisation measures are discussed in later chapters (see especially Chapter 6).

Several methods of transference to private ownership have been used. For example, the Rover Group was sold to the already privatised British Aerospace, and National Freight was sold to its employees. However, by far the most common privatisation route has been by public issue of shares in newly created plcs. Share offers have usually been on favourable terms, enabling purchasers to enjoy a profit, sometimes a substantial one, from quick resale (by 'stagging' the issues, see above page 51) – e.g. British

Table 2.2 Privatisation: major sales of public sector assets since 1981

Year*	Company	Business	Sales proceeds (approx.) (£mn)
1981	British Aerospace	aerospace	400
	Cable and Wireless	telecommunications	1,000
1982	National Freight	road haulage	10
	Britoil	oil	1,050
1983	Associated British Ports	seaports	100
	British Rail Hotels	hotels	50
1984	Enterprise Oil	oil	400
	Sealink Ferries	cross-channel ferries	70
	Jaguar cars	cars	300
	British Telecom	telecommunications	3,900
	British Technology Group	miscellaneous	700
1986	British Gas	gas	5,400
	National Bus Co.	passenger transport	40
1987	British Airways	civil airline	850
	Rolls-Royce	aero-engines	1,000
	British Airport Authority	airports	1,200
1988	British Steel	steel	1,200
	Rover	cars	150
1989	Regional Water Authorities	water	5,200
1990	Regional Electricity Cos.	electricity distribution	⎫
to	Powergen and National Power	electricity generation	⎬ 7,400
1991	Scottish Power and Hydroelectric	electricity generation	3,000
1993 and later	British Rail British Coal Post Office		

*Year when shares first offered

Telecom, British Airways, Rolls-Royce and the electricity company shares, for instance, could be sold at over 50 per cent more than the price paid for them. Holding on to the shares has, however been shown to have been more profitable on average than stagging.[3] Privatisation sales have generally been supported by national advertising campaigns.

The government has been, at times, in a dilemma about how to privatise. On the one hand, selling public utilities as single units, retaining some of their monopoly powers, helps ensure success and maximise revenue from issues. On the other hand, breaking up monopolies before sale should promote efficiency by increasing competition.

Table 2.2 lists the principal industries involved. Figures in the right-hand column are of the monetary values of assets sold. They give an approximate idea of the sizes of individual industries. Note, the table excludes certain 'privatisation' sales such as the government's shares in British Petroleum, and shares in the Trustees Savings Bank, which were never nationalised industries in the sense that the term has been used in this book. However, it includes a number of industries which, though not run as independent public corporations, were none the less state-run businesses. These came into the public sector for special reasons – e.g. unintentionally acquired because they happened to be subsidiary companies of major industries, such as British Rail's Hotels, or because they were temporarily taken over in order to help key industries in short-term financial difficulties, e.g. Rolls-Royce aero-engines.

Privatisation plans for the future are shown at the foot of the Table. In the case of British Rail, it seems uncertain at the time of writing (January 1993) how far the government will proceed with its 'semi-privatisation' programme, as it has been described by prime minister John Major. The intention appears to be to sell off freight operations outright, while offering franchises (see below) to private operators to run passenger services for specific routes on the state-owned track. Successful applicants should be eligible for

3 Note (i) many applicants were allotted only a few shares and (ii) figures in the text ignore dealing costs. See also P. Curwen and D. Holmes, 'Returns to Small Shareholders from Privatisation', *National Westminster Bank Quarterly Review*, February 1992.

government subsidies on social grounds for certain unprofitable lines, e.g. in rural areas. However, the objective of securing effective competition among franchisees is unlikely to materialise unless sufficient private businesses come forward who are prepared to accept open access to their routes from rival firms. Some commentators expressed doubts about this important aspect of the programme, which could persuade the government to revise its proposals as they go through parliament in 1993.

Parcel services of the Post Office are also on the list for privatisation. The coal industry is another matter. At nationalisation, in 1947, there were more than three-quarters of a million workers in the industry. By 1992, the labour force numbered a mere 50,000, and is planned to fall to less than half that figure.

In so far as changes in ownership created privately owned in place of state-owned monopolies, new regulatory bodies have in some cases been set up (e.g. OFTEL, OFGAS and OFWAT). These are discussed in Chapter 6 (see page 213).

Market structures

This chapter has dealt mainly with the institutional framework within which private and public sector businesses make decisions. Economic theory tells us, however, that the behaviour of a firm is affected also by the kind of market in which it operates – in particular, by the number of firms in the industry and the type of product sold, both of which influence the degree of competition.

We shall look at the size and concentration of firms in Chapter 3, but we may say now, in anticipation, that it is not easy to generalise about the degree of competition. The power that a firm can exercise over price, however, can be associated with market structure. Some structures allow the firm to set its own price while others make the firm a price taker, responding to the market forces of supply and demand. Figure 2.5 shows the course of prices for two contrasting products which typify the extreme cases – a popular model of car and silver, a primary product with industrial and monetary uses.

Within the car industry individual manufacturers enjoy a degree of monopoly power arising from the special features of their models, whether real or imagined by buyers. Within limits,

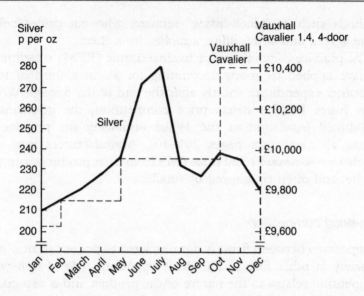

Figure 2.5 Average monthly prices of a Vauxhall Cavalier and an ounce of silver

Sources: *Autocar* and *The Times* (The prices are those of 1991, but are typical of any year)

therefore, the industry is able to set prices for itself. **Administered pricing**, as it is called, can be contrasted with the behaviour of suppliers of many primary products, where the material is homogeneous and there are many producers. One such product is silver, the world price of which fluctuates with changes in supply and demand. Figure 2.5 shows that the price of silver is much more volatile than that of the administratively set Vauxhall Cavalier.

Note, the power of individual manufacturers may extend beyond fixing their own selling prices to setting minimum prices below which retailers, who are their customers, may not resell their products. Price setting may appeal to shopkeepers in so far as it protects them from price competition from other shops. It is not surprising that many manufacturers, acting partly in their own interests and partly in response to requests from retailers, long ago took steps to ensure that their products were sold everywhere at the same price. General conformity to fixed prices used often to be maintained by collective agreement between the appropriate trade associations of manufacturers and distributors, reinforced by methods such as 'black-listing' retailers who cut prices below those agreed and withholding supplies from them.

The practice of **resale price maintenance** (RPM) is estimated to have applied to goods accounting for about a third of total consumer expenditure shortly after the end of the Second World War. Since RPM restricts price competition, the government introduced legislation in the 1960s outlawing the practice in almost all cases (see pages 209–10). Manufacturers may still attach a *recommended* retail price (MRP) to their products, but this can be, and often is, ignored by retailers.

Non-price competition

Competition between firms is not restricted to prices but may take a variety of other forms. The most important type of non-price competition relates to the nature of the product and is associated with advertising, which can increase sales in two ways:

- by spreading information about the existence of a commodity
- by persuading people that an article is worth buying

The way in which persuasion is achieved is not important from the viewpoint of advertisers. Whether you are induced to buy, say, a particular brand of detergent because you are told it contains a substance which has been 'proved' to wash whiter or whether it is because you have seen a picture of a television personality using it, the effect on sales of that detergent may be much the same. The tendency to emphasise persuasion is at the back of much of the criticism continually levelled at advertising. On the other hand, the provision of information, especially about new products, is valuable and may help to build sales to the point where costs begin to fall.

The scale of advertising in Britain, after a period of fairly steady growth, seems to have settled at a level representing around 2 per cent of total consumer expenditure. Most advertising is by manufacturers directed at final consumers, but some is organised by retailers. The press is the most important single medium. In fact, revenue from advertisements is a larger source of income for many newspapers than proceeds from sales.

Questions and exercises

(For key to abbreviations indicating sources, see pages xv–xvi)

1   From the yellow pages of your local phone book, estimate the proportion of the total number of businesses that are limited companies under the following heads: (a) dressmakers, (b) furniture manufacturers, (c) garages, (d) paint manufacturers. How different would you expect your results to be if you had access to figures of the value of sales?

2   For last year collect data relating to large companies' (i) gross trading profits, (ii) dividends paid, (iii) interest paid, (iv) retained profits. Calculate (i), (ii) and (iii) as percentages of (iv). Compare your results with Figure 2.1. (*AS*)

3   From *The Times 1000*, select 15 UK companies among the top 50 ranked by the value of turnover. Rerank them by the value of capital and consider reasons for any differences you find.

4   Using the list of companies in question 3, find out the price of the ordinary shares of each, yesterday and a year ago. If you had invested £1,000 each, would you have shown a profit compared to (i) leaving the money under the mattress, (ii) placing it on deposit with a building society or (iii) the FT 100 share index? (Ignore dealing costs.)

5   Suppose you had invested £250 in each of any five privatised companies listed in Table 2.2 over the same period as in question 4. How profitable would your investment have been compared to the options in question 4?

6   Obtain a copy of the annual balance sheet and profit and loss account of two local or national plcs. (Your public library probably has a selection, or you can write to the company secretary, address in the *Stock Exchange Official Yearbook*). Calculate the proportion of total costs that appear fixed in the two cases. Would the proportions be the same if the accounts were for a half-year only?

Appendix 2

Table A2.1 Retail trade by form of organisation

	Businesses	Outlets	Persons engaged	Retail turnover (inclusive of VAT)
	Number	Number	Thousand	£ million
Total retail trade	242,288	350,013	2,440	118,569
Single outlet retailers	215,613	215,613	837	32,702
Small multiple retailers	25,779	67,678	319	13,976
Large multiple retailers	895	66,522	1,284	71,892
of which				
Co-operative societies accounted for	90	4,691	100	4,200

Source: *Annual Abstract of Statistics*

Table A2.2 Securities quoted on the Stock Exchange

	1981	1986	1991
Total of all securities at market values	375,931	1,247,580	2,195,213
British government and government guaranteed stocks			
Nominal values	85,384	128,850	118,702
Market values	76,079	138,417	121,183
Company securities			
Total	211,267	907,302	1,922,919
Loan capital	3,803	8,680	14,129
Preference and preferred capital	1,836	5,510	32,916
Ordinary and deferred capital	205,628	893,112	1,875,872

Source: *Annual Abstract of Statistics*

Table A2.3 Allocation of income of companies

	1987	1988	1989	1990	1991
Dividend and interest payments:					
Dividends on ordinary and preference shares	11,047	14,984	18,569	20,542	22,093
Interest on building society shares and deposits	12,024	12,817	17,547	20,492	19,837
Other interest	13,113	16,564	27,556	37,242	35,266
Total	36,184	44,365	63,672	78,276	77,196
Current transfers to charities	160	200	284	299	288
Miscellaneous current transfers	24	32	40	35	26
Profits due abroad (net of United Kingdom tax)	7,014	8,611	9,157	6,901	5,721
United Kingdom taxes on income:					
Advance corporation tax	4,869	5,693	6,782	7,661	7,794
Other payments	10,876	12,232	15,290	13,660	9,469
Total UK taxes on income	15,745	17,925	22,072	21,321	17,263
Royalties and licence fees on oil and gas production	1,151	823	556	654	561
Balance: undistributed income after taxation	49,604	50,376	49,240	47,083	44,092
Total	109,882	122,332	145,021	154,569	145,167

Source: *Annual Abstract of Statistics*

3
Structure of British Industry

This chapter deals with the following aspects of UK industrial structure:[1]

- sectors of national output
- productivity
- regional location of industry
- industrial concentration

National Output

Figure 3.1 shows the main industrial groups in the UK in 1991. It confirms the dominance, noted in Chapter 1, of the tertiary (service) sector, which is substantially larger than the combined sums of the other two sectors – secondary (manufacturing and construction) and primary (agriculture and energy), which together account for about two-thirds of total national output. The principal components of national output are shown in Figure 3.1.

1 The structure of industry is the result of market forces and government intervention. For exposition of the economic theory relating to topics discussed in this chapter see Lipsey–Harbury, FP2, Chapters 16–18.

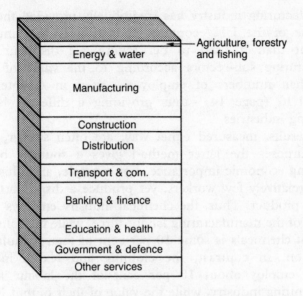

Figure 3.1 Value of national output 1991
Source: *UK National Accounts*

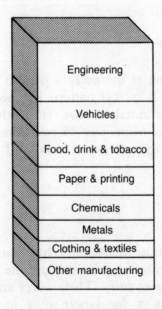

Figure 3.2 Manufacturing production 1991
Source: *UK National Accounts*

Manufacturing industry has traditionally provided the industrial base of the UK economy, though it is very much less dominant than it used to be. Figure 3.2 distinguishes the manufacturing sub-sectors according to the value of output, rather than numbers of employees – used in Chapter 1 for Figure 1.10 (page 14) – thus providing a different basis for comparing industries.

The results, measured either way, are often similar, but for some purposes the latter method gives a sounder basis for comparing economic importance. For example, an industry may employ relatively few workers, yet produce a disproportionately valuable product. Thus, the chemical industry employs about 6 per cent of the manufacturing labour force, while the value of the output of chemicals is some 10 per cent of total manufacturing production. In contrast, the clothing and textile industries together employ about 10 per cent of the labour force in manufacturing industry, while the value of their output is nearer to 6 per cent of the total.

Industrial Change

In addition to looking at the current pattern of production, we should observe also how this pattern has been changing. One significant and substantial change is of the decline of the manufacturing sector, from over 35 per cent of total output in 1950 to barely more than 20 per cent in 1991. See Figure 3.3.

Deindustrialisation

The process of 'deindustrialisation', has caused great concern among some commentators, who deplore the destruction of the industrial heart of the country. Their worry arises partly because manufacturing plays a far larger part in exports than in production, and partly because employment in manufacturing has fallen much more than has output of that sector. Hence, they

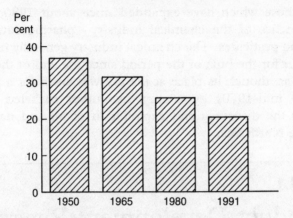

Figure 3.3 Manufacturing output as a share of total domestic production, selected years since 1950
Source: *UK National Accounts*

see deindustrialisation as a cause both of balance of payments problems and of rising unemployment.

Not everyone is alarmed by the undisputed trend. Some rely heavily on the power of market forces which, arguably, should allow sectors to prosper or decline depending on what is happening to cost and demand conditions. They point out that the greater fall in employment than in output in manufacturing is simply the result of productivity rising faster in manufacturing than in the rest of the economy. Moreover, the falling share of manufacturing in total output is not unique to the UK, but has been experienced in other industrialised nations. In the 30 years from 1960, for example, that share fell in France, Germany, Italy and Japan, though to a significantly lesser extent in those countries than in the UK. The explanation for the UK's differential experience is, at least in part, put down to the special opportunities available to the UK for exploitation of oil and gas in the North Sea in the 1970s.

Expanding and contracting industries

While manufacturing industry, as a whole, has been declining, we can pick out sectors which rose or fell in relative importance.

Among those which have expanded since about 1980, we may note branches of the chemical industry – pharmaceutical, cosmetics and pesticides. The chemical industry generally has been a pace setter for the bulk of the period since the end of the Second World War, though its place at the top was taken for a few years from the mid-1970s by energy, as output rocketed upwards following the discovery and exploitation of oil and natural gas under the North Sea.

Box 3.1

Product Development Rewritten

Many of Britain's companies are wasting millions of pounds on R & D and restricting their growth by following outdated product development strategies, according to one report emerging from ESRC's research initiative on the Competitiveness and Regeneration of British Industry. . . .

One of the hallmarks of this new breed of companies is the willingness to create new markets. Canon's entry into the copier market is an outstanding example. At the time, Xerox was king, selling high value copiers direct to offices through a large sales force. Canon spotted a need for cheap, simple and reliable copiers which it could sell through retailers, sidestepping the Xerox sales machine. Canon developed these copiers and went on to grab a large share of the market. It did not try to fight head-on with Xerox, which would have involved a huge and probably fruitless R & D commitment. All it had to do was redefine the market and develop a cheaper product with minimal R & D expenditure.

Annual Report of the Economic and Social Research Council 1990–1991

Industrial change is often, rightly, attributed to changes in costs of production or to changes in demand. This reference to recent research by Professor Johne of City University highlights a different reason.

Among expanding sectors, the following are worthy of mention – electrical, electronic and instrument engineering, including computers for industrial and domestic use and data-processing equipment; aerospace, including satellite equipment, reflecting growing demand in the area of communications and travel; paper and printing; and non-ferrous metals and alloys.

Among industries which have, in contrast, contracted in relative terms are textiles, clothing and motor vehicles, where British industry has suffered from intense competition from foreign producers, but has to some extent been saved by embarking on joint ventures with Japanese car manufacturers, such as Nissan.

Finally, take note of the food, drink and tobacco industry, which tends to keep pace with the average growth rate of industry as a whole as, of course, do many sub-sectors of major groups.

Productivity

Expansion in the volume of output in an industry can be traced to one of two causes:

- increases in the supply of factors of production
- increases in productivity

Increasing productivity (due to improvements in techniques of production) has been a major source of rising living standards in most industrial countries for a very long time. Even an apparently modest rate of increase of output per person of 2 per cent per annum leads to a doubling of output every 35 years, without a rise in the size of the labour force.

The most common way of measuring productivity is by dividing output by the number of employees to give a figure of output per head. Trends in this statistic must be treated with caution because both the numerator and the denominator of the fraction may be hard to interpret. For example, variations in hours worked is an alternative denominator to – in some ways a better one than – numbers of employees. Moreover, quantifying the output numerator is particularly hard for some service trades.

Productivity growth in the UK was sluggish in the 1960s and 1970s but grew rapidly in the 1980s, as Figure 3.4 shows. The reasons for the observed trends are not fully understood. However, a prominent contributory explanation is the decline in the size of the labour force in manufacturing, which we noted earlier. The reduction in overstaffing, which had been a feature of

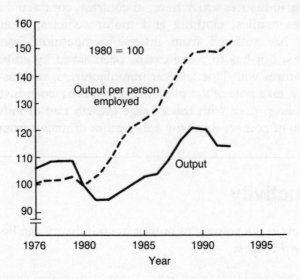

Figure 3.4 Manufacturing output and output per employee since 1976
Source: *Monthly Digest of Statistics*

the two decades prior to 1980, and a more rapid growth in output from 1982 to 1989, were major determinants of the rise in manufacturing output per employee. It must be remembered, too, that overall productivity accompanies changes in the pattern of production, e.g. it rises when high productivity sectors expand at the expense of those where productivity is relatively low.

Productivity varies from industry to industry, partly because of differences in capital investment and the scope for the application of new technology. Computerisation, for example, is more easily applied to the chemical industry than to the services of hairdressers or lawyers.

One component of investment expenditure of particular importance in promoting productivity growth is that on R & D (Research and Development). Less than 2 per cent of UK national product goes on R & D, though about a quarter of this is spent in the field of military defence. R & D expenditure in manufacturing accounts for 80 per cent of the total. Figure 3.5 shows its distribution. Note that a relatively few industries are responsible for a disproportionate amount of the work – electronics, chemi-

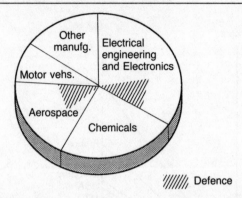

Figure 3.5 Research and development expenditure, manufacturing industry, 1989
Source: *Annual Abstract of Statistics*

cals and aerospace make up about three-quarters of the total. R & D tends to be concentrated in large firms which can afford the high costs involved in modern technological research, not to mention willingness to accept the risks of failure. However, small firms have been responsible for some major innovations.

International comparisons of productivity are instructive and quite commonly attempted. Care must be taken when making them that, as far as possible, one is comparing like with like. A recent careful study found labour productivity in German manufacturing industry to be just over 20 per cent higher than that in the UK.[2] Germany's superiority was greatest in non-electrical engineering, vehicles and metals, and least in food, drink and tobacco and textiles. The differential advantage to Germany was greater in the 1970s, but the gap narrowed in the 1980s. Similar patterns are suggested for comparisons between the UK and other countries as a result of improved economic performance by the UK and a slackening by others in the last decade. Figure 3.6 contrasts the growth over two decades of output per employee of the UK with that of the major industrial countries of France, Germany, Japan and the USA.

2   M. O'Mahony, 'Productivity Levels in British and German Manufacturing Industry', *National Institute Economic Review*, 1992.

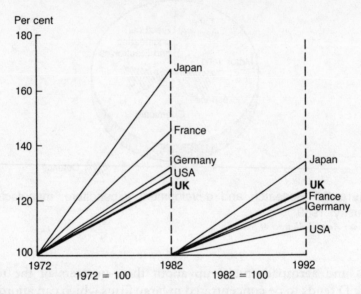

Figure 3.6 Productivity in manufacturing output per employee, 1972–1982, output per employee-hour, 1982–1992, in selected countries

Source: *National Institute Economic Review*

It must be appreciated that measures of productivity of the kind on which Figure 3.6 is based reflect complex factors, including the amount of capital investment, R & D expenditure, the scale of output, and industrial relations.

The level of investment can usefully be expressed as a percentage of the value of total output, as is done in Figure 3.7, which compares the UK with a selection of countries in 1991. The comparison is unfavourable, as it has typically been for many years. British R & D expenditure tends to run at a lower rate than that of Japan and Germany, though closer to France.

Productivity in the Short Term

So far we have discussed long-term trends. Productivity also fluctuates in the short term. Output per person tends to fall at the beginning of downturns in economic activity as firms hold on to

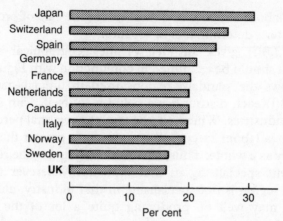

Figure 3.7 Investment as a percentage of GDP 1991, selected countries
Source: *International Financial Statistics*

labour, dismissing the workforce only when the decline in sales is perceived to be lasting. In contrast, productivity typically rises at the start of upturns in output for the opposite reason, as employment rises only some time after increases in output. This pattern is not always strongly exhibited. If you look, however, at Figure 3.4, you may observe falling output per employee in 1990 when the recession began to bite.

The Location of Industry

Economic theory tells us that profit-maximising firms tend to locate their businesses where costs are lowest relative to revenues. This basic underlying principle is relevant to the geographical distribution of industry in the UK, although it needs to be applied in the context of government regional policy (discussed in Chapter 6).

We know something of the regional distribution of the population from Chapter 1 (see pages 5–8). This gives a first approximation to the location of industry too, since the need to be near both labour supplies and markets for the sale of products are two important determinants of location.

Figure 3.8(i) gives an idea of the geographical spread of industry. It should be examined in conjunction with Figure 3.8(ii), which shows the standard regions used in official statistics. In Figure 3.8(i) each district has a column to itself, with spaces for the main industries. Where a • appears, the regional percentage of the total area labour force in that industry is greater than that for the country as a whole. Thus, wherever there is a •, the region is to some extent specialising in that industry. Wherever there is a blank, the region is not specialising in that industry, although, of course, it may well be producing quite a lot of the goods in question.

Northern England

Centred on Tyneside, the Northern region of England used to be particularly dependent on the heavy industries of coal, iron and steel, shipbuilding and chemicals. Forty per cent of the male labour force is still employed in energy and manufacturing, which is now more diversified.

Yorkshire and Humberside

This is another diversified manufacturing region. Its specialisations include chemicals, metal manufacture and textiles.

Midlands

The Midlands is divided into West and East divisions, the former being substantially the larger. Both are relatively heavily concentrated in manufacturing. Both also specialise in metal manufacture. West Midlands is the more important in the field of engineering, including (road) vehicles, much of the heavier sections of which are in what used to be called the 'Black Country' around Birmingham and Wolverhampton. East Midlands industry tends to be lighter and includes more clothing, textiles, and food, drink and tobacco. The East Midlands also has

	Northern England	Yorks & Humberside	East Midlands	East Anglia	South East	South West	West Midlands	North West	Wales	Scotland	Northern Ireland
Agriculture, forestry, fishing			•	•		•			•	•	•
Energy & water supply	•	•	•						•	•	
MANUFACTURING											
Metal manufacturing & chemicals	•	•	•				•	•	•		
Metal goods, engineering and vehicles	•		•			•	•		•		
Other manufacturing		•	•	•				•		•	•
Construction	•	•							•	•	•
SERVICES											
Distribution, hotels and catering			•	•		•					
Transport & communication			•	•							
Banking & finance				•							
Public administration & other services	•			•					•	•	•

Figure 3.8(i) Regional specialisation

Source: *Regional Trends*

Figure 3.8(ii) UK standard regions

a sizeable agricultural sector, as well as taking in the coalfields of Derbyshire and Nottinghamshire.

East Anglia

East Anglia's workforce of three-quarters of a million makes it the smallest region in Great Britain, but the proportion of its labour force in agriculture (over 4 per cent) is the highest after Northern Ireland (which is the smallest region in the UK). East Anglia has a fair share of manufacturing industry of various kinds, especially food processing, and is an important tourist area.

South East

The South East employs over a third of the entire UK labour force. It includes London, which concentrates predominantly on non-manufacturing – hence the specialisation in banking and finance, as many offices of banks, insurance companies and other financial institutions are in the City. London is the pivot of road and rail networks, and the site of many government departments.

The South East is also an important producer in agriculture, engineering and vehicles and employs more than the national average of its workforce in distribution, public administration and other services, which include education and health.

South West

The South West employs more workers in agriculture than any other region, and is second only to East Anglia in being relatively heavily specialised in that sector. Like East Anglia, its industry includes food processing. The industrial centre is Bristol, where engineering and aerospace equipment flourish, while the region's coastal resorts account for the high employment in hotels, catering and distribution.

The North West

The North West, encompassing Manchester and Liverpool, is the second largest region in the UK. It is also strongly industrial, specialising in many of the major manufacturing sectors, especially chemicals. Textiles, the region's traditional strength, has long been overshadowed by other industries, including engineering, much of it heavy.

Wales

Wales is sparsely populated and largely mountainous. However, it has more than the national average percentage of workers in agriculture. South Wales used to be a major coal mining area, although only a very small percentage of the labour force remains in that industry now. Wales specialises in metal manufacture and chemicals, but iron and steel has been on the decline for several years. The range of manufacturing industry has, however, been widening to include engineering, plastics and clothing. Decentralisation of government departments explains some of the specialisation in public administration.

Scotland

Scotland is larger than Wales and has double its workforce. It is also sparsely populated and mountainous. Scotland's agricultural specialisation is less marked than other regions mentioned above in terms of the proportion of employees in that industry. Industry is centred on Glasgow, and exploitation of North Sea oil and gas accounts for the specialisation in energy.

Northern Ireland

Northern Ireland has the smallest labour force of any region in the UK – about half a million – but is the most highly specialised in agriculture. Industry is diversified, and includes food processing, clothing and textiles. The region has, of course, suffered for many years from political unrest, which has not helped the economy, and the unemployment rate is the highest in the UK.

Changes in Location

We have discussed regional specialisation as it exists in the UK today. To understand the reasons for the present pattern, it is necessary to go back to the earlier part of this century, because there has been considerable redeployment of industry among the various parts of the country. The decades between the two world wars were outstanding, and witnessed a striking growth in the relative importance of Southern England and the Midlands at the expense of Northern England, Merseyside, South Wales and Scotland.

Two major factors account for these changes. In the first place, industrialists tended to move southwards when erecting new factories because they were attracted by the growing market of Greater London. Moreover, the development of electricity as a source of power released them from the need to be near coalfields. The second explanation is the one that carries more weight. As we saw earlier, not all industries were expanding at the same rate. Some were, in fact, declining. Most of the expanding new twentieth-century industries, such as engineering, vehicles and electrical goods, were those in which the South and the Midlands were specialising, while the staple industries of the nineteenth century, especially textiles, coal and shipbuilding, largely

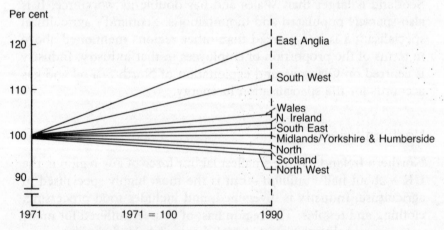

Figure 3.9 Regional population changes, 1971–1990
Source: *Regional Trends*

concentrated in the North of England, Scotland and South Wales, were declining in importance.

The period since the end of the Second World War saw a continuation of the same broad trends, modified by the fact that some of the older 'new' industries began to be replaced by other new ones. The influence of the government's regional policy can also be observed in the changing scene post-1945, especially with regard to stemming the growth in the South East. (See pages 214–15) Figure 3.9 shows the regions which gained and which lost population in the 20 years after 1971. It may be compared with the longer term trends, since 1911, in Figure 1.6.

Industrial Concentration

One of the outstanding features of industrial development since the nineteenth century has been the growth in the size of firms and the increasing concentration of industry in large enterprises.[3] The days when the bulk of output was produced by a large number of small businesses have disappeared. The typical unit is still small but in many industries today output is typically in the hands of giant corporations.

Two of the reasons for this development are of special importance. First, costs per unit of output commonly fall as production expands, therefore favouring larger firms. The second determinant is market power, which leads a firm (or small group of firms) to dominate an industry. In such cases, the firm does not have to accept market price as given, but may be able to manipulate price by controlling output and/or stifling innovations which threaten the demand for its product. A third reason for expansion is to diversify – to spread risks by being in several markets.

---

3 The theoretical issues dealt with in the rest of this chapter are examined in Lipsey–Harbury, FP2, Chapters 17–18.

The Size of Manufacturing Units

A single firm may control one or more companies by owning a controlling interest in the other's voting shares (see Chapter 2, pages 56–7). Such a firm is called an 'enterprise' in the census of production. We leave for the moment the size distribution of controlling business enterprises and begin our discussion at the lower level of companies, whether independent or owned by others. These may operate one or more factories, or plants, and are known as **manufacturing units** in the census of production.[4]

The size distribution of manufacturing units is shown in Figure 3.10. Over 150,000 units operated in UK manufacturing in 1991. Together they employed $4\frac{3}{4}$ million workers. The vast majority of units were small. Two-thirds employed fewer than 10 workers each, and 90 per cent less than 50 workers. The important role played by large units, however, is emphasised by the fact that the

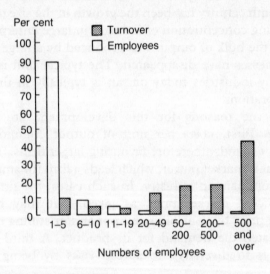

Figure 3.10 Size of business units in manufacturing, UK, 1989
Source: *Economic Trends*, February 1992

4   Prior to 1987, the official reporting unit was the 'establishment', often equivalent to a single company, but sometimes a part of a larger, multi-plant, company located at a single site. Note, too, that census of production statistics are based on forms sent only to firms employing 20 or more workers.

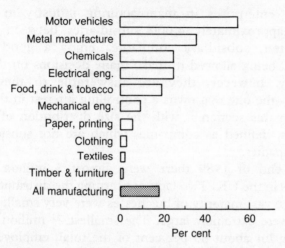

Figure 3.11 Large manufacturing units, UK 1991. Shares of total employment in units with 1,000 or more workers
Source: *Annual Abstract of Statistics*

1 per cent of the total number of companies at the top end of the scale, each of which had 500 or more workers on its payroll, were together responsible for 30 per cent of total employment.

Consider, now, Figure 3.11, which shows that large-scale production is more common in some industries than in others. We see a prime example of large-scale industry in motor vehicles (and other transport equipment), where large units are responsible for the employment of over half of the labour force. In metal manufacture large units account for more than a third of total employment; in chemicals and electrical engineering for about a quarter. The Figure shows, however, that there are industries, such as timber and furniture, textiles and clothing, paper and printing, and even mechanical engineering, where large units are relatively uncommon.

The Size of Business Enterprises

The concentration of industry in large manufacturing units is, as we have seen, considerable. However, a business **enterprise** may own several subsidiary companies. For example, the very largest (top 100) enterprises in manufacturing industry in the UK operated approximately 4,000 subsidiaries between them in 1990. Often, subsidiary companies enjoy a good deal of autonomy, being allowed to make many decisions on their own. Ultimately, however, they are answerable to their parent company – the one that owns a controlling interest in them. Our concern in this section is with the size distribution of business enterprises, defined as companies which are not subsidiaries of other companies.

At the end of 1989 there were almost 3 million business enterprises in the UK. Two facts concerning the distribution stand out: (1) the vast majority of businesses were very small; (2) a few business were extremely large. The smallest $2\frac{1}{2}$ million of them, accounting for about 85 per cent of the total, employed five or fewer workers, but were responsible for less than 10 per cent of the total sales value of turnover. In contrast, the largest 1,000 giant corporations accounted for a tiny fraction of 1 per cent of the total, but were responsible for over 30 per cent of the value of turnover.

Consider now Figure 3.12, which is based on the census of production for 1990 (and therefore excludes the very smallest

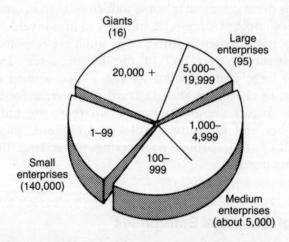

Figure 3.12 Concentration in business enterprises, 1990. Shares of total manufacturing output by enterprises of different size (figures in brackets indicate number of enterprises)

Source: *Census of Production, Summary Tables*, Business Monitor PA 1002

businesses). It must not be confused with Figure 3.10, which relates to manufacturing units.

The concentration of business in large enterprises is particularly marked in the manufacturing sector. Among the very largest businesses were 111 each employing 5,000 or more workers, accounting for almost 40 per cent of the total value of output. At the very top of the tree were 16 megagiant empires, each with 20,000 or more workers on the payroll and producing nearly a quarter of total manufacturing output.

The degree of concentration in individual industries varies as much when we take enterprises as our unit as when we take manufacturing units. Figure 3.13 illustrates some of the differences. It shows, for selected industries, the shares of the five largest enterprises in total sales, known as **concentration ratios** (CRS).

The wide range of CRSs shown – from 9 to 99 per cent – is just one way of depicting the extent of differences in concentration. Thus, while there are highly concentrated industries, such as

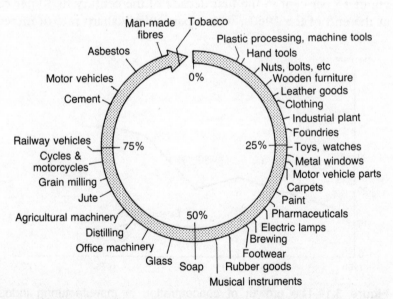

Figure 3.13 Concentration ratios, selected industries, UK, 1990. Percentage of total net output by the five largest enterprises (the percentage for each industry is measured separately, clockwise from the 12 o'clock origin)
Source: *Census of Production, Summary Tables,* Business Monitor PA 1002

tobacco, man-made fibres and asbestos, there are others, such as wooden furniture, nuts and bolts, hand and machine tools and processing of plastic, where the share of the largest five enterprises is much lower. It must be remembered that Figure 3.13 is confined to selected industries. It can, therefore, be used for illustrative purposes only. Moreover, comparisons must be treated with caution. Measured concentration is sensitive to how an industry is defined – the more narrowly the limits are drawn, the higher the degree of measured concentration.

The growth of firms

Attention has so far focused on the present extent of concentration in UK industry. We should also look at trends. Figure 3.14 shows the history of the share of the largest 100 enterprises in total manufacturing output since 1900. We can see that the degree of overall concentration is much higher nowadays than it used to be. The share of the 100 giant manufacturing enterprises rose from about 15 per cent in the first decade of the century to 40 per cent at the end of the 1960s, with a particularly sharp rate of increase

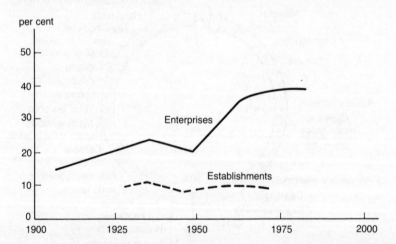

Figure 3.14 The growth of concentration in manufacturing industry since 1911 (share of the largest 100 enterprises and largest 100 establishments in total output)
Sources: *The Evolution of Giant Firms in Britain*, S J Prais (Cambridge University Press, 1981) and *Economic Trends* August 1992

after the Second World War. Since 1970 the level of overall concentration appears to have more or less stabilised.

It is instructive to compare the rising share of the top 100 enterprises with that of the same number of largest establishments, i.e. factories or plants. (The latter data are shown only for the shorter period when concentration among enterprises was rising.) The contrast between the two series is marked. While concentration in giant companies was proceeding most rapidly, the share of the largest establishments was virtually constant, at around 10 per cent. This strongly suggests that, whatever the cause of the increase in concentration, it was not substantially due to firms taking advantage of economies of scale associated with large plants.

The observed trend in overall concentration is broadly matched by changes in concentration within sectors; as far as the time pattern is concerned, however, the size of increases in concentration has been rather less sharp. The postwar decade of most rapid concentration growth was the 1960s. According to one study, average CR3[5] in a sample of 42 industries was 29, 32 and 41 per cent in 1951, 1958 and 1968 respectively. Thereafter, sectoral concentration stabilised, even falling most recently. Note, our summary runs only in terms of average concentration; not all industries move in line together. Some sectors grew at above average rates and, even in the period of rapid growth of concentration, some industries experienced falling concentration (e.g. fruit and vegetable products and agricultural and electrical machinery).

How concentration grows

Firms may grow in two ways – by internal expansion or by merging with other firms. In the latter case, large business enterprises may result from the acquisition of existing companies, and a network of firms built up ultimately under the control of one of them.

5   Concentration Ratio for the three largest firms.

Some company structures are complex, involving a principal, or **holding company** – the 'parent' – owning controlling interests in other companies – the subsidiaries. The subsidiaries may, in their turn, own controlling interests in other companies, which are subsidiaries of subsidiaries. In principle, there is no limit to how elaborate or extensive a pyramid of companies can be created by this procedure. Variable degrees of autonomy may be allowed to subsidiaries, but ultimate control lies with the holding company (so long as its shareholdings are sufficient to give controlling interest – as we saw in Chapter 2, this does not necessarily mean ownership of over 50 per cent of the shares).

Box 3.2

Pearson Profits Slide by 14pc to £34.8m

Shares in Pearson, owner of the *Financial Times* and Madame Tussauds, jumped 20p on the release of interim results yesterday, although pre-tax profits were $14\frac{1}{2}$ pc below last year. Chairman, Lord Blakenham, warned the recession could continue for at least another two years.

During the first half of this year the oil services division dropped 55pc ... Lord Blakenham said exploration had fallen to 'the lowest level due to environmental regulation and more drilling areas being off limits for drilling'. Profits at the Lazards merchant banking arm fell by almost half to £7m because takeover activity has fallen away. The Royal Doulton china subsidiary plunged 59pc to £2.2m as the big Canadian market contracted sharply and margins suffered from competition. But a star performer was the book business, with Penguin boasting 7 of the top 50 bestsellers in America....

Newspapers, which include the Westminster group of provincial papers, benefited from cost-cutting, while *The Economist* increased its circulation. The 16pc stake in satellite television station BSkyB is expected to produce a small return next year.

The Independent on Sunday,
5 September 1992

This press report on the Pearson group plc (see also Figure 3.15), shows its diversity of interests. Risk spreading is particularly advantageous in recessions, when it may help maintain dividend payments to shareholders.

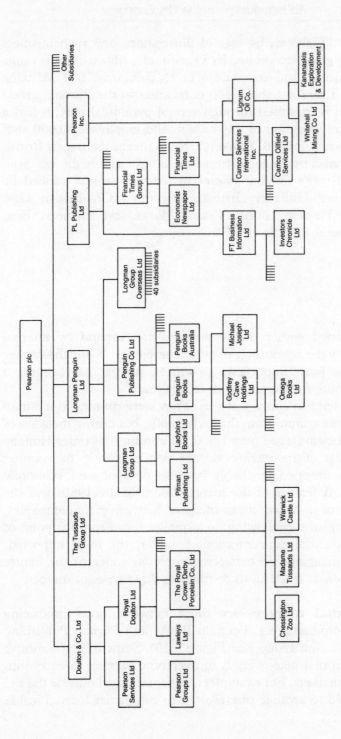

Figure 3.15 Company structure, Pearson plc, 1992

Source: *Who owns whom*

Figure 3.15 shows, by way of illustration, one such business empire, the group controlled by Pearson plc, whose outputs range from publishing and entertainment to chinaware and Madame Tussauds. There are about 400 companies in the Pearson group and control is exercised through several pyramidal tiers; it had a stock market valuation of $£1\frac{3}{4}$ billion, and employed 30,000 staff in the year ending 1990. Pearson is by no means the largest British giant. Its rank, by value of turnover, is just within the top 100. Bigger and more familiar names in the top twenty (ranked by turnover) are Unilever, British Telecom, ICI, British Gas, Sainsbury, Hanson, Ford, Tesco, Marks and Spencer, Esso (UK), General Electric and P&O.

Mergers

We mentioned earlier that businesses can expand by internal growth or by the acquisition of other companies. While the former method has been important, growth by merger has become a common route for expansion in recent years.

Mergers tend to come in waves. They were running at a rate of about 750 per annum from the early 1960s, but during the wave of 1987–89, they averaged over 1,400 per annum – $3\frac{1}{2}$ times as many as the average of the previous decade. More recently, the number of mergers dropped, probably because of depressed economic conditions. A feature of the merger boom of the 1980s was the appearance of so-called 'mega-mergers' between giant companies, rather than giants swallowing up a smaller fish. From the point of view of industrial concentration, however, the most important aspect of amalgamation between companies concerns the nature of businesses. It is useful to distinguish three types of merger.

- **Horizontal mergers** are those between firms producing similar products, e.g. Penguin Books and Pitman Publishing in the Pearson group (see Figure 3.15). Sometimes the motive for horizontal take-overs is to overcome barriers to entry into foreign markets. For example, companies based outside the EC have tried to arrange marriages with companies located inside the EC in anticipation of the 'single market' commencing in 1993 (see below page 161–3).

- **Vertical mergers** involve companies at different stages of the production process, e.g. Royal Doulton (producers of chinaware) and Lawleys (retail outlets), also in the Pearson group (Figure 3.15).

- **Conglomerate mergers** lead to diversification of interests. They are sometimes even given the name 'diversifying mergers'. The Pearson group yet again provides an example; there is little in common between the product lines of some of its companies – publishing, chinaware, oil exploration and Madame Tussauds (Figure 3.15).

It is not always easy to place a particular merger in a single category. Some amalgamations may not appear to have elements of either vertical or horizontal merger about them. They may, however, conceal less obvious matters, such as disposal of by-products or utilisation of expertise in a related field which might explain such otherwise unlikely combinations as detergents, plastics and ice-cream manufacture in the Unilever group.

Horizontal mergers have been the predominant type in post-Second World War Britain, with vertical integration being insignificant. Conglomerate mergers gradually increased in importance after 1960, rising to account for about a third of the total until the end of the 1980s when, with the onset of recession, they gave way to horizontal mergers.

Conglomerate mergers may increase its bargaining power in the financial markets in which a firm raises capital. However, they usually have the prime aim of diversification in order to reduce risks by spreading them. Horizontal, and to an extent vertical, mergers tend to increase the power of a company over its market.

While increasing concentration may be associated with increasing market power, in a curious way greater concentration may heighten competition. This may happen if it leads diversified giant companies to enter each other's markets.

Demergers

It must not be concluded from the previous section that amalgamation always pays off. Studies of the effects of mergers on company profits suggest that it is not uncommon for the financial situation to worsen after a merger.

A business may decide to demerge, i.e. sell off some part of its operations if it finds itself unable to manage them profitably. This may happen if the parent company overextends itself, or has urgent need for cash for current purposes. Selling off subsidiaries occurs more often in depressed economic conditions. In 1992, for example, the Sears group, which had become one of the largest 50 companies in the UK in the late 1980s by diversifying from its original chain of footwear shops (Dolcis, Saxone, and Freeman, Hardy & Willis, etc.), demerged out of menswear retailing by selling 350 shops (Fosters and Your Price).[6]

Inter-firm Co-operation

The emphasis so far has been on common ownership. However, there are avenues of co-operation among firms which do not involve loss of sovereignty, as happens with full mergers.

One such is the joint venture by a consortium of two, or more, firms who collaborate in a limited way in some aspect of business which appears to be in their joint interest. The limits may be for a stipulated time period or product-related. Installing engines from a Japanese manufacturer in the cars of a British producer provides an example of a joint venture which appealed to both parties.

Another device for inter-firm co-operation is the 'interlocking directorate'. A link between firms is contrived by one or more persons becoming directors of several companies. This practice is common in the area of banking and finance, but less so in manufacturing industry.

6 Readers of the previous edition of this book might remember that the Sears group was used as the illustration of company structure taken here by the Pearson group (see page 91).

A different collaborative device is franchising. This permits a large company to avoid vertical integration by licensing independents to perform functions at a different stage of the business. Franchising is most frequently found in retailing, where it offers manufacturers outlets for products without the need to own and manage them. A large company usually provides exclusive marketing rights, know-how and training to franchisees, who own their businesses and maintain a profit motive. McDonald's burger houses provide a well-known example of a highly successful franchise operation.

Some inter-firm co-operation takes place through **trade associations**. This is a wide term and includes any body of employers who have agreements with each other. The functions of trade associations vary from industry to industry, but usually include research and publicity.

Trade associations may organise collusive behaviour for members, e.g. regulating output or fixing the price of products, and organising enforcement machinery. Though now largely illegal to do so, trade associations have behaved as **cartels**, and allocated market shares to constituent firms on a predetermined basis. Arrangements of this kind can have effects similar to complete mergers, although they may be less stable. Because of illegality since the mid-1950s, we have had to go back a long time in history to find a good illustration for this book. However, Figure 3.16 shows the complex set of links that once operated among several separate companies in the electric lamp industry. Secret cartels continue to be discovered from time to time in operation of the government's competition policy (see 207-13).

Multinational Corporations

The bulk of this chapter has been written from a nationalistic point of view. We end with a few observations to put the discussion into a wider perspective.

According to the census of production, roughly 20 per cent of the value of UK output is by firms which are foreign-owned, in that parent companies are incorporated outside Britain. Interest-

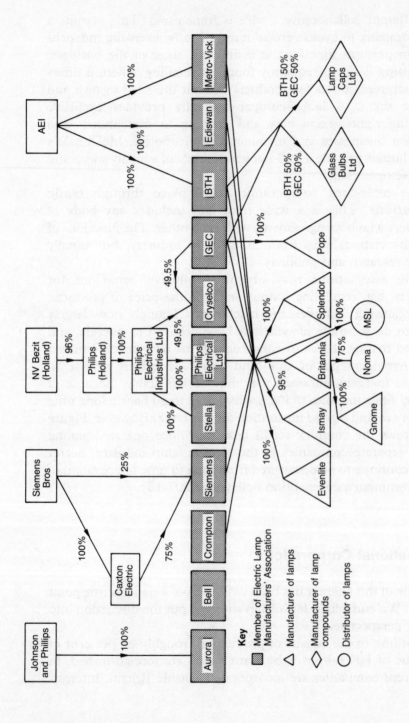

Figure 3.16 Links between members of the Electric Lamp Manufacturers' Association, 1951

Source: *Report on the Supply of Electric Lamps*, Monopolies Commission, HC Paper 287, 1950–51

ingly, both labour productivity and capital expenditure per head are, on average, substantially higher in foreign-owned than in domestically owned UK businesses. It is, of course, true also that UK companies own others overseas. For example, B.P. has subsidiaries in well over 50 foreign countries.

International megagiants are known as **multinational** or **transnational** corporations. They normally dwarf the typical large domestic enterprise. Thus, the value of turnover in the world's largest company (Sumitomo Corporation of Japan) in 1990 was £86 billion – more than fifty times that of the Pearson group described earlier. Even the smallest of the top 25 multinationals (Matsushita Electrical Industrial Co. Ltd) was 15 times the size of Pearson. Of the top 50, over 30 had their HQ in either Japan or the USA. Only one was UK-based (British Petroleum), 7 were German, 4 French, 1 Swiss, 1 Italian, and 2 Anglo-Dutch (Shell and Unilever).

For a variety of reasons, recent trends in international investment flows have greatly increased the importance of transnational corporations. Among explanations for this is a desire by companies to circumvent tariff and other barriers to international trade (see Chapter 5.) Thus, the acquisition in 1988 of the UK-based chocolate manufacturer Rowntree by the Swiss giant Nestlé was an early example of a company in a non-EC member nation (Switzerland) seeking to avoid discrimination when the 'single market' arrived in 1993 (see pages 161–3). The 1991 US take-over of the Italian Plessey SpA is a more recent example.

Another advantage enjoyed by multinationals is the ability to distribute the fruits of technological advance amongst subsidiaries, and to locate production of components where costs are lowest. A potentially disturbing aspect of this power is that the multinationals are, by the same token, able to manipulate their global tax bills. This they do by what is known as 'transfer pricing' – selling components among subsidiaries in different countries at prices which result in accounting profits being highest where tax rates are lowest. From the viewpoint of economic policy for a single nation, multinationals may cause intractable problems, though country groupings such as the EC may be better placed to take appropriate action.

Questions and exercises

(For key to abbreviations identifying sources, see pages xv–xvi)

1   Prepare a table to show what has happened to the share of the manufacturing sector in total national output (use GDP) over the past 10 years. Compare and contrast any differences in your results measured by (i) numbers of employees, and (ii) the value of output. Do your findings make you optimistic about the future for the UK economy? (*AS* and *UKNA*)

2   Construct a table listing the 10 industries which expanded most and the 10 which expanded least over the past five years. Do you find the results at all surprising ? Why or why not? (*AS*)

3   Ask a group of 20 people (friends or relatives perhaps) how many employees they think there are in the firm they work for: (a) less than 10; (b) 10–49; (c) 50–199; (d) 200–10,000; (e) over 10,000? Compare the results with Figures 3.10 and 3.11.

4   Arrange a visit to a local factory. Ask:

   (a)   How long it has been where it is.
   (b)   Why it started up where it did.
   (c)   Whether it is an independent or subsidiary company.
   (d)   How many employees it has on the books.
   (e)   How output per employee compares with last year.

   Would you judge the company to be a good investment prospect?

5   From the world section in *The Times 1000* list the top two Japanese, US, German, French and UK companies. Rank the pairs by the value of turnover. From *Who Owns Whom*, find out which, if any, have subsidiaries in the UK.

6   Prepare a table showing for each of the standard regions of the UK numbers (a) of employees, (b) in the population. What implications do your results suggest for regional policy?

Appendix 3

Table A3.1 UK output* 1981 and 1991 (£ million)

	1981	1991
Agriculture, forestry and fishing	4,839	8,772
Energy and water supply	23,521	28,273
Manufacturing	54,826	104,283
Construction	13,027	33,686
Distribution, hotels and catering; repairs	27,469	73,024
Transport and communication	16,182	34,755
Banking, finance, insurance, etc.	25,013	88,179
Public administration, defence and social security	16,287	34,786
Education and health	20,618	49,643
Others	16,973	41,600
Total	218,755	497,001

*Gross Domestic Product at current prices

Source: *UK National Accounts*, 1992

Table A3.2 Industrial output, UK 1981–1991

	Energy	Manufac- turing	Metals	Building materials	Chemicals	Engineering and allied	Food, drink, tobacco	Textiles, clothing	Other manufac- turing	Construction
1981	73.0	91.0	94.1	94.2	83.5	88.3	97.3	91.0	94.1	82.9
1982	83.2	91.2	91.5	96.1	83.7	89.3	98.8	89.6	91.7	89.4
1983	91.2	93.8	94.2	96.8	90.9	92.6	99.5	92.6	93.6	95.2
1984	97.3	97.4	92.9	100.4	96.7	96.5	100.5	96.1	98.4	99.6
1985	100.0	100.0	100.0	100.0	100.0	100.0	100.0	100.0	100.0	100.0
1986	101.2	101.3	100.3	101.3	101.8	100.2	100.8	100.7	104.5	104.5
1987	98.6	106.6	108.6	106.8	109.0	103.7	103.2	103.7	115.0	112.8
1988	90.1	114.1	122.3	117.3	114.2	112.3	104.7	102.0	126.6	122.9
1989	73.4	118.9	124.7	120.1	119.4	119.9	105.6	98.3	132.3	130.4
1990	73.4	118.5	121.3	113.4	118.3	119.7	106.3	95.9	133.2	131.8
1991	74.9	112.2	110.0	103.0	121.5	111.0	106.1	87.7	126.1	120.3

Source: *National Institute Economic Review*

Table A3.3 Labour productivity, UK, 1981–1991

	Output per employee		Output per person-hour in manufacturing
	Whole economy	*Manufacturing industries 1985=100*	
1981	89.2	79.2	82.2
1982	92.6	84.5	86.7
1983	96.7	91.8	93.4
1984	97.4	97.0	97.5
1985	100.0	100.0	100.0
1986	103.5	103.5	103.8
1987	106.3	109.8	109.4
1988	107.2	116.2	115.3
1989	106.9	120.8	120.2
1990	107.3	121.7	121.6
1991	107.7	121.6	123.1

Source: *National Institute Economic Review*

Table A3.4 Size of business units and business enterprises, 1989

	Analysis by number of employees (thousands)							
	1–9	10–19	20–49	50–99	100–199	200–499	500–999	1,000 and over
Number of business units	105,125	15,952	18,003	7,883	4,855	3,318	905	408
Total employment (thousands)	307	225	555	548	675	1,010	613	806
Enterprises								
Number of business enterprises	134,797				2,471	1,495	520	587
Total employment (thousands)	1,201				342	460	366	2,506

Sources: *Annual Abstract of Statistics* and *Business Monitor*, PA 1002

Table A3.5 Gross output per employee, 1980–1990

	UK	Japan	France	Germany	Italy	USA
			1980 = 100			
1980	100.0	100.0	100.0	100.0	100.0	100.0
1981	103.7	102.6	101.7	100.7	100.3	100.7
1982	107.8	104.8	103.9	101.4	100.8	99.3
1983	113.5	106.2	105.4	104.9	101.6	101.9
1984	115.1	110.1	107.5	107.9	103.9	103.9
1985	117.7	115.0	109.6	104.9	106.1	105.0
1986	121.9	117.1	112.0	105.7	108.7	105.7
1987	127.2	120.9	114.2	106.3	112.3	106.2
1988	128.7	126.4	118.3	109.2	115.5	107.9
1989	129.4	130.0	121.6	111.9	118.8	108.4
1990	130.1	134.1	123.1	114.0	119.2	108.8
1991	130.9	137.4	124.2	115.7	119.9	108.5

Source: *National Institute Economic Review*

4
Distribution

The previous two chapters in this book have concentrated on a number of aspects of UK output. However, economics is concerned not only with the production of the goods and services which constitute the national 'cake', but also with how the cake is divided up among individuals. In dealing with this latter subject economists refer to the distribution of income.[1] Distribution is important for two reasons. In the first place, people's incomes (together with their wealth) are key determinants of what they are able to consume – their standard of living. In the second place, the prices of factors of production, wages, rent, interest and profit rates influence employment.

Distribution of Income

The forces of supply and demand operate in the markets for factors of production, thereby affecting the way income is distributed. There are many distributions of interest – e.g. between men and women, and among different regions of the country – but two are of special importance:

- distribution according to the size of incomes
- distribution among factors of production

1 The theory of distribution is covered in Lipsey–Harbury, FP2, Chapters 20–1.

Size Distribution

We look first at the degree of inequality in income distribution in the UK. Figure 4.1 presents this information in a convenient, though unusual, way. It makes use of what is known as a **Lorenz curve**.

A Lorenz curve shows how much of total income is received by given proportions, or percentages, of the population. The percentages measured on both axes are cumulative. Hence, as we move rightwards from the origin along the horizontal axis, we observe the bottom 1 per cent, 2 per cent, etc., of the population. We then read shares from points on the Lorenz curve on to the vertical axis.

We can illustrate with Figure 4.1, which shows the distribution among households. Point 'a' on the Lorenz curve indicates that the bottom 40 per cent of households received 9 per cent of total

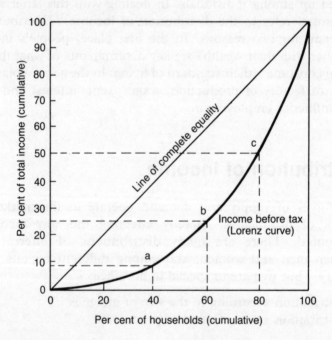

Figure 4.1 Distribution of household income, UK, 1988
Source: *Social Trends, 1992*

income. To see this, start from the 40 per cent point on the horizontal axis, and follow the dotted line upwards to point 'a' on the Lorenz curve and then along the dotted line to cut the vertical axis at 9 per cent. Point 'b' on the Figure shows that the bottom 60 per cent received about 25 per cent of income, point 'c' that the bottom 80 per cent received half of total income, and so forth.

We can compare the Lorenz curve with the line of absolute equality. This is the diagonal going through the origin of the diagram. It indicates absolute equality because all points along it show that a given percentage of the population receives exactly the same percentage of total income, i.e. the bottom 1 per cent receive 1 per cent of total income, the bottom 5 per cent receive 5 per cent, etc. Hence the further away the Lorenz curve bends below the diagonal, the greater the degree of inequality.

The simple single line of the Lorenz curve gives a full description of the distribution of income among households. It is clear from Figure 4.1 that a considerable degree of inequality exists in Britain. Both the top 20 per cent and the bottom 80 per cent of households receive the same percentage of total income (50 per cent each).[2] Why should this be so?

The answer to this question is complex. The distribution of income is the result of several influences – economic forces, the socioeconomic system of the country, and action by the government. We shall consider the last of these in Chapter 6. Here we concentrate on the influence of market forces. They are relevant because a part, at least, of the income of most individuals comes as a reward for their services as factors of production.

Factor Shares

Chapter 1 of this book began by explaining that economists classify resources, or factors of production, into three main categories – land, labour and capital. Each factor receives an

---

2 The shares of the top percentages of households are not directly observable from the diagram. They are residuals – what is left by subtracting the shares of the bottom percentages of households from 100 per cent.

income – known respectively as rent, wages (and salaries) and interest. There is also a fourth kind of income, called profit, earned by a factor, which is sometimes given the name **enterprise**, or entrepreneurship. Of course, a single individual may receive income from several sources, e.g. wages from employment, interest on capital, and profit from the running of a business.

The factor (or **functional**) distribution of income is shown in Figure 4.2. It must be emphasised that the divisions in the diagram (derived from published statistics) do not correspond precisely to the concepts used in economic theory, though they come closest in the case of income from employment. Gross trading profits include interest on capital as well as pure profit; self-employment income contains an element of labour income as well as interest and profit; while rent is the return on land and buildings rather than pure economic rent. (**Economic rent** is a payment to any factor of production in excess of its transfer earnings – some data relating to this concept are given in Figure 4.15 below).

The largest share, about two-thirds of the total in 1991, accrued to labour in the form of wages and salaries. The remaining third consisted mainly of profits and self-employment income, with rather less than 10 per cent being rent. Note, the gross trading profits of the private and public sectors are the pool from which dividends and interest are paid. In the diagram, profits are shown

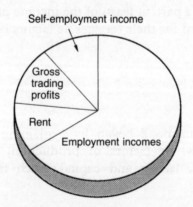

Figure 4.2 Factor distribution of income, UK, 1991
Source: *UK National Accounts*

before any deduction for depreciation (see page 43). All proportions are gross, i.e. inclusive of income due in taxes. Self-employment income is a mixture. Part represents income for work done and part a return on capital invested, either in a business or in education and training to acquire the qualifications without which such professional earnings would not accrue.

Trends in the shares of factor incomes

Figure 4.2 shows the shares of the chief factors of production as they existed in one particular year, 1991. These shares fluctuate. The share of capital tends to be high in years of prosperity, when profits are high. Labour's share falls accordingly in boom periods and rises, for the opposite reason, in recessionary times. That is not to say that wages tend to be high in depressions, only that the *share* of employment income is large. In absolute terms, wages may be high or low.

Apart from short-term fluctuations, certain long-term trends are observable in factor shares. If we look as far back as the 1870s, we see a fairly stable share of wages, which persisted until about the middle of the present century. It should be added, however, that the proportion of wage earners was falling at the same time. Taking account of all incomes from employment, the share of wages and salaries rose by about 10 per cent over this long period, although towards the end there may have been a slight fall.

The share of self-employment income is more complex to analyse. The long-term historical trend was naturally downwards during the period of growth of joint stock companies. In more recent times, self-employment income has accounted for between 8 and 12 per cent of the total. One reason for variation lies in the way in which taxes are levied. There have been changes from time to time in the advantages that accrue from being treated for tax purposes as a self-employed person rather than as a wage earner or the owner of shares in a company. Another is the level of unemployment. When it is high, people may try to start up small businesses, often assisted by payments made in compensation for being declared redundant. There was a substantial increase in the number of self-employed persons during the 1980s (from 2 to 3 million, of which half a million are part-time), though this was reflected in only a modest 2 percentage points increase in the share of self-employment income in the total.

The income of a factor and its share in total income depend on the price that is paid for it, and on the amount that is used. Economic theory tells us that the forces of supply and demand determine the prices of factors of production just as they do those of goods and services, although, as usual, government intervention can affect the final outcome. The remainder of this chapter will examine the background within which market forces work.

The Supply of Labour

The number of persons in the community able and wishing to work depends in the first instance on the size of the total population and its age (and to some extent its sex) distribution.

Population Size

We saw in Chapter 1 that the population of the UK grew rapidly during the nineteenth and early twentieth centuries, and is now around 57 million.

The size of the population depends on:

- **birth rates**
- **death rates**
- **the balance of migration movements**

Birth rates

The birth rate (defined as the number of babies born per thousand of the population) is determined by the number of women of child-bearing age in the population and by family size. Statistics on both these matters are shown in Figures 4.3 and 4.4. They are put in historical perspective by placing data for the most recent year alongside those for the late nineteenth century. Figure 4.3 brings out the substantial difference between the Victorian period and the

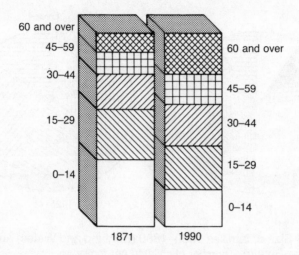

Figure 4.3 Age distribution of the female population 1871 and 1990
Source: *Annual Abstract of Statistics*

present. Not only was the proportion of women in the fertile age group much higher in the Victorian period of rapid population growth, but the numbers in the 0–14 age group, coming up later to fertility, were also very much higher.

Figure 4.4 shows that by the interwar years family size had also changed dramatically from that of the nineteenth century. The contrast between the two periods is startling. Whereas every fourth Victorian family had at least 9 children, only 1 in 40 in the later period had as many. The reasons for this tremendous fall in the size of families are interesting even if they are not all understood. They are clearly associated with increasing knowledge and use of contraceptive techniques, which in turn reflect other changes – the growth of the middle classes (who tend to have fewer children), the emancipation of women, and changing attitudes towards family life and parental responsibility.

The trend in the birth rate in the present century has shown a fairly steady fall. It almost halved from a rate of 29 per thousand of the population in 1900 to one of 16 per thousand in the 1930s. The rate picked up after the end of the Second World War as servicemen returned home to raise families deferred during the war. It dropped once more in the 1960s, to a minimum of under

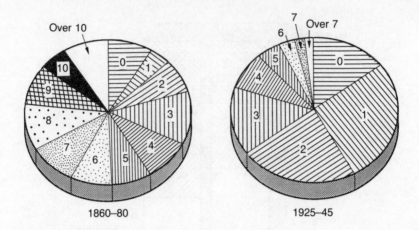

Figure 4.4 Size of families 1860–1880 (England and Wales) and 1925–1945 (Great Britain) – number of children per family
Source: *Report of the Royal Commission on population*, Cmnd 7695, 1949

12 in 1977, since when it has hovered around the 12 to 13 per thousand mark.

Death rates

The second determinant of population size is the death rate. This is linked to advances in health care and to the age distribution of the population. Death rates have remained fairly constant throughout the present century, reflecting the opposing influences of an aging population and of a decline in mortality rates for most age groups. The current situation may be summarised as that the average baby can expect to live to be $72\frac{1}{2}$ if a boy, or 78 if a girl. By comparison, average life expectancies at the beginning of the century were 49 and 52 respectively.

Migration

Throughout the nineteenth century, migration was an important restraint on the growth of Britain's population; the range of opportunities, particularly in North America, ensured that emigrants greatly outnumbered immigrants. Towards the end of the century immigration into Britain had also assumed sizeable proportions, but in the 60 years after 1871 there was a net loss from migration of the order of 4 million.

In the 1920s most foreign countries erected barriers to immigrants and the balance of movements between the censuses of 1931 and 1961 was reversed, to become one of a net gain of some half a million people. This figure conceals the fact that after the Second World War, Britain reassumed its traditional role as a country of emigration, chiefly to the Commonwealth (especially Australia and Canada). At the same time the movement was more than offset in the late 1950s by increasing numbers of immigrants, mainly from the West Indies, India and Pakistan. Net immigration around 1960 approached 150,000 per annum.

As a result, the government passed the Commonwealth Immigration Acts, the first in 1962, which gave it power to restrict immigration from the Commonwealth. A sharp fall in the number of immigrants followed, and for the next 20 years there was a net loss of more than three-quarters of a million people through migration. After 1973, when the UK joined the European Community, migration increased to and from other EC member countries. However, since 1980 the total numbers of immigrants and emigrants have almost exactly balanced each other.

Activity rates

The **working population**, or the labour force, comes largely from those in the age group 16–65, and, as we observed in Chapter 1, involves only about half the total population – about 27 million.

The size of the labour force in a given population depends on many factors, including conventional views as to the proper age of retirement, the level of pensions, attitudes towards family life and responsibilities, the legal minimum school-leaving age, the popularity of further education, and the general economic state of the country.

The ratio of the working to the total population aged 16 or over, expressed as a percentage, is known as the **activity rate**, or the **participation rate**. Current activity rates are 75 per cent for men and 43 per cent for women. The lower female rate is partly explained by the longevity of women and their earlier entitlement to state pensions. It is also a result of the tendency for many women to leave work for at least a few years while bringing up young children. However, changing social attitudes have brought about a major upward shift in the participation rate for married women, which has nearly tripled (from 20 to 59 per cent) in a generation. The activity rates for almost all groups in the population dipped slightly in 1991, confirming the influence of the economic recession.

Occupations

Men and women are not evenly represented in the various occupational groups. On the one hand, manual work accounts for over half of men's jobs but less than a third of women's. There are men in most occupational groups. On the other hand, women tend to be concentrated in service industries (a fact that is true of almost 90 per cent of part-time women workers). Figure 4.5 selects occupations where either men or women predominate.

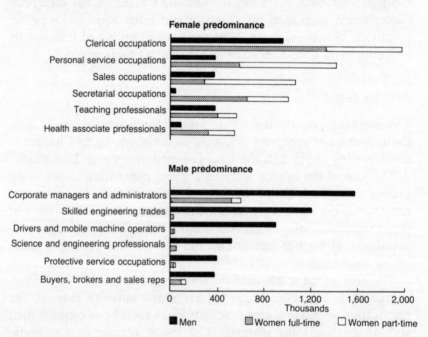

Figure 4.5 Female and male workers, selected occupations, 1991
Source: *Employment Gazette*, September 1992

Thus, women outnumber men as clerks, secretaries, nurses, teachers, shop assistants and in personal service including catering, cleaning and hairdressing. Men, in contrast, predominate in managerial and administrative jobs, in science and engineering, and as salesmen, as well as in more obvious 'heavy' occupations such as protective services and truck driving.

Note, that the occupational structure in Britain has been changing considerably in recent years. Technological advance has led to the replacement of an increasing number of manual jobs by machines; and growth of the service sector in the economy and professionalisation of more and more skills has taken place.

Unemployment

The reader could be excused for assuming that the term 'working population' comprised people actually at work. That is not the case. The term includes all members of the labour force even if they happen to be unemployed for any reason.

Several types of unemployment are distinguished in economic theory. Two are of special relevance here:

- **frictional** unemployment, associated with the turnover of labour as people move from one job to another.

- **structural** unemployment applies when mismatches occur as workers are made redundant in declining industries, but they are not employable in expanding industries, at least not without retraining and/or relocating.

Before we look at the extent and characteristics of unemployment in the UK, we must explain that the level of unemployment, measured as a percentage of the total labour force, is sensitive to definitions of (i) who is to be counted as unemployed and (ii) who is to be included in the totals on which percentage rates are calculated. Unless you know precisely how the unemployment rate is defined you can hardly interpret it sensibly.

Trends in the UK unemployment rate in the 1980s have been particularly difficult to interpret because of a number of changes in the ways in which the statistics are prepared. Since all but one of the changes had the effect of reducing the measured level of unemployment, some observers (not all with political axes to grind) have been suspicious that the changes, justifiable though they may be on other grounds, may have been partly politically motivated.

The most important innovation was a redefining of who was to count as unemployed. In 1982, the definition was altered from those registering for work to those claiming benefit. The change resulted in an immediate drop of nearly a quarter of a million in the numbers officially jobless. The main difference between the new and the old bases relates to those (mainly married women) who do not claim benefit on losing their jobs because they are not entitled to it.

Fortunately the ILO (International Labour Office, which functions in collaboration with the United Nations) devised a standardised unemployment rate for international comparisons. The UK government publishes statistics of the ILO rate as well as the official UK rate. The comparisons are interesting. In 1991, for example, there were 2.08 million unemployed by the UK government's count of claimants for benefit. The equivalent number according to the ILO was 2.3 million. The deficiency was entirely due to the count of unemployed women – 0.87 million rather than 0.5 million. The deficiency of 57 per cent by the UK government's statistics arises because the ILO counts people as unemployed if they are without paid jobs, available for work and have sought work at some time during the four weeks prior to being interviewed.[3]

The method of calculating the unemployment rate will concern us again when we deal, in Chapter 9, with economic policy for a low aggregate level of unemployment. In this chapter, we are interested in the pattern of unemployment within a given total. We consider now variations in unemployment relating to different

3 The official reason for continuing to base the unemployment rate on benefit claimants is that the ILO method involves costly surveys which take time to process and do not offer the range of detail of their own method. However, the government admits that the claimants method 'is not ideal for every purpose, e.g. to measure the number of people who would like to work, but cannot find a job, or a measure of social hardship'. *Employment Gazette*, July 1992, page 348.

regions, different ethnic groups, different occupations, the age and qualifications of employees, and length of time without work.

Regional Unemployment

As we saw in Chapter 3 (see pages 77–81), regions tend to specialise in different industries. Hence, it is not surprising that when the structure of industry is changing, frictional and

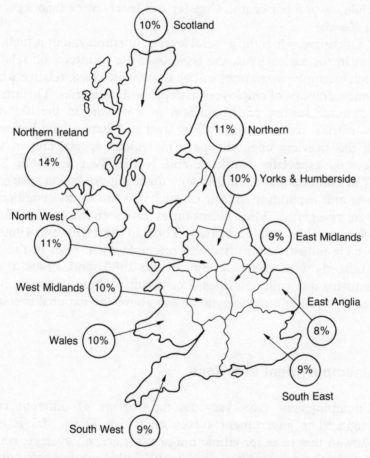

Figure 4.6 Regional unemployment rates (percentages) 1992
Source: *Monthly Digest of Statistics*

structural unemployment tend to vary among regions because of mismatches between the location of job vacancies and of unemployed seeking work.

Figure 4.6 shows unemployment rates for each of the standard regions of the UK. The lowest level was in East Anglia followed by the East Midlands, the South East and South West. The highest level was in Northern Ireland, followed by the North and North West. It must, of course, be appreciated that these are regional averages. Looking at smaller localities one can find much greater variation. For example, in 1992 the unemployment rate was as high as 24 per cent in Strabane, and 16 per cent in Hartlepool, while it was 5 per cent in Crawley and barely more than 3 per cent in Kendal.

Of course, when the general level of unemployment is high, as it was in the early 1990s, the regions of the country with relatively high unemployment rates will be those which have relatively heavy concentrations of employees in depressed industries. The interwar economic history of Britain was of a decline in the old staple industries, such as shipbuilding, steel and textiles, and hence also of the heaviest unemployment in regions specialising in those sectors, especially Northern and North West England, South Wales and Scotland. At the same time, regions hosting the (then) new and expanding industries, such as vehicles and engineering, were prospering. More recent times have seen the decline of some of these 'older new' industries. Thus, in the 1950s and 1960s the vehicle industry flourished and unemployment rates in the West Midlands were relatively low. In the 1980s and 1990s, the car industry was suffering intense competition from overseas, so the region's rate of unemployment was above the national average.

Unemployment and Race

Unemployment rates vary among workers of different ethnic origin. The government survey on which Figure 4.7 is based showed that rates for ethnic minorities were, on average, roughly double those for whites. Pakistani/Bangladeshi workers suffered particularly severely, with Indians the least badly affected.

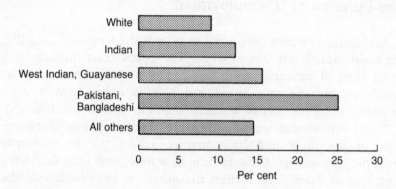

Figure 4.7 Unemployment rates by ethnic origin, 1991
Source: *Employment Gazette*, April 1992

Although some part of the differentials in the diagram may be explained by differences in qualification and region, a significant disadvantage to ethnic minorities remains when these factors are taken into account.

Unemployment, Age and Qualifications

Unemployment is strongly associated with age. The highest rates occur among the young under-26 age bracket, while the middle 25–52 category have the lowest rates.

There is, too, a relationship between age and qualifications, and a strong association between the possession of qualifications and unemployment rates. Those of you, readers of this book, who attain GCSE, A-levels, or even degrees, will be reassured to know that they will significantly reduce your chances of being unemployed. For example, take the age group 25–44; in 1992 the unemployment rate for those with no formal qualifications was 11 per cent, for those with GCE O-level (or equivalent) the rate was $5\frac{1}{2}$ per cent, for those with A-levels the rate was $4\frac{1}{2}$ per cent, and for those with higher qualifications than A-level, the rate was $2\frac{1}{4}$ per cent.

The Duration of Unemployment

A final feature of unemployment to note is the length of time that the unemployed stay out of work. The social consequences of a given level of unemployment differ if it is shared more or less evenly among the workforce, and if it is borne heavily by a relatively small number of workers – the chronically unemployed.

There are several ways to measure unemployment duration. Two of the most important involve asking (a) the currently unemployed, and (b) those finding new jobs, how long they have been out of work. The former measures uncompleted, and the latter completed, spells of unemployment. The former is used in Figure 4.8, which shows, therefore, the distribution of uncompleted spells of unemployment in 1992. The extent of chronic unemployment is brought out by the diagram. About a third of unemployed men and a quarter of unemployed women were out of work for over a year. This pattern has prevailed since 1980. In the previous decade, when the general level of unemployment was much lower, the incidence of long-term joblessness was much less as well.

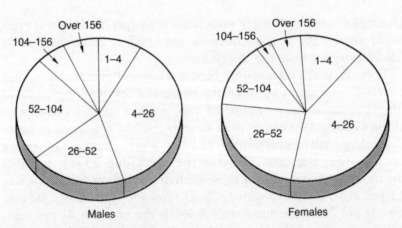

Figure 4.8 Duration of unemployment 1992 (number of weeks out of work)
Source: *Employment Gazette*

Wages

Economic theory suggests that the supply and demand for labour affects its price – the wage rate. The theory also suggests that market forces will tend to equalise wages, provided that no barriers to labour mobility exist, and that everyone is equally skilled at all kinds of work. Of course, the world is not like this. Some workers are more efficient than others, and there are many barriers to movement. Some are natural, e.g. those stemming from difficulties in moving from one part of the country to another. Others are artificial, e.g. there is evidence of the existence of what has been called a dual labour market – a primary market, where pay and employment prospects are good, and a secondary market with high unemployment and low pay – and little movement between them, with many low-paid workers trapped in the secondary market.

We cannot examine all conceivable kinds of wage difference in this book, so we shall concentrate on the following:

- differences among occupations
- differences among industries
- differences by age and sex
- differences among regions

Occupational Wage Differences

To a large extent occupational wage variations may be attributable to the skills needed to perform particular jobs. For example, the head chef at the Savoy Hotel is paid more than the unskilled cleaners and dishwashers there. It is hardly surprising that people with innate talents, and others who take the time and trouble to acquire skills, should earn higher incomes. But how much higher should these be?

That is not an easy question to which a general answer can be given, because there is no unambiguous way of measuring the relative skills needed for different occupations. A first attempt to throw light on the subject might make use of the distinction used in official statistics between skilled manual and unskilled manual workers. A crude measure of the extra rewards paid for skills is to compare the earnings of manual and non-manual workers. In 1991, the average hourly earnings of adult male manual workers was £5.43, while that of non-manual workers was £8.10. Of course, these are average figures and conceal both larger and smaller differentials for specific skills.

So far we have looked at present differentials. There is also some evidence about long-term trends which is worth repeating. Figure 4.9 shows the earnings of men in certain occupational groups, expressed as percentages of average earnings in 1913 and 1978.

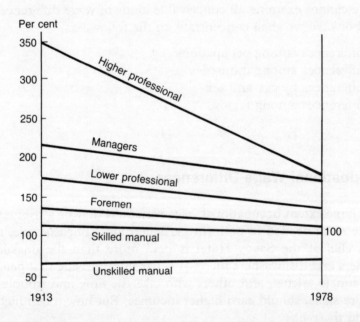

Figure 4.9 Occupational wage differences (males) 1913 and 1978 (earnings for each occupation are shown as a percentage of average earnings)
Source: *Report No 8 of the Royal Commission on the Distribution of Income and Wealth*, Cmnd 7679, 1979

Box 4.1

The Distribution of Earnings

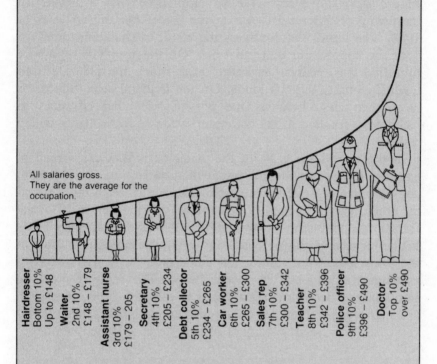

All salaries gross.
They are the average for the
occupation.

Hairdresser
Bottom 10%
Up to £148

Waiter
2nd 10%
£148 – £179

Assistant nurse
3rd 10%
£179 – 205

Secretary
4th 10%
£205 – £234

Debt collector
5th 10%
£234 – £265

Car worker
6th 10%
£265 – £300

Sales rep
7th 10%
£300 – £342

Teacher
8th 10%
£342 – £396

Police officer
9th 10%
£396 – £490

Doctor
Top 10%
over £490

The Figure shows (all decile*) ranges of gross weekly earnings in April 1992. For each of these it depicts an occupation whose average earnings (for men and women together) are within each (decile) range, and which can be considered representative of that tenth of the earnings distribution. The heights of the employees are proportional to their earnings. The illustration is based on a chart using 1991 data which was published in *The Independent on Sunday* in March 1992.

Employment Gazette, November 1992

*Decile means tenth, e.g. the top 10 per cent of the distribution is illustrated by the earnings of a doctor.

The diagram is based on sample data published by a Royal Commission asked to report on the distribution of income and wealth.[4]

Too much should not be read into evidence that extends over so long a period when many conditions were changing. The data in Figure 4.9, however, serve to emphasise that a long-term narrowing of differentials was taking place over the 65 years to 1978. The trend was doubtless the result of changing forces on both the supply and demand sides. On the supply side, labour mobility was rising, as more and more people acquired qualifications of various kinds. On the demand side, the forces have been less obvious. One possibility is that advances in technology resulted in the computerisation of some highly skilled tasks.

In the period since 1978, the evidence is that the spread of earnings has been widening rather than narrowing. To illustrate, consider two representative employees, one close to the top and the other near the bottom of the earnings distribution. In 1977, the former was paid almost exactly double that of the latter. By 1991, the better paid employee's earnings were over three times those of the lower paid. We cannot tell you exactly why the spread of earnings has widened in recent times. The reasons must be something to do with characteristics of the post-1980 years, such as a higher general level of unemployment than had existed for 50 years, and increased scarcity of certain kinds of skilled labour.

Industry Wage Differences

Wage differences are related to the industry in which people work. Figure 4.10 shows details of the weekly earnings of workers in a selection of industries in 1991. The average weekly pay of adult male manual workers at the time was about £260. Compared to these averages, workers in some industries were clocking up 20 per cent more, while others in industries at the bottom of the table were getting 20 per cent less.

4   Full reference details given in Figure 4.9.

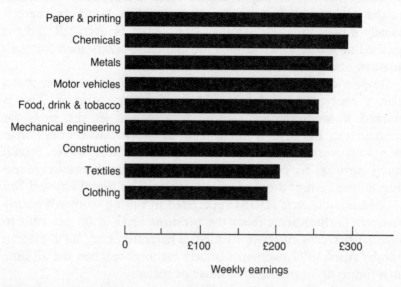

Figure 4.10 Average weekly earnings of full-time adult male manual workers in selected industries, October 1991
Source: *Employment Gazette,* April 1992

There are two reasons for the ordering of industries in the diagram. The first relates to the conditions prevailing in an industry at the time, e.g. the proportions of skilled to unskilled workers and of men to women, in hours worked, in firm and plant size, and in the relative strength of trade unions. The second reason concerns industry differentials over time. It must be remembered that businesses expand and contract, and that changing wages may reflect alterations in the underlying conditions of supply and/or demand.

Age and Sex Wage Differences

It is commonly believed that people tend to be paid more as they get older. This is true up to a point. The average earnings of male manual workers aged 18–20 are less than two-thirds of the average for all workers. What happens later on in life depends very much on the job – and it is dangerous to generalise. However, there is usually a plateau when earnings stop rising, or even fall. This is reached at younger age groups for manual workers than for non-manual, and earlier for women than for men.

Despite legislation aimed at equal pay, it remains the case that a man is likely to earn considerably more than a woman. This is marked if average *weekly* earnings are used as the basis for comparison, because women tend to work fewer hours than men – on average, about four hours a week less. However, even if *hourly* earnings are compared, those of female workers average less than 80 per cent of those of male workers. The Equal Pay and Sex Discrimination Acts (1975) succeeded in raising women's hourly earnings fairly quickly from the previous level of 63 per cent to over 70 per cent of those of men. Thereafter, they hit a plateau but, by April 1992, women's hourly earnings reached the all time high figure of 79 per cent of those of men.

The reasons for sex wage differences are complex and may still reflect an element of discrimination against women. However, part of the explanation lies in the fact that women tend to be concentrated in relatively low-paid occupations and industries. Additionally, some women may be less career-oriented than men, because of stronger feelings of family responsibility. They are under-represented in higher education, they tend to spend less (or to have less spent by employers) on vocational training, and they are less likely to join trade unions. Finally, the shorter hours that women, work, on average, not only keeps down their weekly earnings, but also means that they work fewer hours paid at high overtime rates.

Regional Wage Differences

The final source of differences in wages is the region in which one works. Wages tend to be highest in Greater London. Figure 4.11 shows the average hourly earnings for manual workers in each region as a percentage of those in the capital city. Variations are considerable, with most regions having averages below 80 per cent

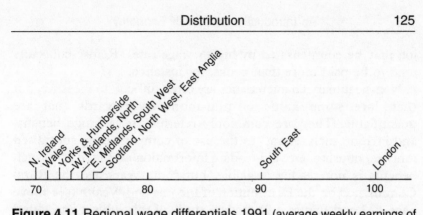

Figure 4.11 Regional wage differentials 1991 (average weekly earnings of full-time adult male manual workers. Each region shown as a percentage of those in Greater London)
Source: *Regional Trends*

of those in London. Regional wage differences are, in the main, no more than a reflection of the basic forces discussed earlier. Behind the statistics lies the fact that regions differ in the proportions of their labour forces in different industries. We have observed something of the extent of variations in earnings by industry, and these obviously affect the regional statistics. Earnings differentials reflect also the state of local labour markets. It is no accident, for example, that earnings are highest in Greater London and lowest in Northern Ireland.

Non-Pecuniary Advantages and Disadvantages

The discussion of wage differences has centred on money earnings. However, this is not the whole story. An economist once coined the term 'non-pecuniary advantages and disadvantages' of different occupations. He did so to emphasise that some people are happy with relatively low-paid jobs if there are compensating, non-pecuniary, advantages to go with them. An outdoor job appeals to many people more than one in an office or factory; an interesting one (e.g. teaching!) more than a routine one; a job with long holidays more than one with short; and so on. The argument holds, too, in the opposite direction. An unpleasant job may be compensated by higher wage rates. Refuse collectors tend to be paid more than cooks, for instance.

Non-pecuniary characteristics are often difficult to measure, but there are some kinds of non-monetary rewards that are quantifiable. They are commonly referred to as fringe benefits and include such 'extras' as the use of company cars, subsidised lunches, housing, etc. Up-to-date information on the scale of such benefits is not readily available, but some years ago the Royal Commission on the Distribution of Income and Wealth (see above page 122 and Figure 4.9) made a study of this subject and found benefits over and above monetary remuneration to run from around a fifth to a third of total pay, on average, in 1978. Note, benefits may have been high that year, which was one when the government was engaged in a policy of pay restraint.

Trade Unions

Our discussion of the supply of labour and wages made a passing reference to trade unions.[5] It is time to consider them in more detail.

Historical Development

Trade unionism had its origins in the pitifully low standard of living of the average nineteenth-century worker and his family. The explanation of the standard of living throughout the world lay in the small size of the total national output relative to the population. In 1800, even in the wealthiest of countries, an equal division of national income among all families would have left everyone in poverty by present standards.

Poverty had existed for centuries. It was accentuated by the twin processes of urbanisation and industrialisation. The man who was

5 See Lipsey–Harbury, FP2, pages 199–201, for economic analysis of trade unions.

moderately content working his land usually became restive when he moved into a grimy nineteenth-century city, took employment in a sweatshop or a factory, and settled with his family in a crowded, insanitary slum. (Of course, many moved because they had no choice, having been driven off their land by the enclosure movements. Urban life was simply preferable to starvation.) Stories of suffering during the industrial revolution could fill volumes. One example will illustrate some of the conditions that lay behind the drive for change and reform:

In the cotton-spinning work, these creatures [the workers] are kept, fourteen hours in each day, locked up, summer and winter, in a heat of from *eighty to eighty-four degrees*.... The door of the place wherein they work, is *locked, except half an hour*, at tea-time, the work-people are not allowed to send for water to drink ... even *the rain water is locked up*, by the master's order.... If any spinner be found with his *window open* he is to pay a fine of a shilling!... for a large part of the time, there is the abominable and pernicious stink of the *gas* to assist in the murderous effects of the heat ... the notorious fact is that well constitutioned men are rendered old and past labour at forty years of age, and that children are rendered decrepit and deformed, and thousands upon thousands of them slaughtered by consumption [tuberculosis], before they arrive at the age of sixteen ...[6]

Out of these conditions came the range of radical political movements from Marxism to Fabian socialism. Out of them also came the union, which was to some extent a club providing protection for unemployed, disabled or retired workers, and to some extent a negotiating agent. For a long time unions were vigorously resisted by both employers and government.

Union organisers perceived that 10 or 100 men acting together had more influence than one man acting alone. The union was the organisation that would provide a basis for confronting the power of employers with the collective power of workers. However,

6   *Political Register*, Vol. LII, William Cobbett, 20 November 1824, as quoted by E. Royston Pike in *Human Documents of the Industrial Revolution in Britain* (London: Allen & Unwin, 1966), pages 60–1.

employers did not accept organisations of workers passively. Those who tried to organise workers were often dismissed and blacklisted, in some cases physically assaulted or even killed. In order to create effective power over the labour market, it was necessary to control the supply of labour and to marshall financial resources to outlast employers. There was no 'right to organise', and the union usually had to force a hostile employer to negotiate with it. Since early unions did not have large resources, the employer had to be attacked where he was weakest.

These considerations explain why it was highly skilled and specialist types of labour union that first met with success – it was easier to control the supply of skilled than unskilled workers. Moreover, a union of a small number of highly skilled specialists could attack the employer's weakest spots. Even then unions had their ups and downs. When employment was full and business booming, the cost of being fired for joining a union was not so great. During times of depression and unemployment, however, the risks were greater and we can observe cyclical swings in

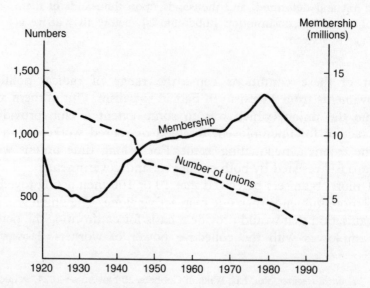

Figure 4.12 Numbers of trade unions and members since 1920
Source: *Annual Abstract of Statistics*

membership with gains in booms and setbacks in slumps – a pattern that has persisted to the present day (see Figure 4.12).

There was a substantial drop in the number of unionised workers during the depressed interwar years. More recently, membership fell again in the 1980s, when unemployment was high, from a peak of $13\frac{1}{4}$ million in 1979 to less than 10 million in 1990. Part of the decline can also be explained by changes in the structure of the economy, and reduced employment in industries where unionism has traditionally been strong, e.g coal mining and manufacturing.

Trade Union Membership

Total union membership is less than 40 per cent of total employment in the UK. However, there are sectors which are strongly unionised and others which are weak. Figure 4.13 illustrates the variations by industry, though it must be viewed in the light of the fact that some of the largest unions have members extending over several industries.

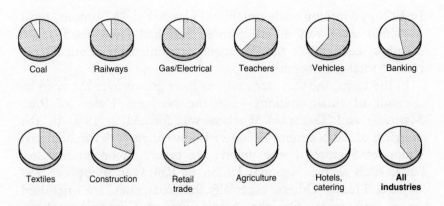

Figure 4.13 Trade union membership 1990 (trade union members as a percentage of numbers employed in selected industries)
Source: *Employment Gazette*, April 1992

The diagram is based on full-time workers only. It shows unionism is especially strong in coal mining, the railways and the supply of power (gas and electricity). In contrast, unionism is especially weak in retail distribution, agriculture, construction, and the hotel and catering trades.

Additionally, union membership is higher among full-time than part-time employees, among men than women, among manual than non-manual occupations (though more white-collar and professional workers have joined trade unions in recent years), and among large than small firms.

High union membership is a source of power for unions when negotiating with employers. This used to be greatly helped by the institution of the closed shop. This is an arrangement, agreed with employers, where only union members may be employed. About a quarter of the workforce were in closed shops in the early 1980s. The proportion had fallen to a tenth by the end of the decade as a result of discouraging legislation, culminating in the 1990 Employment Act, which made it illegal for an employer to decline a job to an applicant who neither was, nor wished to be, a union member.

Trade Union Structure

In 1990, 10 million trade unionists belonged to 287 unions, most of which were very small. Almost half had fewer than 1,000 members each, while the 24 largest accounted for about 80 per cent of total membership.

In the main, the very large unions have grown over the years as a result of amalgamations – e.g. the National Union of Rail, Maritime and Transport Workers was formed in 1990 by the merging of the National Union of Railwaymen with the National Union of Seamen. Some unions are organised on an industry basis, such as the National Union of Knitwear, Footwear and Apparel Trades. Others, especially the older ones, are organised on a craft basis, like the Association of Cinematographers, Television and Allied Technicians. However, the largest unions of all are either general unions covering a wide range of

industries and/or occupations, such as the Transport and
General Workers' Union with nearly $1\frac{1}{4}$ million members, or
multi-craft unions like the Electrical, Electronic Telecommuni-
cation and Plumbing Union.

The central body of the trade union movement is the Trades
Union Congress (TUC), to which most unions, especially the
large ones, are affiliated. The TUC is often regarded as the voice
of trade unions, and it negotiates with the government and
national employers' associations. However, its formal powers are
limited. Individual unions are not obliged to observe decisions
taken at its annual conference. The standing of the TUC suffered
a blow in 1988 when one large union, the electricians' EETPU,
was expelled for poaching members from other unions. The union
was, however, readmitted in 1992.

Collective Bargaining

Trade unions are concerned with all aspects of the employment of
their members, especially wages, hours and conditions of work,
and unemployment; and some provide benefits for members,
financed out of subscription income. However, the main function
of unions is to engage in collective bargaining with employers.
Negotiations usually take place at least annually, leading to 'wage
rounds' of pay increases. Comparability with workers in similar
industries or occupations, and the profitability of the business, are
generally the major issues discussed.

Negotiations are usually successful, in that the bargaining
sessions produce an agreed package, sometimes associated with
productivity commitments on the part of unions. Negotiations
take place at many levels and can cover a variety of subjects.
Wages are usually the central issue, but hours and conditions of
work, redundancy, allegations of victimisation of individual
workers by management, etc., may also be involved.

Trade Disputes

If the parties fail to agree, an industrial dispute follows; the union may call on its members either to strike or to take other action, such as refusing to work overtime. Employers, on the other side, may threaten to dismiss staff, to implement their offer even when it has not been agreed, or even to close the business.

Disputes, of course, involve loss of production and Figure 4.14 shows the numbers of days lost as a result of stoppages of work since 1920. The first point to make is that the average number of days lost has been substantially lower in the postwar period than it was in the 1920s. It began to rise again in the 1970s, though falling once more in the second half of the 1980s. The second point is that a high proportion of the total number of days lost is often attributable to a very few disputes. An outstanding example of this occurred in 1984 when 22 million of the total of 27 million days lost can be put down to the strike in the coal industry. Moreover, strikes tend to come in waves, and when they do their effects can be widespread and serious, particularly if they involve disruption

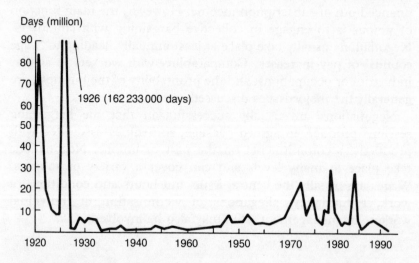

Figure 4.14 Industrial disputes since 1920 – number of working days lost as a result of industrial disputes
Source: *Annual Abstract of Statistics*

of power and communication services, threatening indirectly both industry and the home.

Half a dozen Acts of Parliament were passed between 1980 and 1990, greatly limiting the power of unions to engage in industrial action. They included action against the closed shop, already mentioned, against secondary picketing (involving sympathetic actions by workers in firms not actually involved in a dispute) and the enforcement of postal and secret ballots before strikes could be called. Certain union practices were made unlawful, and employers were given powers to sue unions for damages.

Box 4.2

Britain's Tamed Trade Unionists Find Solidarity is Not Forever

The *Workplace Industrial Relations Survey* [is] one of the few widely accepted pieces of research about how industry uses and regulates its labour.... Studiously neutral politically, its findings show how far the Conservative government achieved its aim of making the notoriously rigid UK labour market more flexible through a combination of economic, legal and social changes....

The survey confirms how savagely the trade unions have been hit.... Union density – the proportion of employees who are members – fell from 58 per cent in 1984 to 48 per cent in 1990.... Non unionism – having no unions at all in the workplace – is sharply up. Now 36 per cent of establishments have no unions compared with 27 per cent in 1984 ... the proportion of workers whose pay and conditions are settled in this way [by collective bargaining] may be less than 40 per cent.... Conservative legislation has brought about the virtual disappearance of closed shops.... Across much of British industry, strikes are largely a thing of the past.

The Times, 25 September 1992

The team writing the above survey concluded that 'many of the changes that occurred in the 1980s are irreversible'. Do you agree? Which of the changes do you think (a) most and (b) least desirable? What effects do you think the changes might have on the structure of earnings in the UK?

Prior to the legislation mentioned in the previous paragraph, the incidence of strikes had become a prominent political issue.

Britain's strike record was also often regarded as something of a national disgrace. However, the picture was not quite as dreadful as some may have thought. Although the UK has not had the best record in the international league table, when compared with such countries as Japan, the Netherlands, and Germany, neither has it usually been at the bottom. Canada and Italy, in particular, have worse records on average than the UK.

Other Factors of Production

The bulk of this chapter has been devoted to a discussion of labour as a factor of production. This is not unreasonable, because incomes from employment take by far the largest proportion of the total, and because of the great importance of labour in the economy as a whole. In a sense, too, some of the material in the preceding sections is also illustrative of productive factors generally.

Although there are special features related to the incomes of other factors of production, especially to rent and profits, it is a little difficult to find much descriptive material that is useful for economic analysis on such matters. None the less, we end this chapter by highlighting some features concerning rent and profits.

Rent

To an economist rent is not just the return received by the factor of production, land; it is a surplus that accrues to any factor of production which possesses a characteristic that others do not. A common example is the so-called 'rent of ability' earned by leading golfers, tennis players and film stars, which greatly exceeds their potential earnings in other occupations. Figure 4.15 is an attempt to illustrate the differential nature of the earnings received by individuals with diverse abilities. The figures are in no way precise measurements of the economic rents accruing to distinctive skills. It could be forcibly maintained that at least some of the differentials are part of the returns for undergoing

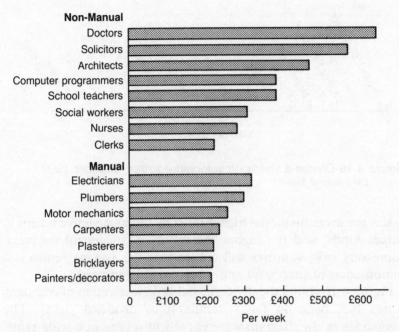

Figure 4.15 Average gross weekly earnings of adult men, selected occupations 1991
Source: *New Earnings Survey* (Department of Employment)

education and training to acquire skills. However, the limited supply of entrants to certain trades and professions is probably due to a shortage of talents, or even to artificial restrictions. Hence, some part of the high earnings are of the nature of economic rent.

Profit

What the man or woman in the street calls profit, economists call the return on capital. When someone buys shares on the stock exchange, the return on their investment usually contains an amount that would be earned on a riskless investment and something which could be described as a risk premium. The

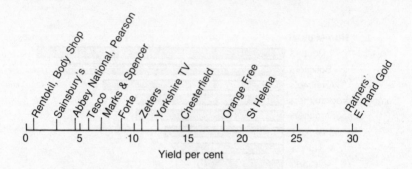

Figure 4.16 Dividend yields on selected equities, October 1992
Source: *The Financial Times*

riskier the investment, the higher must be the prospective return to attract funds, and the higher the profit on successful ventures. Some very risky ventures will fail, so that the average return is a combination of successful and unsuccessful ventures.

Figure 4.16 shows the dividend yields on a selection of company shares (see page 44 for a definition of dividend yield). The companies in the diagram were chosen to represent a wide range of degrees of risk. They have, correspondingly, a wide range of dividend yields. Among the riskiest shares are those of some mining companies where output in future years is something of a gamble. Another currently risky investment was in Ratners, a retail jewellery chain, which was in such dire straits that it was asking the landlords of its shops to defer rent demands so that it might manage to continue trading.

Among shares shown in the Figure with low yields are those of companies with steadily rising profit records such as Body Shop, Sainsbury's and Abbey National. (We should warn you that high yielding shares are not necessarily wonderful investments which one should rush out to buy. The market assessment of risk ought to be such as to make a portfolio of investments in several stocks equally profitable – whether in mining shares and/or 'safe' companies.)

Questions and exercises

(For key to abbreviations indicating sources, see pages xv–xvi)

1   The annual *Social Trends* publishes statistics on the distribution of household income. Use the latest edition and one from 5–10 years ago to plot Lorenz curves as in Figure 4.1. How has income distribution changed, if at all? Why? Would you rather have seen other changes?

2   Construct a table comparing the age distribution of the current population and the projected distribution for the furthest future years given. Comment on the economic consequences.(*AS*)

3   Calculate (i) activity rates and (ii) unemployment rates for the UK for (a) the population aged 16–65 including unemployed and (b) the employed workforce. How different are your results in each case? Which would you prefer to use? (*AS*)

4   Which groups of workers had (a) the highest, (b) the lowest rise in earnings over the past (i) 5, (ii) 10 years? Were your answers the same to (i) and (ii)? If they were not, do you know why not? Even if they were the same, why might they have differed? (*EG*)

5   Which industries had (i) the highest and (ii) the lowest differential disadvantage to women, as measured by average hourly earnings in the most recent year for which you can find statistics? List all possible explanations. (*AS*)

6   Suppose you had bought £1,000 worth of shares in each of the stocks listed in Figure 4.16. Which would have brought you the highest and the lowest gain (in terms of changed share price)? If possible find a share with a higher and a lower dividend yield than any in Figure 4.16. If it was not possible, why was this so? Even if it was possible, why might it not have been? (*FT* or *T*, or other daily newspaper which carries stock exchange prices).

Appendix 4

Table A4.1 Regional male unemployment rates (per cent), UK, 1992

North	15.4	Scotland	12.5
West Midlands	13.8	South East	12.2
Yorkshire and Humberside	13.4	Northern Ireland	18.8
North West	14.4	Greater London	13.4
East Midlands	11.8	South West	12.1
Wales	13.1	UK	9.7
East Anglia	9.9		

Sources: *Monthly Digest of Statistics, Economic Trends* and *Regional Trends*

Table A4.2 Population, unemployment and household income, 1990

	Population (mn)	Unemployment* (%)	Average household income (£)
North	3.1	10.4	140
Yorkshire and Humberside	5.0	8.7	135
East Midlands	4.0	7.2	149
East Anglia	2.1	5.8	152
South East	17.5	7.0	183
South West	4.7	7.1	149
West Midlands	5.2	8.6	155
North West	6.4	9.4	155
Wales	2.9	8.4	144
Scotland	5.1	8.7	147
Northern Ireland	1.6	13.7	123
UK	57.4	8.1	158

*1992

Source: *Regional Trends*

Table A4.3 Average weekly earnings of manual workers (full-time workers on adult rates of pay), UK, 1991 (£s)

	Food, drink and tobacco	Mineral extraction	Chemicals and allied industries	Metal manufacture	Mechanical engineering	Metal goods	Electrical engineering	Motor vehicles
Males	264	262	295	279	259	240	241	277
Females	179	163	189	163	183	166	173	221

	Textiles	Clothing and footwear	Timber furniture, etc.	Paper, printing and publishing	Energy and water	Construction	All manufacturing
Males	206	190	219	317	260	311	264
Females	137	128	168	207	161	223	179

Source: *Employment Gazette*

Table A4.4 Industrial stoppages, UK, 1971–1991

(i)

Year	Number of stoppages	Working days lost
1971	2,263	13,551
1972	2,530	23,909
1973	2,902	7,197
1974	2,946	14,750
1975	2,332	6,012
1976	2,034	3,284
1977	2,737	10,142
1978	2,498	9,405
1979	2,125	29,474
1980	1,348	11,964
1981	1,344	4,266
1982	1,538	5,313
1983	1,364	3,754
1984	1,221	27,135
1985	903	6,402
1986	1,074	1,920
1987	1,016	3,546
1988	781	3,702
1989	701	4,128
1990	630	1,903
1991	369	761

(ii)

Industry	Working days lost			
	1985	1987	1989	1990
Coal extraction	4,142	217	50	59
Other energy and water	57	9	20	39
Metals, minerals and chemicals	167	60	42	42
Engineering and vehicles	481	422	617	922
Other manufacturing industries	261	115	91	106
Construction	50	22	128	14
Transport and communication	197	1,705	624	177
Public admin. sanitary services and education	957	939	2,237	175
Medical and health services	33	6	151	345
All other industries and services	54	53	167	20
Total	6,402	3,546	4,128	1,903

Source: *Employment Gazette*

5
International Trade and Development

No modern nations exist in isolation.[1] They engage in trade in goods and services and in financial transactions of many kinds. International payments and receipts for all purposes are recorded in a country's balance of payments, which will be discussed in Chapter 7. For the present, we ignore purely financial transactions and concentrate on the international allocation of resources and patterns of trade in visible goods and services.

The Basis for Trade

International specialisation is no different in principle from interregional specialisation, which was examined in Chapter 3. We saw there how different parts of the UK tend to concentrate on certain lines of economic activity. The reasons for specialisation relate to natural and acquired endowments of factors of production – the size and quality of the labour force, the quantity and fertility of the land, the mineral resources below it, and the amount of capital equipment that has been accumulated.

In one important respect international variations in factor endowments are of greater significance than are interregional variations – factors of production are much more freely mobile within countries than between them. Some of the reasons are

1 The theory related to the issues discussed in this chapter is covered in Lipsey–Harbury, FP2, Chapter 22.

linguistic and political, stemming from the existence of national frontiers which impede factor movement. Others are social and psychological barriers reflecting national life styles, which discourage labour, in particular, from moving in search of the highest paid employment. Moreover, the existence of national governments and national currencies often leads to state intervention to protect industries from foreign competition.

Most international trade is based on relative scarcities, or abundances, of factors of production, which in turn give rise to relative cost advantages and disadvantages in the production of particular goods and services. Occasionally, a disadvantage may be extreme, so that a country may be totally incapable of producing some product. In the main, however, extreme cases stem either from the uneven dispersion of minerals over the world, or from climatic conditions. Canada, for example, is rich in nickel deposits, Spain and Italy in mercury and South Africa in gold, while Britain has virtually none of these metals. Moreover, with a temperate climate Britain cannot grow tropical and subtropical products such as coffee, tea, cotton, rubber or cocoa. The only way in which Britain can obtain these and similar products is by importing them from abroad in exchange for British exports.

Most trade is between countries who have what is known as a comparative advantage in the production of some goods, which they export, and a comparative disadvantage in the production of others, which they import. This means that, although a country could produce most goods that it imports, the relative costs are such as to encourage specialisation in some and importation of others.

The Major Trading Nations

We start to put the UK in perspective by noting the major world trading nations. Figure 5.1 shows the values of total imports and exports of the 10 leading trading nations, which are together responsible for about 60 per cent of all international trade. It is apparent that there are great differences even among the leaders. The scene is dominated by the United States, Germany and Japan,

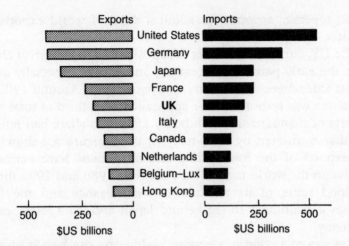

Figure 5.1 Major trading nations; values of exports and imports in US dollars, 1991

Source: *International Financial Statistics (IMF)*

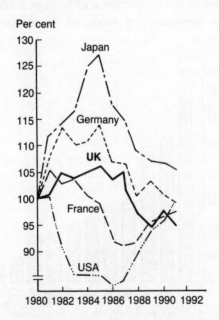

Figure 5.2 Exports performance of leading trading nations since 1980 (the series for each country shows the volume of exports relative to the world total)

Source: *National Institute Economic Review*

which together account for about a third of world exports and imports.

The UK currently occupies fifth position. This is a great change from the early part of this century, and earlier, especially on the export side where this country was paramount. Around 1900, the UK alone was responsible for approximately a third of total world exports of manufactured goods. By 1950 that share had fallen to less than a quarter; by 1990 to 7 per cent. Figure 5.2 shows how the exports of the five leading trading nations have performed relative to the world total. Thus, between 1980 and 1992 the UK regained some of its position *vis-à-vis* France and the USA, though it continued to lag behind Japan and, to a lesser extent, Germany.

The size of a country's exports or imports can be a misleading guide to the significance of foreign trade to that nation. A large country can have an extensive foreign trade which is, nevertheless, proportionately small compared to that of a more modest nation. A useful measure of the importance of foreign trade to a country is the relationship between the value of its imports and its total national product.

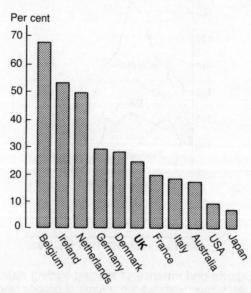

Figure 5.3 Imports as a percentage of national income (GDP), selected countries 1991
Source: *International Financial Statistics (IMF)*

Figure 5.3 shows the wide variations which exist between some representative nations. The USA, for example – the world's leading importing country – depends much less on imports than almost all the others. Only 11 per cent of its total income is spent on imported goods, while a relatively small country, Ireland, spends about half its income on imports. Belgium is even more dependent on trade: no less than two-thirds of its income is spent on goods imported from abroad. Britain spends about a quarter. Thus, a decline of, say, 50 per cent in foreign trade by the United States would make a big hole in the total volume of world trade, but it would make comparatively little difference to the United States itself. In contrast, the complete cessation of imports by Ireland would lower world trade by under 1 per cent, but it would gravely disrupt the Irish economy.

The Trade of the UK

The ways in which trade impinges on economic life can be seen by studying the pattern of trade, especially two aspects:

- commodity composition
- geographical distribution

Commodity Trade

The commodity composition of UK trade in 1991 is shown in Figure 5.4. Note that this composition is not typical of earlier periods. Chapter 1 described the major shifts that have taken place in British overseas trade during the present century – the reader is urged to review that section, and in particular Figure 1.11 and Figure 1.12.

The pattern of imports today is one where manufactures and semi-manufactures account for about three-quarters of the total, whereas prior to the First World War their share was less than a quarter. The traditional, nineteenth century, picture of the UK,

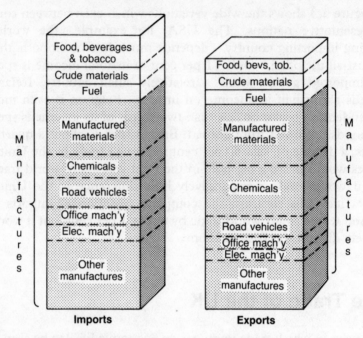

Figure 5.4 Commodity trade of the UK, 1991
Source: *Annual Abstract of Statistics*

exporting manufactured goods in exchange for imports of primary products, has been eroded over the twentieth-century, at first gradually and then at an accelerating pace after the 1960s. British foreign trade now consists predominantly of the exchange of manufactured goods with other countries. The only raw material whose import increased significantly for a limited period was fuel, although Britain became a fuel exporter as a result of the oil discoveries in the North Sea in the 1970s and, as can be seen from Figure 5.4, trade in fuels is now more or less in balance.

Although manufactures remain the solid backbone of Britain's exports, there have been substantial shifts in their composition. These reflect, in part, changes in the structure of British industry itself, noted in Chapter 3. Textiles and iron and steel, for example, made up approximately half of total exports in 1913. By 1991 their place had been taken by machinery, chemicals and vehicles, and their share had dropped to about 5 per cent – too small to be shown on Figure 5.4.

Import and export penetration

Two aspects of commodity trade worthy of attention are:

- the extent to which foreign imports compete with domestically produced goods
- the relative importance of exports to home production

Figure 5.5 throws light on both these matters for a selection of industries. The top, lightly shaded bars show the percentages of UK sales which go to export markets; the lower, darker bars show the percentages of UK markets which draw their supplies as imports from overseas.

The large share of some British markets taken by foreign suppliers is not necessarily a cause for concern. One should look also at the export performance of British industries. We find that many of the industries where there is heavy import penetration are

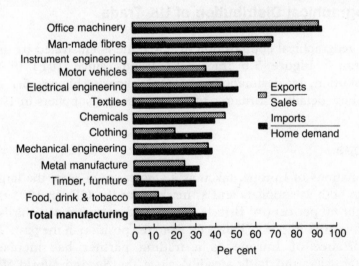

Figure 5.5 Exports/sales and imports/home demand, selected industries, UK 1991
Source: *Annual Abstract of Statistics*

also ones where exports account for high proportions of output by UK firms. For example, the manufacturers of office machinery (which includes data processing equipment) sell over 90 per cent of their output overseas – almost the same proportion as foreign firms take in the UK market. The export/sales ratio exceeds the imports/home demand ratio in chemicals, and in several industry groups the import and export penetration ratios are not too far apart.

Figure 5.5 presents only a snapshot of the situation in a single, recent, year. It should be added that the trends in import penetration and export/sales ratios have been of steady and appreciable increases in both figures. For manufacturing industry as a whole, import penetration rose from 17 to 37 per cent between 1971 and 1990, while exports as a percentage of sales rose from 19 to 30 per cent over the same period. In the previous section, we described British foreign trade as being characterised nowadays by an interchange of manufactures. We see now that this applies as much within industry groups as to exports of manufactures as a whole.

Geographical Distribution of UK Trade

The geographical composition of UK trade is illustrated by three diagrams: Figure 5.6 traces the trends since 1913 in the distribution, by destination, of British exports; Figures 5.7 and 5.8 show details of Britain's main markets and suppliers in 1991.

Europe

The nations of Europe, taken as a whole, are at once the largest group both as suppliers and as markets for the UK. In 1991 they bought 60 per cent of British exports and provided two-thirds of the country's imports. This is far from the position in the past. The importance of Europe as a trading partner has increased substantially, and fairly steadily, since the Second World War. The growth can be attributed, in the first place, to the changed structure of UK trade – the fall in importance of imports of

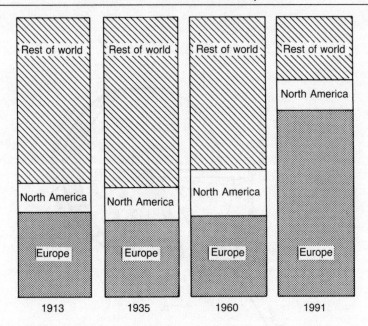

Figure 5.6 UK exports (percentage distribution by destination), selected
years 1913–1991
Sources: *Abstract of British Historical Statistics*, B R Mitchell and P Deane Cambridge
University Press, 1962), and *Annual Abstract of Statistics*

primary products relative to manufactured goods – and to
declining trading links between Britain and the Commonwealth,
which used to occupy the dominant trading position. In the
second place, the postwar trend towards increasing European
trade received a massive boost when, in 1973, the UK joined the
European Community (see below).

Figures 5.7 and 5.8 divide Europe into two parts – members of
the EC, and the rest. The former can be seen to be much the more
important; in 1991 the EC accounted for nearly 60 per cent of UK
exports and over 50 per cent of imports. The situation may be
compared with the 1960s when those proportions were less than a
third.

Within the EC, Germany is Britain's major market and supplier
of imports (mainly machinery and manufactured goods including
cars and chemicals). Next is France (which sends Britain
manufactures and food) followed by the Netherlands (dairy
produce and other foodstuffs), Italy, Belgium and Ireland. The

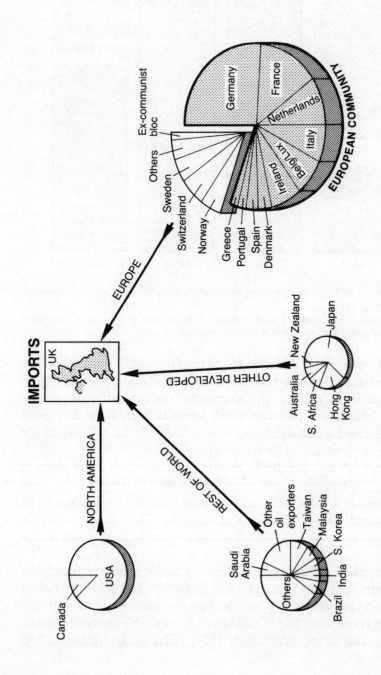

Figure 5.7 UK imports by origin 1991
Source: *Annual Abstract of Statistics*

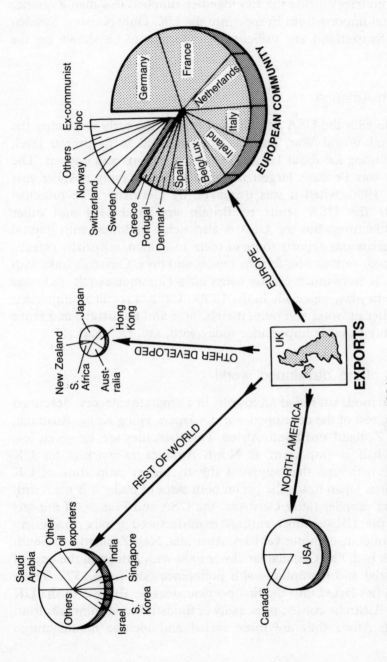

Figure 5.8 UK exports by destination 1991
Source: *Annual Abstract of Statistics*

shares of the other EC member countries can be seen in Figures 5.7 and 5.8.

Countries outside the EC together supplied less than a quarter of total imports from Europe into the UK. Only Norway, Sweden and Switzerland are sufficiently important to be shown on the diagram.

North America

Trade with the USA and Canada rose in the early years after the Second World War, but has now reverted to its prewar level, accounting for about 12 per cent of UK exports and imports. The USA was Britain's largest market for almost every postwar year until 1990, when it was overtaken by Germany. The principal goods the USA sends to Britain are machinery and other manufactures, but the USA is also richly endowed with natural resources and exports some of them to Britain, especially cereals, tobacco, cotton, non-ferrous metals and ores. Canada's links with the UK were much greater when intra-Commonwealth trade was in its heyday, especially in the 1930s. Canada is still an important supplier of wood and pulp, metals, ores and foodstuffs, and ranks roughly equal in importance today with, say, Denmark.

Rest of the 'developed' world

Five nations sit, rather arbitrarily, in a separate category, described as the rest of the developed world – Japan, Hong Kong, Australia, New Zealand and South Africa. Together, they are, however, less than half as important as North America as markets for UK exports, though they supply a slightly higher proportion of UK imports. Japan heads the list on both sides of trade; it is the fourth largest supplier (after Germany, the USA and France) of imports into the UK – almost entirely manufactured goods, machinery and, of course, motor vehicles. Australia, New Zealand and South Africa had, like Canada, far closer links with Britain in the days of Imperial and Commonwealth preference (see page 157). These trade ties lasted into the first postwar decade. Exports to the UK from Australia consist principally of foodstuffs and minerals; from South Africa they are more varied and include manufactured goods as well as cereals, metals, fruit and vegetables; from New Zealand they are substantially foodstuffs.

Developing countries

The final group of countries are usually described as 'developing' countries, or less developed countries (LDCs). So-called oil-exporting countries are included in this category. They first sprang into prominence in 1973–4 when the group known as OPEC (standing for Organisation of Petroleum Exporting Countries) succeeded in quadrupling the price of crude oil. Thereafter, they grew in importance, both as oil suppliers and as growing markets for UK exports, until British exploitation of North Sea oil. By 1991, this group of countries (of which Saudi Arabia is the largest) supplied only about 2 per cent of UK imports, but took double that proportion of exports.

A host of other developing countries are included in the 'others' section in Figures 5.7 and 5.8. The only ones large enough to appear in the diagrams are India, South Korea, Taiwan, Malaysia, Singapore, Brazil and Israel.

The terms of trade

Trading patterns result from the actions of many forces. Prime among them are the prices of goods in different countries. Prices are affected by the rates at which currencies exchange for each other, which will be discussed in Chapter 7. We make a start on this subject here by looking at the terms of trade, which relate the prices of imports to those of exports. The terms of trade are calculated by dividing an index of export prices level by an index of import prices.[2]

Movements of the UK terms of trade since 1970 are plotted in Figure 5.9. The diagram shows the sharp deterioration which followed the oil price shock of 1973-74, referred to earlier, when

2 The terms of trade is a dynamic concept. It shows how export prices *are changing* relative to import prices.

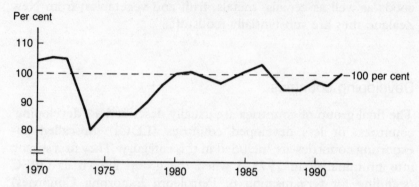

Per cent

Figure 5.9 Terms of trade, UK since 1970 (quantity of imports obtainable for a fixed quantity of exports) – an upward movement corresponds to an improvement in the UK's terms of trade
Source: *Annual Abstract of Statistics*

the prices of many other primary products which the UK imports (cocoa, zinc, etc.) also rose substantially. The general trend thereafter was of a gradual improvement in the UK's terms of trade, with a short-term deterioration in the late 1980s.

Export competitiveness

The terms of trade are an expression of the relative prices of imports and exports. To ascertain the competitiveness of British goods requires a comparison of UK export prices relative to those of producers in competing countries. This requires consideration of exchange rates between currencies and relative inflation rates,

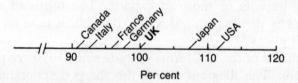

Per cent

Figure 5.10 Export competitiveness; changes in export prices, relative to the world average, selected countries, 1980–1991. Note, the higher the figure the less competitive are exports
Source: *National Institute Economic Review*

as well as the terms of trade. In the 1970s, the net outcome of these factors worked unfavourably i.e. against the UK compared with the USA, Japan, Germany and other EC countries. However, since 1980 the competitiveness of UK exports has steadied (see Figure 5.10), though with an improvement in the earlier years and a deterioration later on. (The reader is warned that the figures on which the diagram are based are particularly sensitive to the choice of base year for the comparisons. You are advised to attempt question 4 at the end of this chapter.)

Trade Restrictions

International trade does not take place in completely free markets. Most governments take some actions designed to discourage certain imports and to encourage certain exports. Since one country's imports are another country's exports, it follows that the net effect of all measures is to lower the volume of world trade and reduce the scope for gains from trade based on comparative advantage. Three methods of restricting imports may be distinguished:

- **tariffs**
- **quotas**
- **non-tariff barriers**

Tariffs

The traditional means of restricting imports is through tariffs (also called import duties). These are taxes placed on imported goods which raise their prices in the levying country's domestic market above those in international markets.

Quotas

Quotas set limits to the quantities of certain goods that are allowed to be imported in a stated period.

Non-tariff barriers (NTBs)

Non-tariff barriers refer to all other measures that reduce imports. (Strictly speaking quotas are NTBs, but we follow tradition in listing them separately.) Major non-tariff barriers include **Voluntary Export Restraints** (VERs), one of a group of Voluntary Restraint Arrangements, in which one country agrees to restrict its exports to a second country (often to avoid more severe import restrictions which the second country might otherwise impose). A different set of NTBs involves harassment of goods at frontiers by unnecessarily complex and costly entry procedures, or the application of stricter standards for safety, quality, etc., than are applied to similar goods produced domestically.

Measures to encourage exports

The two most common practices designed to encourage exports are dumping and export subsidies. **Dumping** is defined as sales in a foreign market at artificially low prices. Export subsidies are moneys given to exporting firms, allowing goods to be sold abroad at reduced prices. Both practices have been employed to try to drive competitors out of business or to get rid of unwanted surpluses.

Importing countries attempt to offset 'unfair' dumping by levying anti-dumping duties, and/or countervailing duties to offset export subsidies by foreign governments. Properly used, such 'trade remedy laws' do not distort trade. Misused, they can become potent non-tariff barriers, restricting trade. Partly because tariff barriers were drastically reduced during the decades that followed the end of the Second World War (see below), increasing use has been made of anti-dumping duties in the more recent past in situations when the exporting country was not engaging in obviously unfair practices. Other non-tariff barriers were also increasingly used over this period.

UK Commercial Policy

UK commercial policy should be examined in two contexts – global and regional. The first looks at the UK *vis-à-vis* the world as a whole; the second *vis-à-vis* particular groups of countries.

The most helpful description takes a historical starting point with Britain's mid-nineteenth-century stand in support of free trade. This lasted, with a few relatively minor exceptions, until the early 1930s. Thereafter, world economic depression caused a collapse in the volume of international trade. In 1932, the UK introduced protective tariffs on all imports, barring some foodstuffs and raw materials. Later the same year, the idea was born of giving favoured tariff treatment to countries of the British Empire – Imperial, later Commonwealth, Preference.

The Imperial Preference system led to a substantial increase in intra-Commonwealth trade. During the Second World War, however, new markets were generated and, after the war, the UK turned to develop links with Western Europe.

The European Community (EC)

The prime regional group with which the UK is linked is, of course, the European Community, the origins of which are to be found in the disruption caused by the Second World War, in subsequent US (Marshall) aid to the stricken countries, and in the establishment of the Organisation for Economic Co-operation and Development (OECD).

The first move towards closer economic links in Europe came in 1948, but this was limited to the three nations of Belgium, Luxembourg and the Netherlands (Benelux). The three then joined France, (West) Germany and Italy in 1952, to form the European Coal and Steel Community, designed to create a unified market in these products. Five years later, the 'Six', as they then were, signed the Treaty of Rome establishing the **European**

Economic Community (**EEC**, now simply EC) and outlining a programme for the elimination of tariffs among member nations and a unified schedule of import duties for outsiders.

The UK was at first reluctant to join the EEC, partly on political grounds and partly because of traditional links with the Commonwealth. Instead, the UK made an agreement with Austria, Denmark, Norway, Portugal, Sweden and Switzerland (and subsequently Finland) to set up the **European Free Trade Association** (EFTA) in 1960. The aims of EFTA were more modest than those of the EEC (with which free trade in industrial products was, incidentally, later agreed). In one particular way they were attractive for Britain. Although tariffs were to be abolished within the Association, a common external tariff was not included. This allowed the UK to continue Commonwealth preferences.

Meanwhile, EEC countries were mostly enjoying more favourable conditions with regard to living standards, inflation and the balance of payments than was the UK. At the same time Britain's trade with the Commonwealth was declining. The UK therefore sought EEC membership. One application was turned down, in 1962 (effectively by the French); another was successful, in 1973. Denmark and Ireland joined at the same time; Greece, Spain and Portugal joined subsequently, to turn the 'Six' into 'Twelve'. The formal structure of the Community consists of four institutions:

- The **European Commission**. This is made up of 17 Commissioners appointed by member governments – one from each of the smallest member nations, and two from each of the five largest. The Commission, currently presided over (for two four-year terms) by the Frenchman Jacques Delors, is the body which administers EC policies.

- The **European Council of Ministers**. This consists of 12 ministers, one from each member state. The ministers who actually attend Council meetings are determined by its business. They might, for example, be ministers of transport or of agriculture. When major policy issues are on the agenda, it is the practice for heads of state to attend.

- The **European Parliament**. This is composed of European MPs (MEPs) who are directly elected from constituencies within EC nations.

- The **European Court of Justice**. This settles matters affected by Community law.

The political and administrative processes of the EC are beyond the scope of this book, though the importance of such matters as the procedures and powers of the institutions mentioned above can be crucial. So too can be the voting arrangements, e.g. whether policy decisions are based on unanimity, simple majority or more complex rules.

Economically speaking the EC represents a major world power grouping. Its total output is approximately equal to, and its total population is some 30 per cent greater than, that of the USA. The relative sizes of member states is shown in Figure 5.11, which focuses on the prime characteristics of population, output and foreign trade. Other details appear at appropriate places in the book, e.g. investment as a percentage of total output [page 77] and income per head [page 166]). The Figure brings out the dominance of Germany within the EC. The largest four member nations, Germany, France, Italy and the UK, account for three-quarters or more of total EC population, output and trade.

The EC operates in numerous areas of economic and social life. Several are referred to elsewhere in the book, e.g. agricultural and competition policies in Chapter 6. A common unit of currency – the ECU – has been introduced for accounting purposes, and institutions have been set up with the aim of providing stability in the rates of exchange between the currencies of member countries.

These last mentioned, financial, matters were at the heart of the **Treaty of Maastricht**, signed by the representatives of the governments of participating nations in 1992. The Maastricht programme was designed to take the Community towards full economic integration, including monetary union and the eventual adoption of a single currency to replace the currencies of all member states. The Treaty raised extremely sensitive issues of national sovereignty, especially with regard to foreign policy and the overall management of the economy. We return to this subject in Chapter 9.

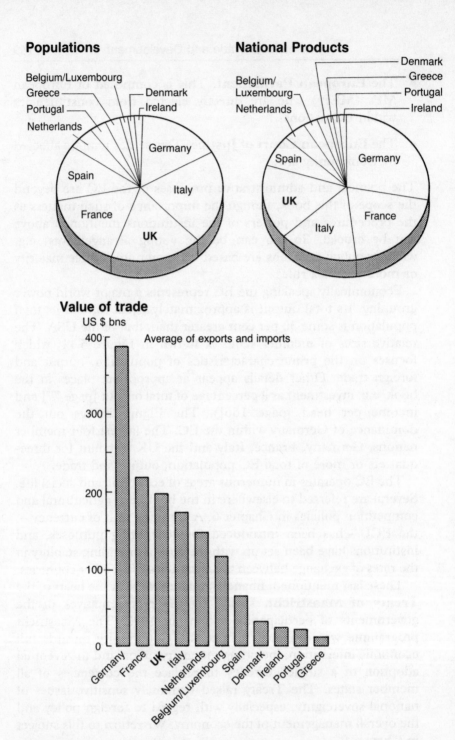

Populations

Belgium/Luxembourg
Greece
Portugal
Netherlands
Denmark
Ireland
Germany
Spain
Italy
France
UK

National Products

Belgium/
Luxembourg
Netherlands
Denmark
Greece
Portugal
Ireland
Spain
Germany
UK
Italy
France

Value of trade
US $ bns

Average of exports and imports

400

300

200

100

0

Germany
France
UK
Italy
Netherlands
Belgium/Luxembourg
Spain
Denmark
Ireland
Portugal
Greece

Figure 5.11 European Community, population, output, and trade 1991
Source: *Eurostat* (EC) and *International Financial Statistics* (IMF)

The electorates of Denmark, France and Ireland were asked in referenda whether they wished their governments to ratify the Treaty. Denmark voted against ratification, France and Ireland voted in favour, the former with the slenderest of margins. At the time of writing, the future of Maastricht is uncertain. There is a chance that events might move either in the direction of amending the Treaty to keep membership of the EC intact, or in a split into a 'two-speed' Europe, with one group of members pressing faster than the other towards full economic union.

In the present chapter, we are concerned with the limited issue of trade in goods and services. The original intentions of the Six in this respect, were to create a customs union with free trade internally, and to impose a common external tariff on goods imported from the rest of the world. Rates of import duty were gradually lowered, however. As far as the UK is concerned, they were finally eliminated in 1977. Tariffs affecting the latest joining nations, Portugal and Spain, are due to be phased out by 1993 for industrial commodities, later for certain agricultural products.

The Single European Act 1992

EC development entered a new phase in 1985, when member states signed an agreement which called on the Commission to organise a detailed programme for 'completing the common market'. The background to the new phase was the realisation that European integration had been limited in many ways – not least because of the focus on tariff reductions – and that the time had come to move further. A package of reforms for a 'single market', the **Single European Act** (SEA), was drawn up, to be introduced by 31 December 1992.

Two kinds of restriction were addressed in the SEA. One related to trade in services, as distinct from trade in visible commodities. The UK is not the only EC country to have experienced a decline in the relative size of its manufacturing sector and its replacement by services of one sort or another. Yet, trade in services was restricted by a host of rules which impeded competition among suppliers within the EC. For example, there were financial regulations which interfered with trade in banking and insurance; and there were restrictions relating to personal qualifications, which hindered consumers in one EC country from buying the services of professionals and tradesmen resident in others.

The second kind of non-tariff trade restriction relates more to goods than to services. Frontier formalities both delay and interfere with trade. Freedom to buy and sell in the best market is hampered by countless inter-country differences. Thus, domestic standards of safety, security and health can, accidentally or deliberately, discourage imports. So can domestic taxes and laws related to patents and trade marks. There are also anti-competitive practices whereby governments in their contracts for purchases (so-called public procurement) give preferential treatment to domestic suppliers.

The Single European Market targets barriers such as those mentioned above. The principle of 'mutual recognition' built into the SEA provides an example of how such barriers can be tackled. This principle followed a judgment by the European Court of Justice in the 'Cassis de Dijon' case, which involved Germany prohibiting imports of the drink cassis from France. The French won the case. The principle now generally denies the right of any member state to ban imports of another member state's goods so long as they have been legally produced elsewhere in the Community.[3] Other ways of 'completing the single market' include 'harmonisation' of taxes – e.g the UK had to substitute VAT for its own purchase tax.

Note, the achievement of a single market is not easy, cost-free or even necessarily desirable. It entails compromises, whereby countries make changes that they would prefer not to, in return for concessions by others, and/or financial compensation from Community funds. It also tends to involve a degree of loss of sovereignty for national governments, who may be precluded from adopting policies that depart from EC guidelines. This is a consequence of particular importance in the field of fiscal and monetary policies, discussed in Chapters 8 and 9.

3 Exceptions are allowed for cases where health, safety or consumer protection is concerned.

It should not be inferred that full integration of the EC necessarily implies a strict free market rather than an interventionist approach within the economic systems of members. It does imply, however, that all countries in the Community accept a similar balance in their economic systems. An interventionist policy (such as there has been towards agriculture, discussed in the next chapter) is as consistent with the Single Market as is a free market orientation. It is up to member states through the political institutions to determine what the balance should be.

Finally, on the question of the desirability of full integration within the Community, one should look separately at two distinct implications. On the one hand, there are the relationships among EC members themselves. On the other hand, there is the relationship between EC members and the rest of the world. The former question may be guided by the economic theory that analyses the benefits that accrue to nations under free trade. This rests on countries specialising in the production of goods in which they have a comparative advantage, and of reaping the economies of large-scale production that were unattainable because of the limited size of domestic markets.

The second question of the effects of integration within the EC on its trade with the rest of the world is also guided by economic theory, that of trade creation and diversion. If, as some people fear, 'Fortress Europe' should become too isolationist, the world as a whole might become worse off, as more regional trade groupings do less trade with each other.

World Trade Liberalisation

Since 1945, trade liberalisation – reducing trade barriers – has operated on two bases, regional and multilateral. Regional trade liberalisation is restricted to individual blocks of countries, such as the EC, discussed above. There have been other regional groupings, including the recent USA–Canada Trade Agreement, which is scheduled to phase out tariffs on the world's largest bilateral flow of trade in goods and services between 1989 and 1999.

Multilateral trade liberalisation is worldwide. The most important international institution fostering global reduction of trade barriers is the GATT, standing for General Agreement on Tariffs and Trade.

GATT

GATT acts as a forum for discussion on ways of lowering trade restrictions and for settling disputes among its members. It has also developed a number of 'codes' governing world trade and investment. GATT is, arguably, the most successful of the international organisations set up in the aftermath of the Second World War. It presided over a major liberalisation of international trade, reducing tariffs from the very high levels to which they had been pushed during the Great Depression of the 1930s. The average level of tariffs among participating nations is estimated to have fallen from the first to the last completed 'round' of negotiations' (Geneva to Tokyo, see next paragraph) by as much as 95 per cent.

The main devices for reducing tariffs under GATT's auspices have been international negotiating conferences. Initially, participants to the negotiations bargained bilaterally (in pairs) while agreeing in advance to extend tariff concessions multilaterally to all nations in GATT. In most recent rounds, general percentage reductions in all tariffs have been agreed to by members. Seven meetings have been held from the first in Geneva, in 1947, to two very successful ones in the early 1960s and late 1970s, called the 'Kennedy Round' and the 'Tokyo Round' respectively. The eighth, 'Uruguay Round', involving 105 participating nations began in 1986 and was scheduled to end by 1990, but negotiations were at a critical stage by late 1992.

The Uruguay Round was expected to extend liberalisation to invisible trade in services, and to tackle some of the non-tariff barriers that have replaced tariffs. Failure to reach agreement as deadline after deadline passed, however, was largely due to problems over agriculture which dominated discussions. Friction between the USA and the EC over export subsidies for farm products has been at the heart of the dispute. Indeed, the state of deadlock led the USA to walk out of negotiations in October 1992. In November the same year, the USA announced the imposition of retaliatory tariffs on imports from the EC. A grave risk appeared that a trade war might develop with dire consequences for the level of world trade. A serious political crisis ensued within the Community, involving (especially French) farmers and the resignation of the EC Commissioner for Agriculture, their chief GATT negotiator. At the time of writing (January 1993) the issue has not been settled, but hopes of resolving it have risen as a new president of the United States takes up office.

Although some of the poorest developing countries gain from subsidies for their food imports, others lose because government policies in the agricultural sector have turned them from major importers to large-scale exporters of agricultural products. Agriculture accounts, on average, for some 15 per cent of national output (GDP) in less developed countries (compared to 2 per cent in developed countries), hence the concern over the subsidisation of EC exports is understandable. The governments of LDCs cannot afford lavish subsidies, so their products lose out to European competition even though their production costs are lower.

One particular agreement made at the start of the Uruguay Round was for a standstill and rollback of VERs (see above), i.e. no new ones are to be entered into and existing ones are to be phased out. As far as the UK is concerned, membership of the EC means that its VERs with Japan could not have been continued after 1992 anyway, though the EC negotiated with Japan to restrict certain exports to EC markets until the end of 1999.

Economic Development

One outstanding characteristic of the international economy is the inequality of the distribution of income among countries. More than half of the world's population of 5 billion live in countries where income per head in 1990 was less than $500 (US) per year. In stark contrast, 15 per cent of the population live in the rich countries, where average per capita income was $20,000 per annum.

Figure 5.12 shows the income per head of the population for a selection of countries. It is shaped like a pyramid because there are relatively few countries with high average incomes but many with low ones. It is intended only as a rough guide and must be treated with caution for a variety of reasons, some of them technical in nature. Moreover, income per head is not by any means the same thing as 'happiness' – a subject beyond the boundaries of economics, involving questions of life styles in different countries. It would be presumptuous to suggest that someone in Britain watching a video-recorded colour TV programme was more or less 'happy' than an Indian listening to a local village singer.

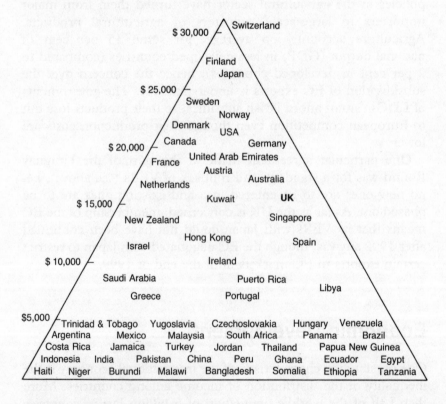

Figure 5.12 Average income per head selected countries, 1990 (estimated GNP per capita in US$)
Source: *World Bank Atlas*

Bearing these reservations in mind, we can examine Figure 5.12 for evidence of what is called the development gap – the discrepancy between the standards of living in countries at either end of the distribution. Some of the differences in income per head are so enormous that they can hardly be explained by statistical errors. Countries at the top of the scale enjoy per capita incomes 50 to 100 times those of the LDCs at the bottom.

The reasons why some countries have low and others high incomes per head are complex. They relate in part to the natural resources with which nations are endowed. Incomes per capita are also affected by the size of the populations in different countries. It can scarcely be an accident that many of the poorest countries are those with large populations. China and India alone have nearly 40 per cent of the total world population, double that of the whole of Europe and North America put together.

With the passage of time some countries have lifted themselves out of poverty. However, the overall inequality between rich and poor is increasing rather than diminishing. This is because rates of economic growth tend to be low for the poorest countries, many of which also have rapid population increases to cope with. Moreover, the economic health of many LDCs, especially in sub-Saharan Africa, deteriorated drastically over the last 20 years as a result of the enormous debts they had accumulated (see pages 333–5).

Aid

The consciences of rich countries are pricked by the growing gap in living standards between themselves and the poor countries of the 'Third World' and by the large number of nations at the bottom of the scale. However, action to help the less developed countries has not been on the massive scale necessary to make a substantial impact on income inequality. The United Nations Organisation set a target of 0.7 per cent of national income for developed countries to contribute as aid for their poorer neighbours, though few have achieved that level in recent years (see Box 5.1).

Box 5.1

UN Aid Figure Sets Rich and Poor Nations Squabbling

A small figure, 0.7, is beginning to obsess the two camps of countries, the rich and the poor, now squaring up to each other as the Earth Summit in Rio de Janeiro enters its final stage. The figure represents the percentage of national wealth that has been the longstanding official United Nations target for annual foreign aid donations by the industrialised countries, including Britain. Sixteen of the principal aid donors accept the target – the United States and Switzerland do not – but only the Nordic countries and the Netherlands have managed to meet it. Britain's contribution has been steadily falling over the past 13 years, from 0.51 per cent in 1979 to 0.27 per cent in 1990.

Agenda 21 aims to channel eco-nomic growth along an environmentally friendly path.. The Group of 77, the developing nations attending Rio, have spent ten months of the summit preparatory process demanding more aid ... refused point blank by the donor countries.... A promise to match the UN aid target of 0.7 per cent of gross national product by a fixed date, such as 2000, offers the best possibility of compromise.

Britain has accepted the target in principle, while declining to attach any timetable to it.... 'Focusing on the totem pole of 0.7 is actually misleading' said Baroness Chalker, the overseas development minister ... 'the quality and targeting of aid, and what it is spent on, are as important as how much is spent.'

The Times, 12 June 1992

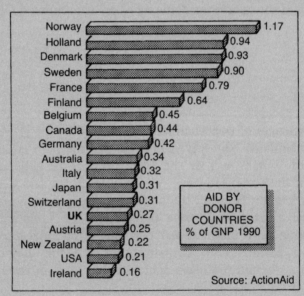

AID BY DONOR COUNTRIES % of GNP 1990

Source: ActionAid

Having regard to the evidence in Figure 5.12 and Table A5.3 in the Appendix, what do you make of the attitude of the nations at the Earth Summit ? How relevant is the estimate that for Britain to achieve 0.7 per cent would require more than a penny to be

The World Bank

In addition to private charities (such as Oxfam and Bandaid) targeted at the relief of Third World poverty, there are international organisations specifically concerned with economic development. The most important is the World Bank, which comprises four agencies:

- the International Bank for Reconstruction and Development (IBRD), which makes loans for economic development to 'better-off' developing countries, at something like market rates of interest
- the International Development Association (IDA), which lends at much lower rates to poorer LDCs (those with per capita incomes below $[US]750)
- the International Finance Corporation (IFC), which lends to the private sector
- the Multilateral Investment Guarantee Agency (MIGA), which offers insurance against political risk in order to encourage private investment

IBRD makes the biggest contribution, $16 billion of new lending in 1991, compared to $6 billion by IDA. Some loans are project-related, others focused on infrastructure, i.e. designed to improve the economic climate generally in order to encourage economic development.

Preferential trading arrangements

An alternative to aid, favoured by those who mistrust the governments who dispense it, is to develop trading links. The prime international organisation concerned in this area is UNCTAD (the United Nations Conference on Trade and Development), established in 1964 under the auspices of the United Nations Organisation. High-sounding resolutions have been passed at UNCTAD conferences and a 'north–south dialogue' has attempted to integrate the economies of some Third World countries more closely with those of the developed nations, especially in Europe. Under the auspices of UNCTAD, a general system of preferences (GSP) was introduced to give the exports of manufactured goods from LDCs preferential access to markets in developed nations.

Some preferential treatment for less developed countries has been negotiated under GATT, and more is still hoped for in the current Uruguay Round. The European Community has also made similar concessions, first under Yaoundé agreements, and then under Lomé Conventions. The latter gives nearly 70 African, Caribbean and Pacific developing countries virtually free access to the markets in the Community for industrial products. The scale of these arrangements is relatively small and less helpful for some recipients than if the concessions were for agricultural products.

Questions and exercises

(For key to abbreviations identifying sources, see pages xv–xvi)

1 Divide the categories of commodities in Figure 5.5. according to whether there was an excess of imports or of exports. Compare your results with Figure 5.4. Are they at all surprising?

2 Record the countries of origin of goods coming from abroad that your family bought last week. What proportions came from (i) the EC, (ii) the USA and (iii) the rest of the world? How similar are the proportions to those in Figure 5.7?

3 Prepare two graphs showing the course over the past five years of the following index numbers:

   (i) the volume of UK exports (*NIER*) and the price of exports (*UKNA*)
   (ii) the volume of UK imports (*NIER*) and the price of imports (*UKNA.*)

   How can you interpret your results?

4 List for three years ago and six years ago the export competitiveness of exports of the following countries: France, Germany, Italy, Japan, the USA. Compare your results with Figure 5.10. Can you explain any differences? (*NIER*)

5 Calculate the average growth rates for developed and for developing countries in Table A5.4 in the Appendix. Allocate developing countries into three lists according to whether they are relatively

catching up, lagging behind, or standing still. Obtain a recent copy of *BER* from Barclays Bank and update the Table in the Appendix. Do the population figures in the *Review* help explain which of your three lists countries fall into?

6   Find out for the following countries how far they became more or less export-oriented over the past 10 years: France, Germany, Italy, Japan, the USA and the UK. Use index numbers of gross product and of the volume of exports. (*NIER*)

7   Repeat question 6 for the same countries and dates, but focusing now on the volume of *imports* and its relationship to national income. Rank the countries according to the extent to which imports become more (or less) important over the period. Compare this list with one based on exports from question 6. How do they differ: Have any idea why they might differ? (*NIER*)

Appendix 5

Table A5.1 Geographical distribution of UK visible trade, 1981 and 1991 (£ million)

| | 1981 | | 1991 | |
	Exports	*Imports*	*Exports*	*Imports*
European Community	21,119	21,718	59,256	61,321
Other Western Europe	6,341	7,799	8,641	14,287
Eastern Europe	1,130	1,015	1,255	1,694
North America	7,131	7,588	13,124	15,749
Other Developed Countries	3,558	4,528	6,284	11,119
Oil-exporting countries	5,932	3,667	5,752	2,795
Other countries	5,787	4,854	10,506	11,906
Total	50,998	51,169	104,818	118,871

Source: *Annual Abstract of Statistics* and *Monthly Digest of Statistics*

Table A5.2 Commodity composition of UK visible trade: 1981 and 1991
(£ million)

| | 1981 | | 1991 | |
	Exports	Imports	Exports	Imports
Food & live animals	2,339	5,785	4,717	10,390
Beverages & tobacco	1,312	752	3,032	1,936
Crude materials	1,248	3,737	1,920	4,679
Fuel	9,617	7,166	7,145	7,581
Animal & vegetable oils	65	263	96	387
Chemicals	5,550	3,597	13,782	10,978
Manufactures, classified by material	7,719	8,936	15,575	20,521
Machinery and transport equipment	16,784	13,399	43,600	43,128
Other manufactures	4,845	6,061	13,143	17,560
Other goods	1,521	1,472	1,808	1,714
Total	50,998	51,169	104,818	118,871

Source: *Monthly Digest of Statistics*

Table A5.3 World exports by volume

	World	US	Japan	France	West Germany	Italy	UK
			1980 = 100				
1978	93	81	83	89	104	99	96
1979	99	91	83	97	104	108	99
1980	100	100	100	100	100	100	100
1981	98	98	110	104	107	105	99
1982	97	88	108	101	110	106	102
1983	100	84	116	105	109	109	104
1984	108	89	134	112	120	116	113
1985	112	91	143	115	128	125	119
1986	120	94	142	113	129	127	124
1987	127	104	143	118	132	130	131
1988	139	124	149	128	141	136	135
1989	148	138	157	140	153	149	140
1990	154	148	163	148	156	154	149
1991	159	158	167	158	158	154	151

Source: *National Institute Economic Review*

Table A5.4 Real growth rates, developed and developing countries, 1991 (per cent change in GDP compared with 1990)

Developed countries		Developing countries (estimated)	
United States	−1.2	*Africa and the Middle East*	
Japan	4.4	Côte d'Ivoire	−1.5
Germany	3.2	Egypt	2.3
France	1.3	Ghana	4.0
United Kingdom	−2.5	Kenya	4.0
Italy	1.2	Morocco	5.0
Canada	−1.7	Nigeria	4.3
		Saudi Arabia	5.0
Australia	−1.1	South Africa	−1.0
Austria	2.8	Tunisia	3.5
Belgium	1.5	Zambia	−0.8
Denmark	1.0	Zimbabwe	3.0
Finland	−6.5		
Greece	1.5	*Eastern Europe*	
Iceland	0.9	Czechoslovakia	−15.0
Ireland	2.3	Hungary	−7.0
Luxembourg	3.1	Poland	−8.0
Netherlands	2.0		
New Zealand	−2.1	*Far East*	
Norway	1.6	China	7.0
Portugal	2.2	Hong Kong	3.9
Spain	2.4	India	1.0
Sweden	−0.7	Indonesia	6.0
Switzerland	−0.5	Malaysia	8.8
Turkey	1.5	Philippines	−0.1
		Singapore	6.7
		South Korea	8.5
		Taiwan	7.3
		Thailand	7.9
		Latin America	
		Argentina	5.5
		Brazil	1.2
		Chile	5.5
		Colombia	2.1
		Ecuador	2.6
		Mexico	3.6
		Peru	1.0
		Venezuela	9.2

Source: *Barclays Economic Review*

6

Government and Resource Allocation

The allocation of resources in the UK is influenced by two sets of forces – those of the market, following from the interaction of supply and demand, and those induced by government intervention.[1]

The Goals and Instruments of Economic Policy

We start by considering in general terms the chief goals of economic policy and the instruments available to pursue them.

Goals

Governments decide to intervene in the economic life of a country in pursuit of two sets of objectives:

- **macroeconomic objectives**
- **microeconomic objectives**

1 The material covered in this chapter is complementary to that covered in Lipsey–Harbury, FP2, Chapters 23 and 24.

Macroeconomic objectives are concerned with the overall performance of the economy. They relate to aggregates, especially the growth of total output, the general level of employment and unemployment, and the behaviour of the average price level. These matters will be discussed in the final chapter of this book. This chapter deals with the microeconomic goals, which concern what is called the allocation of resources, e.g. how factors of production are combined to yield output and how many resources are devoted to each of the millions of goods and services that are produced. There are two basic microeconomic goals of policy:

- **equity**
- **efficiency**

Equity is a matter of how the national cake is divided up – the distribution of income and wealth. The government tries to influence this distribution on grounds of equity, i.e. fairness. Government intervention on the grounds of efficiency can be for one, or both, of two reasons:

- The desire to ensure that outputs of goods and services are produced at minimum real costs, by using the most efficient techniques and combinations of factors of production.
- The desire to ensure that the goods and services produced are those which best satisfy the needs of the community.

Under favourable conditions, free markets can lead to an efficient allocation of resources. However, they may not always do so. There are several causes of market failure. One set of causes relates to goods which are collectively consumed; a second set relates to goods which indirectly affect persons other than those directly involved in their production or consumption; a third set is due to consumers not always being sufficiently well informed, or otherwise capable, of deciding for themselves what goods benefit them most; a fourth set is due to imperfect competition arising from concentrations of economic power.[2]

2 Causes of market failure are discussed in Lipsey–Harbury, FP2, pages 85–91 and 226–7.

Policy Instruments

Governments have three main sets of instruments, or tools, with which to implement economic policies. Two – taxation and expenditure – relate to the government's budget. Non-budgetary policies involve the use of rules and regulations, including changes in ownership, e.g. nationalisation and privatisation.

Policy can be implemented at different levels. UK policy is substantially in the hands of the central government; some is devolved to local authorities; and some is subject to directives of the EC in Brussels.

We start by looking at the income and expenditure budget of the government in the UK.

Government Revenue and Expenditure

Figure 6.1 sets out the main sources of UK government revenue. The decisions which give rise to the sums on which the Figure is

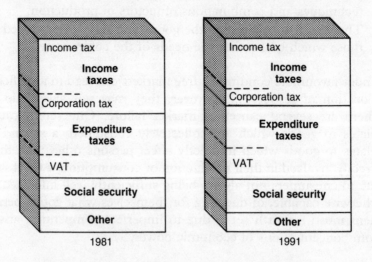

Figure 6.1 Government income 1981 and 1991
Source: *Economic Briefing* 1992

based come from the government's budget, introduced annually to Parliament by the Chancellor of the Exchequer. This used to be a March event but, from 1993, the date is to be changed to December.[3]

Government Revenue

By far the most important source of government income comes from taxation, as Figure 6.1 shows. There are two principal types of taxes: direct taxes on income and indirect taxes on expenditure. At present, the latter are slightly the more important revenue raisers – the opposite of the case 10 years earlier, as the Figure shows. The switch is the result of UK government policy since 1980, which steadily lowered rates of income tax, while raising rates of tax on expenditure, such as VAT (see below).

Taxes on income

Taken together, taxes on the incomes of individuals and businesses account for about a third of the tax revenue of central government in the UK. Easily the most important is income tax, levied on income. It is important to distinguish between the tax base and the rate of tax charged.

The tax base for an individual, his/her **taxable income**, is gross income minus certain deductible allowances. Chief among them is a personal allowance, but there are others such as that on mortgage interest on loans up to £30,000 (1992–3) for house purchases, for contributions to approved pension schemes, and for persons aged 65 on relatively low incomes. Married couples receive additional allowances, though wives began to be taxed independently from their husbands in 1990.

The tax base may be set in nominal terms, by stating the allowances in monetary units, or in real terms by 'indexing'. Since 1977, allowances have been indexed, although not necessarily by

3   Prior to 1983, revenue and expenditure were put up for parliamentary approval at different times, the former in the spring budget, the latter in the autumn.

exactly the amount to compensate for rises in the price level. In 1992–3,the personal allowance was £3,445, and the married couples' additional allowance was £1,720.

Tax rates charged on income have been greatly simplified in recent years. A sliding scale of rising rates for different bands of taxable income was employed – at one time running from 25 per cent to 80 per cent and higher, with an additional Investment Income Surcharge levied until 1984 on what was then called 'unearned' income above a threshold. Since then, tax rates have been lowered and the number of bands reduced. From 1988–9 there were only two rates of income tax (25 and 40 per cent) until 1992–3, when a lower rate of 20 per cent was brought in applicable to the first £2,000 of taxable income The top 40 per cent rate comes into force when taxable income exceeds, approximately, £20,000. The government's goal for the basic rate is said to be 20 per cent.

Since a minimum gross income is exempt from tax, and because the rate rises when incomes reaches the higher rate threshold, the proportion of gross income paid in taxes (known as the average tax rate, ATR) rises steadily with income once gross income has passed the level of allowable deductions. Individuals with incomes below allowances pay no tax. Such a system is called **progressive**. In contrast, a system where the proportion of income paid in taxes falls as income rises is called **regressive**.

In 1944, PAYE (pay as you earn) was introduced. Since then, tax payable by employees has been deducted at source by the employer, who passes it to the Collector of Taxes.

In addition to conventional income taxes, since 1962 a **capital gains tax** has been levied on *increases* in the value of assets held by a person. Gains in the value of such assets are equivalent to income, since they can be spent without reducing the value of accumulated wealth. The tax on net realised gains (i.e. after deduction of realised losses from the sale of other assets) was levied at a flat rate of 30 per cent until 1988–9. Thereafter, capital gains tax was incorporated into the income tax, with the effect that gains are added to a person's taxable income and taxed at the rate corresponding to her or his personal circumstances. Certain assets, such as one private house and chattels, are exempt, as are gains below a stated limit (£5,800 in 1992–3). Since 1984, this exemption has been indexed, along with personal allowances under the income tax, i.e. adjusted to allow for inflation.

Taxes are levied on the income of companies as well as of persons. This is because companies are separate legal entities from their shareholders. **Corporation tax** has to be paid on profits and capital gains. Companies also act as agents for the Inland Revenue and deduct income tax from the sums that they pay as dividends, etc.

Companies do not, of course, qualify for personal allowances but they are permitted to deduct all expenses properly incurred in the earning of profits, and to offset sums allocated to provide for the depreciation of capital assets. Standard depreciation allowances are given, and investment allowances are permitted for industries and regions where the provision of such help is part of government policy. At one time (1976–84) an important allowable deduction was for the increase in the value of stock held by businesses in excess of 15 per cent of gross trading profits.

The rate of corporation tax is fixed in the budget. It was 52 per cent in 1984, and reduced to 33 per cent by 1991, with a lower rate of 25 per cent for small companies. There is no difference in the rate of tax, whether profits are distributed to shareholders or retained in the firm. This contrasts with a much earlier system (ended 1975) whereby distributed profits were taxed more heavily. That practice (intentionally) discriminated in favour of profit retention and was introduced to encourage investment. However, it tended at the same time to create difficulties for new and growing companies to attract outside capital – hence the policy change.

Other taxes on income have been levied in the past and may be introduced. For example, there is a **petroleum revenue tax** (PRT) on the profits earned from oil and gas exploitation in the North Sea; and a **development land tax** was charged (until 1985) on the difference between the proceeds of land sales and their purchase price.

Taxes on expenditure

As their name implies, taxes on expenditure are based on the goods and services bought by individuals. It is, in principle, possible to avoid paying such taxes by refraining from buying taxed goods, but as the range of goods covered by such taxes is extremely wide, this is not a seriously practicable proposition. A more important difference between income and expenditure taxes is that the former tend to be progressive (see above), while at least some of the latter tend to be regressive, i.e. have the opposite incidence in so far as they take a higher proportion of the income of the poor than of the rich. The chief revenue earners among expenditure taxes are duties on petrol, tobacco and alcohol; in 1991, these duties brought in well over a third of receipts from taxes on expenditure.

In addition to the taxes on specific commodities, the government also levies a general expenditure tax. It was introduced in 1973, when the UK started to bring taxes into line with those of other members of the European Community. **Value Added Tax** (VAT) is levied on the amount firms add to the value of the goods they produce, i.e. on the difference between sales revenue and the cost of purchasing intermediate goods and services from other firms. (See Table 7.1 in the next chapter for further clarification.) Intermediate goods and services are inputs of the firm that are outputs of other firms. Such goods and services will already have been subjected to VAT earlier in the production process.

VAT is essentially a tax on consumer spending that is levied in instalments. For example, the manufacturers of a starter motor for a car pay tax on their 'added value'; when they sell the motor to a car manufacturer, the price they charge reflects the tax already paid. The firm producing (i.e. assembling) the car is permitted to deduct the cost of this VAT from its revenue from the sale of cars when calculating its liability to VAT.

When first introduced, VAT carried a flat rate of 10 per cent on all goods and services other than certain 'essentials' (such as food, children's clothing, books and buildings), on which the rate was zero. Certain other intermediate goods, including education, health and insurance, were classified as 'exempt' from the tax, which means that traders do not have to charge it to their customers but are not entitled (as they are with zero-rated goods) to reclaim tax paid by earlier suppliers. In 1974, the VAT rate was lowered to 8 per cent and a higher rate of 25 per cent was introduced first for petrol and then extended to 'luxuries', such as furs and cameras. Both were amalgamated into a standard rate of 15 per cent in 1979, which persisted until 1991 when it was raised to $17\frac{1}{2}$ per cent.

The tax has become an important source of revenue for the government, with a yield greatly in excess of that of any single tax other than income tax, as can be seen from Figure 6.1.

VAT replaced two earlier taxes, a 'purchase tax' on sales of certain luxuries and semi-luxuries, and SET (selective employment tax) on employers of labour. SET was a 'payroll tax', which was also selective in that it favoured manufacturing businesses in the hope of promoting economic growth. Eligible firms in the manufacturing sector of the economy were allowed refunds of SET. Additionally, the SET system was used to help manufacturers in declining areas of the country by granting them a regional employment premium (REP), based on numbers on the payroll.

There are many other goods and services subject to tax, e.g. betting, entertainment and television advertising. Licences must be bought to operate a television set, to run a motor-cycle or a car, and there are legal documents which require the affixing of a special tax stamp.

Unlike direct taxes, the majority of expenditure taxes are collected by the Board of Customs and Excise. **Customs duties** are imposed on articles imported from overseas (these days this means outside the EC). The remainder are known as **excise duties**. All taxes on expenditure are liable to change at any time, especially those fixed in money terms, such as the duties on petrol, tobacco and alcohol.[4]

Capital taxes

Taxes on capital, as distinct from those on capital gains (see above), yield little revenue for the state, partly because of various legal devices for avoiding tax. This does not, however, mean that they are of little significance.

4   Some representative rates in April 1992 were: petrol 27.8p per litre (23.4p unleaded); cigarettes £1.35 per 20; beer 23.4p per pint, spirits £5.55 per 75cl bottle.

Death duties have operated for many centuries, but the modern estate duty was introduced into the UK almost a hundred years ago, in 1894. Estate duty, levied on the value of property left on a person's death, continued until 1975, when **capital transfer tax** (CTT) replaced it. CTT, which lasted until 1986, introduced an important new feature in capital taxation – the extension of liability to tax of *lifetime gifts* in addition to death transfers (though the latter were subject to lower duty rates).

Inheritance tax (IT) replaced CTT in 1986. Rates of duty under all three systems varied with the size of estate until 1988–9, the year which saw the culmination of a process of lower rates and simplification, as happened with income tax (see above). In 1983, rate bands ranged from 30 to 75 per cent (on transfers above £2 million). Since 1988–9, IT has been charged at a single rate of 40 per cent regardless of the size of transfer. There is a threshold, £150,000 in 1992–3, below which tax is not payable. The progressivity built into estate duty was drastically reduced when only a single rate was levied, though an element of progressivity remains because of the tax threshold. Liability to IT may be alleviated by taking advantage of exemptions (such as for transfers between spouses, or in consideration of marriage). One of the easiest ways of reducing IT liability is by using the seven-year cumulation period for lifetime gifts, which are entirely tax-free if the donor survives for seven or more years (regardless of the sum involved).

It is worth mentioning another capital tax, although it has never been levied in Britain. This is an **annual wealth tax** assessed on the total value of all assets owned by an individual. Such a tax has been proposed by past governments but never introduced. Rates suggested have been low. One suggestion was for 1 per cent on property worth £100,000, and between $2\frac{1}{2}$ and 5 per cent on that worth over £5 million. These rates may not seem high, but a tax of 3 per cent means that someone must earn a post-income tax return on capital of at least that rate to avoid a depletion of his or her capital.

Local authorities' finances

Local authorities spend about a fifth of the total of all branches of government. They used to raise a substantial proportion of their financial needs themselves, while obtaining the rest from central government. Their independence has been significantly reduced in recent years. In 1991, three-quarters of revenue came as grants from central government, and spending limits have been imposed on authorities in some instances.

Until the end of the 1980s, the chief source of independent income for local councils came from a species of property tax, as **rates** levied on the owners of land and buildings (unless used for agricultural purposes). Property was given a rateable value (by the Inland Revenue) and the rate was expressed as 'poundage', i.e. pence per pound.

The importance of rates as a source of revenue varied from district to district – the larger the amount of valuable property in a region, the more important the income from rates. This was partly offset by grants from central government, which were larger for authorities where there was relatively little valuable property but there were heavy needs for services, e.g. education, because of a large number of children in the community.

The rating system gave local councils considerable financial autonomy. It had, however, been under review for some time, partly for political reasons, e.g. dissent between Labour-controlled local councils and Conservative-controlled Parliament in White-hall. Several committees scrutinised local government finance, and considered alternatives to rates, such as a local income tax, used in some other countries. However, the outcome was the introduction, in 1990,[5] of a new **community charge**, to replace rates on domestic property.

The government had favoured the community charge because it claimed that it established a strong link between domestic ratepayers and recipients of services provided by local government (pointing out that only about 15 million property-owners paid rates, whereas about 35 million adults enjoyed the benefits

5 Introduced in 1989 in Scotland.

that the rates were used for). The community charge was soon known widely as the **'poll tax'**, a term which describes a tax which bears equally on all local inhabitants. This was not strictly true, since persons on low incomes paid at a reduced rate. However, the tax proved expensive to administer and extremely unpopular, not least because it was regarded as unfair that tax liability should be the same for households with a few adult members living in expensive property as for households comprising several adults living in small, cheap dwellings. Indeed, many persons liable to the tax refused to pay it. The central government had to rescue several local councils and provide funds to help out (this was the reason for the rise in VAT to $17\frac{1}{2}$ per cent mentioned above). The tax was short lived and is about to be replaced (1993) by another new tax, the **council tax**.

The council tax is similar to the rates in that it is partly based on property values. Properties are placed (by the Inland Revenue) into one of eight ranges of value, so that those taxpayers in any one tax band pay the same tax. Tax liability is, however, also related, to an extent, to household size and to income. Single occupants receive a 25 per cent discount, and persons with low incomes are eligible for rebate up to 100 per cent. Each local authority is responsible for setting the rate for council tax for the properties in its area. Central government will provide supplementary grants where needs differ, as with the rating system. Grants will be based on 'Standard Spending Assessments' – what Whitehall thinks a local authority ought to spend.

Note, the demise of domestic rates (and their replacement by the community charge) did not extend to business property, though local authorities lost the right to choose the rate for themselves. The central government sets a uniform business rate for the nation, the proceeds of which it disburses to regions on a per capita basis.

National insurance contributions (NICs)

A further source of government revenue is national insurance contributions. When first introduced in 1948, NICs were levied at a flat rate on all employees. They went into a special National

Insurance Fund to pay social security benefits for the unemployed, disabled, retired, etc.

The flat rate operated as a regressive income tax and the idea of relating NICs to earnings first came in 1961. Today, NICs (and benefits) are earnings-related – with an exempt threshold and ceilings of about £2,700 and £20,000 a year respectively). The National Insurance Fund is not self-financing but augmented by subsidy where necessary, to pay what are regarded as the proper rates of social security benefits. Non-contributory benefits, such as Family Credit, for working families with children, and Income Support (formerly Supplementary Benefit) for other categories in need, are financed from general taxation.

National insurance contribution rates vary with earnings, and according to whether individuals choose to 'contract out' of the state scheme and make private insurance arrangements to provide for pensions on their retirement.

Other income

The miscellaneous category shown as 'other' income in Figure 6.1 covers many different items, including trading surpluses, royalties from North Sea oil, receipts from the European Community, and proceeds of the privatisation sales of state-owned assets.

The National Debt

Total government income and expenditure never balance each other exactly. When expenditure exceeds income, the difference is met by borrowing.

Government borrowing has, at times, been on a very large scale, e.g. to finance wars and to pay compensation to industries taken into public ownership. The total outstanding balance is known as the national debt. After the Second World War and the extensive nationalisation programme of the Labour Government, the debt stood at a figure of about £25 billion in 1950. Compared with the size of the national income, this was an all-time high – approximately 250 per cent. By 1991, the outstanding debt was approximately £200 billion. This represents a dramatic fall in relative terms to well under half the size of the national income. The fall is partly the result of the inflationary rise in the money value of the national income (see next chapter, pages 243–4) and partly due to asset sales in the privatisation programme in the 1980s.

The net change in the national debt measures the amount the government needs to borrow to finance an excess of expenditure over income in any year. It is known as the **Public Sector Borrowing Requirement** (PSBR). When the government's revenue is greater than its expenditure, the PSBR is negative, and is known as the PSDR (**Public Sector Debt Repayment**). We shall consider the relevance of the PSBR again in the context of fiscal policy in Chapter 9.

International Comparisons of Tax Burdens

The level of taxation as a proportion of national income, as we saw in Chapter 1, has been rising considerably during the present century. It is of some interest to compare the situation in the UK with that in other developed countries. Figure 6.2 shows that the UK occupies a middle position. It is less heavily taxed than Sweden, Denmark, Norway, Netherlands, France and Belgium, though notably more so than Switzerland, the USA, Japan and Greece.

In interpreting Figure 6.2, note that countries differ greatly in the relative importance of taxes and social security contributions in their budgets. Some, such as France and the Netherlands, derive high proportions of income from social security contributions, while others, including the UK, take a much lower proportion.

Countries vary also in their choice of methods for achieving given objectives. This can cause the figures to be misleading. For example, to help low-income families there is a choice of giving tax allowances or making cash payments. The former keeps the state budget smaller than the latter, though the effects may be similar.

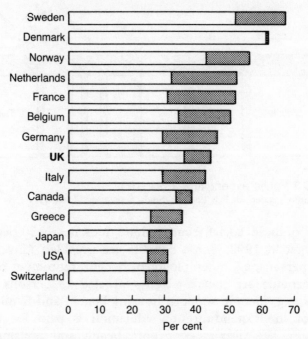

Figure 6.2 Taxes and social security contributions as a percentage of GNP, selected countries, 1989 (shaded areas are social security contributions)
Source: *Economic Trends*, 1992

Note, too, that Figure 6.2 deals with average tax burdens, which may conceal different tax treatments for particular groups.

Government Expenditure

The grand total of public expenditure by both central and local governments absorbs about 40 per cent of national income. The principal categories are shown in Figure 6.3. There are several ways of classifying them; the method used for the diagram is based on function, i.e. for social security, defence, etc.

The social services are by far the largest category, accounting for well over half the total expenditure if the term is defined widely to include health, education, housing and social security benefits.

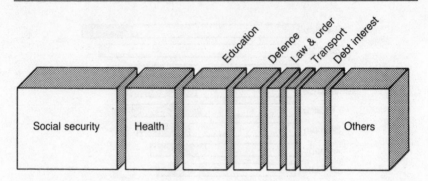

Figure 6.3 Public expenditure 1991–1992
Source: Autumn statement Feb 1992, *Statistical Supplement* (Treasury)

The last of these, social security alone, took nearly 30 per cent of the budget in 1992. Some benefits are provided universally to eligible persons, e.g. unemployment benefit, retirement pensions. Other benefits are means-tested – targeted to persons on low incomes, e.g. income support, housing benefit and family credit. Much of the expenditure on education is paid for by local authorities. We discuss education, health and housing policy below.

The controversial question with cash benefits (e.g. for children) is whether they should be targeted, i.e. restricted to those intended to benefit, or universal, i.e. given to everyone with families in order to ensure a floor below which no families should fall. Those in favour of targeting stress the efficiency advantage in terms of cost to the taxpayer. Those against it point to the low take-up of benefits that are available only on application by the poor, who are put through the indignity of means-testing. The choice between targeting and universality has, of course, strong political connotations.

Defence remains a substantial category, despite the reductions that started after the end of the cold war; it still took nearly a tenth of public expenditure in 1991–2. Interest payments on the National Debt (see above) account for another 7 per cent, the liability varying with the amount outstanding and the rate of interest payable on it. The other items of expenditure are for varied functions, including law and order, the construction and maintenance of roads, overseas aid, support for industry, environmental services, research and development, arts and libraries.

As previously stated, the method used for classifying items of government expenditure for Figure 6.3 is not the only one possible. We could alternatively distinguish between **current expenditure**, such as retirement pensions and drugs for use in hospitals, and **capital expenditure**, such as the provision of new schools or prisons. Current expenditures have immediate effects on the allocation of resources or the distribution of income. Capital expenditures, in contrast, have delayed but lasting effects.

A third classification could distinguish between what are known as **transfer payments** and **exhaustive expenditures**. Exhaustive expenditures are those on goods and services, such as roads and hospitals, where the state decides directly how the money should be spent. In contrast, transfer payments, which include personal grants such as pensions and income support, permit individual recipients to allocate the proceeds as they wish. Transfer payments have grown greatly relative to exhaustive expenditures in recent years.

A fourth and final classification could distinguish between goods and services which benefit the community generally and those that are provided for individuals. The former are referred to as **public goods** and include roads, courts of law and environmental services. The latter comprise all transfers, as well as hospital beds specifically for the sick and schools for the young. Many classes of government expenditure have an element of a public nature about them. For example, it is usually claimed that education benefits society generally, as well as the individuals who take advantage of it.

Budget of the European Commission

At the beginning of the chapter we mentioned that, as a member of the EC, the UK government is to an extent subject to decisions made in Brussels. In fact, the EC has its own budget, agreed annually by the Council of Ministers.

Figure 6.4 shows the main items on the revenue and expenditure side of the budget. EC income comes from four sources, the most important of which is related to the revenue each member government receives from its VAT. A second component, about a quarter the size, also contributed by member governments, is related to each of their national incomes (GNPs). The third substantial revenue source is customs duties and taxes on imports from non-EC nations. The small remainder consists of levies on agricultural imports, designed to raise EC prices to the, normally, lower prices on world markets.

The principal expenditure item in the EC budget has for many years been to help farmers in the **Common Agricultural Policy** (CAP). Agricultural price support took over half of the total budget in 1991. Its great size was a major reason why measures were taken to reform the CAP (see pages 216–17). Other expenditures include help for less developed regions in member countries and training for young persons through the European Social Fund.

The UK has been a regular net contributor to the EC budget, though, following an alteration to the accounting rules agreed at a meeting at Fontainebleau in 1984, Britain's real financial position in the EC has improved in relative terms.

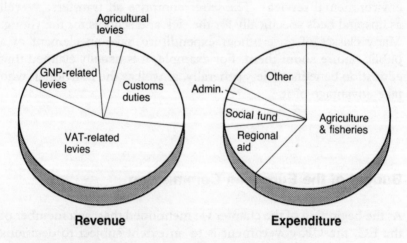

Figure 6.4 Budget of the European Community 1991
Source: *Economic Briefing*, 1991

The focus of this chapter so far has been on financial matters. We shall now consider some of the ways in which government economic policies are employed in pursuit of the goals of equity and efficiency. We deal first with equity in the distribution of income and wealth; following with competition, regional and industrial policy and the specific sectors of education, health and housing. Note this division is useful but inevitably artificial. Virtually all the tools of policy have implications for both equity and efficiency. For example, taxation policy designed to redistribute income can affect resource allocation and growth; competition policy directed at monopolies almost certainly influences the distribution of income.

Government and Equity

Both sides of the government's budget, as well as rules and regulations, are available to influence the distribution of income. The goal is *equity*, i.e. a distribution which is regarded in some sense as fair. This is not synonymous with *equality*. It is unusual to seek absolute equality; rather it is commonly accepted that a degree of inequality, commensurate with the reward of effort, is desirable, so that a compromise distribution is sought. Moreover, equity has several dimensions. People differ in a variety of ways and have diverse needs. Interest attaches to equity between the sexes, between ethnic groups, between families, etc.

Redistribution and Income Tax

Taxation is the most obvious policy instrument, though it is not always the most important quantitatively. Certain taxes are designed expressly to bear more heavily on higher income groups than on lower ones. Outstanding in this connection is income tax, which was especially progressive in the 1970s, when it was levied at a very wide range of rates, rising to 83 per cent on the highest income groups (on top of which a surcharge raised the tax rate on incomes from investment to 98 per cent). The very high rates were heavily criticised, not only on grounds of equity, but also because of incentives, including that of tax avoidance.

In 1992–3, there were only three tax bands. The lowest 20 per cent rate applied to the first £2,000 of taxable income only. The top 40 per cent rate applied on *taxable* incomes in excess of £23,700, affecting only some 5 per cent of taxpayers. Income tax was, nevertheless, progressive, but largely because of existence of personal (and other) allowances which meant that the tax rate on the lowest incomes was zero.

Figure 6.5 illustrates the progressiveness of income tax in 1992–3. Note (i) that it is based on assumptions correct for that year as to rates and allowances then obtaining. The tax burden is expressed as a proportion of total income for different income classes. Note (ii) that it refers to a single person enjoying only the minimum allowance of £3,445. A different diagram could be drawn for any individual or family with different circumstances. For example, the tax burden would be lower for a married couple, or someone buying a house on a mortgage, because of other tax allowances to which they would be entitled. Note (iii) that the only tax that enters the calculations is income tax – national insurance contributions and indirect taxes are excluded (see below).

The picture emerging from Figure 6.5 is, nevertheless, reasonably representative of the progressiveness of income tax in Britain.

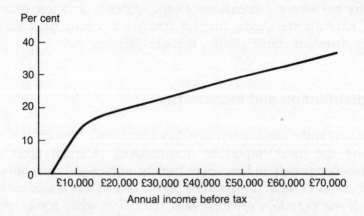

Figure 6.5 Income tax for a single person as a percentage of gross income, 1992–1993

It shows that the proportion of income paid in tax (the average tax rate, ATR) rises with income. ATR is zero until the personal allowance has been used up. It then rises, at first quite sharply, to 10 per cent on incomes of about £7,000, and 15 per cent on those of about £10,000. The top marginal tax rate of 40 per cent comes into effect only for gross incomes in excess of £30,000, but the ATR rises slowly, reaching 30 per cent when income tops £50,000.

Income Redistribution and the Government's Budget

Income tax is one of several budgetary instruments for income redistribution. Other substantial deductions from gross income are national insurance contributions (NICs) and indirect taxes. There are also cash and other state benefits. Estimating the full effect of government requires the inclusion of all redistributory measures. This is not easily done. It calls for an assessment of the incidence of taxes on expenditure and, most tricky of all, judgements about how government expenditure on health, education, etc., benefits different income groups.

Figure 6.6 gives an idea of the effect of all government budgetary measures, other than those which are especially difficult to estimate for reasons just mentioned. Note, therefore, that this diagram excludes the effects of non-cash benefits (education, health, etc.). The Figure shows the shares in total income of (non-retired) households, grouped by income size. The groups are in ranges of 20 per cent, known as quintiles; i.e. the richest 20 per cent of households, the next richest quintile and so on. In Part (i) of the Figure, the share of each quintile group is shown at four stages:

(a) *original income*, before any state intervention
(b) *original income plus* – (a) *plus* state cash benefits (e.g. retirement pensions)
(c) *disposable income* – (b) *minus* income tax and NICs
(d) *purchasing power of income* – (c) *minus* indirect taxes

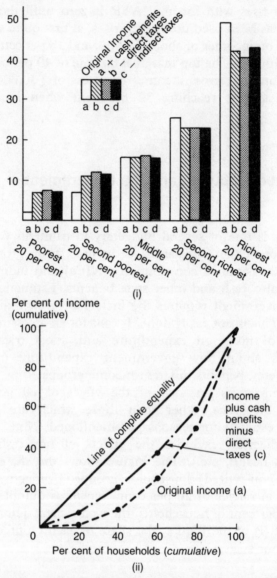

(i)

Per cent of income
(cumulative)

Line of complete equality

Income
plus cash
benefits
minus
direct
taxes (c)

Original income (a)

Per cent of households (*cumulative*)

(ii)

Figure 6.6 Government redistribution 1989. Shares of quintile* groups in total income before and after tax and cash benefits (*quintile means a fifth or 20 per cent)
Source: *Economic Trends,* January 1992

The evidence in Part (i) of Figure 6.6 throws light on the effect of government on the poorest, richest and middle-income groups. Look at these in turn, starting with the poorest 20 per cent of households. Note, first, that their share rises from 2 to 7 per cent of total income after all taxes and cash benefits are taken into account. Note, second, that the provision of cash benefits is the prime reason for the improvement in their position. Income tax is insignificant, because the poor pay little or no income tax. This conclusion applies, though with less force, to the second lowest quintile group.

The share of the top 20 per cent of households, as you might expect, falls – from 49 to 43 per cent after all taxes and cash benefits are included. The prime cause of the falling share of this richest group, in contrast to those at the lower end of the scale, is income tax. It is among this group that you find households who pay some tax at the 40 per cent rate.

Part (ii) of Figure 6.6 provides a summary view of the data in Part (i) using the form of Lorenz curves (see above, page 104). The two Lorenz curves for (a) and (c), as we have defined them, compare original income with disposable income- i.e. income available for households to spend, *net* of direct taxes but inclusive of cash benefits. We see the effect of state intervention is to shift the Lorenz curve nearer to the diagonal representing complete equality – especially for the poorest groups.

You may have noticed that little was said about indirect taxes, which were even omitted from Part (ii) of the Figure. This is because they are the least redistributive of the various measures examined – see Part (i) of the Figure. Such, neutral, taxes are nearer to being proportional to income than progressive or regressive. That does not mean that they cannot be used to finance redistributive *spending*.

Finally, let us remind you that we have said nothing about the redistributive effects of non-cash benefits supplied by the state. Although it should be possible, in principle, to allocate these and determine the full impact of the whole state budget, in practice it is too difficult to produce reliable quantitative estimates. This is mainly because there is no sure way of ascertaining how the benefits of each category of expenditure accrue to different income groups. Moreover, there are some benefits, like defence and the police, which can only be allocated on an arbitrary basis. Despite all these reservations, we feel that we can confidently state that the expenditure side of the government's budget is a more important instrument for helping the lowest income groups than is taxation.

Non-Budgetary Redistribution

The discussion so far on the impact of the state on income distribution has been limited to budgetary measures. However, there are other ways that the state may expressly, or by implication, affect income equality and inequality. They include all interventions in the market place, such as price controls, import duties, regulations affecting the regional distribution of industry, etc. Some will be referred to later, and we cannot deal with them all here. Two which concern earnings directly, however, are of particular importance.

We can be brief about the first because we met it in Chapter 4. We saw then that women's earnings used to be significantly below those of men. In an attempt to reduce the differential, two Acts of Parliament were passed in 1975–6. The Equal Pay Act stipulated that men and women doing the same work should receive equal pay for doing so. The Sex Discrimination Act forbade discrimination in employment between the sexes. The hourly earnings of women rose fairly quickly from their 1960s level of 63 per cent of those of men to over 70 per cent, currently reaching an all time high of 79 per cent (April 1992).

The second non-budgetary measure concerns government intervention in wage settlements. We know (also from Chapter 4) that, in many industries, settlements result from bargaining between trade unions and employers. However, the public claims an interest, as well as the parties involved, in negotiations being conducted in a reasonable manner and settlements being fair. Intervention in the field of industrial relations includes other goals, e.g. the avoidance of strikes, discussed in Chapter 9. We should also mention Wages Councils, bodies that fix minimum wages for adult workers in industries where negotiating machinery is regarded as inadequate, such as retailing, catering and clothing (with similar arrangements in agriculture). In 1992, the government announced that the 20 Wages Councils would be abolished on the grounds that minimum wages cause unemployment.

In addition to Wages Councils, targeted at the lower paid, Review Bodies have been set up to make recommendations on the pay of higher paid professional workers and public sector employees, e.g. for the forces, doctors and dentists and those earning 'top salaries' (senior civil servants, judges, etc.). For a brief period there was even a standing Commission on Pay Comparability, set up by a Labour government in 1979 and abolished by a Conservative one in 1980. At the national level, governments from time to time issue 'guidelines' for wage settlements as part of their anti-inflation policies. In late 1992 a 2 per cent ceiling for workers in the public sector was announced, and a press report suggested that the government was considering dropping the pay review bodies. Further discussion of these matters is deferred to Chapter 9.

Trends in the Size Distribution of Income

Most of the previous discussion has focused on the current distribution of income. We must also consider trends.

Comparisons of income distribution over time are difficult to make. The subject was regarded as sufficiently important for the government to set up a Royal Commission on the Distribution of Income and Wealth in 1974 to report on the facts.[6] The Commission's reports identified a long-term decline in the pre-tax share of the highest income groups between the late 1940s and the 1970s. Those in the top percentile, i.e. with incomes in the top 1 per cent of the population, suffered a virtual halving of their share, from about 11 per cent to $5\frac{1}{2}$ per cent of the total. Those in the top 10 per cent (including the top 1 per cent) suffered a fall in their share from a third to a quarter of total income.

Results from a more recent study are shown in Figure 6.7. The figures on which it is based ignore taxes but include state-provided cash benefits. The diagram shows the changed shares of two

6   It was known as the Diamond Commission, after the name of its chairman.

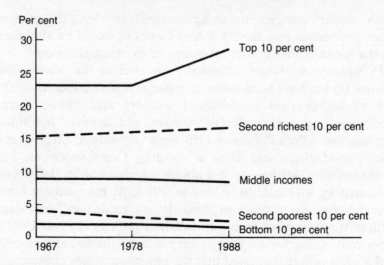

Figure 6.7 Shares in total income by richest, poorest and middle-income households, 1967, 1978 and 1988
Source: *S. P. Jenkins Fiscal Studies Vol 12 No 1 1991*

groups at the top, two at the bottom and one middle-income group at three points in time, 1967, 1978 and 1988. The groups here are deciles (tenths) – top 10 per cent, second top 10 per cent, bottom 10 per cent, etc. The main conclusions are (i) that there was little change in the distribution over the first decade, and (ii) that the decade after 1978 was one of increasing inequality. The shares of the four top deciles rose over the second period, while those of the bottom deciles fell. The biggest gainers were those in the top 10 per cent, whose share of total income was almost 29 per cent, compared to $23\frac{1}{2}$ per cent 10 and 20 years earlier.

Poverty

The bottom 10 per cent of the income distribution suffered a drop in share from $2\frac{1}{2}$ per cent in 1967 to $1\frac{1}{5}$ per cent in 1988. This group usually receives special attention because it includes those who might be described as being in poverty.

Any definition which attaches a precise meaning to the word poverty is inevitably arbitrary. A poverty line can be drawn below which people may be described as 'poor' in a technical sense. For example, a line might be the level of income necessary to sustain life itself. However, the poverty line is more commonly related to 'minimum living standards'. This is where arbitrariness comes in. What sort of diet is acceptable for the minimum? And do minimum living standards require, for example, a tv set, some sort of car, etc.?

We may leave the experts to make estimates of the numbers 'in poverty', though we should not be surprised to learn that surveys of the extent of measured poverty can lead to conflicting conclusions. Less controversial is the identity of the poor. Three groups figure prominently – the old, the unemployed and children, whether resulting from large or from single-parent families. The old have been the largest group of poor for most of the time since the end of the Second World War, and they may be so in the next century as the proportion of the population aged 65 and over rises, as projected. However, the gradual rise in the numbers of single-parent families and the growth in the numbers unemployed in the late 1980s and early 1990s have brought these groups more prominently into the category of those we call poor. This explains the importance attached to benefits linked to means, e.g. family credit for working families with children. Note, however, that only a proportion, about 70 per cent, of those eligible for means-tested benefits actually claim them – whether from pride or from ignorance.

Income Distribution and Price Changes

One influence on the distribution of income not often discussed is that of changes in relative prices. Movements in the average level of prices are commonly measured by the **Index of Retail Prices**, as it is officially called (more commonly referred to as the RPI, or the Retail Price Index). The index shows what is happening to the cost of living, as represented by the prices of a typical 'basket' of goods and services bought by an 'average' household. In the basket are the goods most commonly consumed, with 'weights' attached to them representing their average importance in household budgets.

Index of retail prices

Movements in the RPI record changes in the cost of living between two dates for an average family. Such a family spends about 15 per cent of its income on food, 15 per cent on transport, 18 per cent on housing, 11 per cent on alcohol and tobacco, 11 per cent on household goods and services, 7 per cent on clothing, 7 per cent on leisure, 5 per cent on fuel and about 10 per cent on everything else. The average family is, of course, a statistical artefact. For any individuals or groups the index may not accurately portray their cost of living. That will depend on their own expenditure patterns because all prices do not move in line together.

Figure 6.8 shows price level changes for different commodity groups between 1987 and 1992. At the later date the RPI was about 40 per cent higher than at the earlier one. However, prices had risen more than average for some commodities, especially housing, and less than average for others, such as fuel and light and clothing.

The effect of wide variations in the rate of inflation for different commodity groups on the distribution of income depends, of course, on the relative importance of each item in household budgets. To illustrate, Figure 6.9 shows how households at three different income levels were affected. For example, the prices of two classes of goods which rose more than the average between 1987 and 1992 (housing and tobacco) and one class that rose less than average (fuel and light) were relatively more important in the budget of low-income groups than in that of high ones.

Given the information in Figure 6.9, it would still require careful study before one might conclude that changes in relative prices had affected the distribution of real income in an egalitarian or inegalitarian direction. Furthermore, redistribution should be considered not only from the point of view of groups distinguished

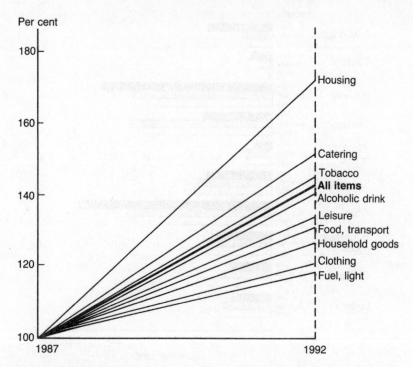

Figure 6.8 Retail price index (percentage increase of major classes of goods and services 1987–1992)
Sources: *Annual Abstract of Statistics* and *Employment Gazette*

by income level. Consumption patterns are affected by other considerations, among which family size and age are important.

The government publishes regular indices of the cost of living for pensioner households, as well as the general RPI. The pensioner price indices give greater weight to items such as food and fuel and less to motoring, alcohol and tobacco, which feature less in the budget of the average pensioner. Over the period from 1987 to 1992, the RPI rose by about 35 per cent compared with 32 per cent for pensioner households. Hence, there appears to have been a very slight improvement in the purchasing power of the pound for pensioners compared with the population as a whole. The difference was, however, marginal. At other times, the cost of living index for pensioners has risen faster than the RPI.

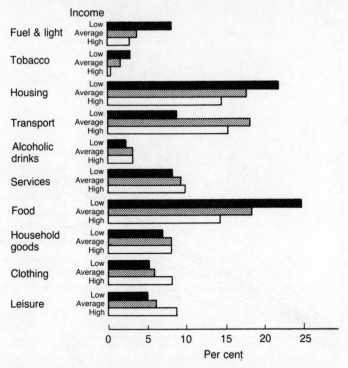

Figure 6.9 Household expenditure at different income levels (percentage of total expenditure on commodity groups) 1990
Source: *Family Expenditure Survey*, Department of Employment

The Distribution of Wealth

Another dimension of equity as a policy goal concerns the distribution of wealth. Inequality in this distribution can explain why some people have higher incomes than others. The reason is that relatively few individuals receive a disproportionately high share of income derived from the ownership of capital. For example, those in the top 1 per cent derive 23 per cent per cent of their income from investment – more than double the percentage for the average income recipient. Hence, even if earned incomes were evenly distributed, total incomes from all sources would still not be equally distributed, because of the distribution of wealth. What then are the facts?

A census of personal wealth has not been taken in modern Britain, so it is necessary to rely on estimates of the shares of different groups in the total. This is a difficult exercise and produces results that are not simple to interpret. It was one of the tasks given to the Diamond Commission (see above, page 199), which failed to provide an unambiguous statement on the ownership of personal property. One difficulty is that of quantifying the property of the lowest groups of wealth-holders. Another is that of deciding whether pension rights should count as wealth, despite their not being 'marketable' assets that can be sold. The case for including pension rights can be illustrated by comparing two persons – one with zero marketable wealth in real (or financial) assets but a guaranteed pension, and another person with zero pension but sufficient assets to provide her/himself with a similar pension.

Estimates of the distribution of personal wealth can be calculated, based on different assumptions about what to include and exclude. Figure 6.10 uses figures chosen from among them. The lines showing shares in total wealth in the Figure are, therefore, deliberately drawn with a broad brush. The measured shares of wealth size groups are sensitive to the choice of

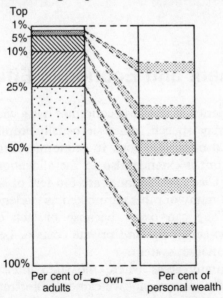

Figure 6.10 Distribution of personal wealth, 1989
Source: *Social Trends*

assumptions about what is included. For example, the diagram suggests that the *average* share of the top 1 per cent of adults in total personal wealth is 15 per cent. The range from which this average is calculated is 11 to 28 – the lower figure results from counting only marketable wealth; the higher figure from including pension rights. Both figures are useful; the appropriate one to use depends on the issue being addressed. For some purposes, only marketable wealth is relevant – e.g. for bequeathing wealth to the next generation (because pension rights are normally neither marketable nor transferable).

Inequality in wealth distribution is the result of many factors, of which inheritance and the tendency for people to accumulate wealth during their working lives and decumulate it after retirement are important in the long term, while changing prices of assets (e.g. houses, land and shares) can have substantial short-term effects. A long-term reduction in the degree of inequality, as measured by a declining share of the top 1 per cent of wealth-holders in total wealth during the present century, is discernible in Britain. To an extent this has been offset by an increasing share of other wealth-holders within the top 20 per cent. It may, therefore, indicate a spread of wealth within families rather than a general redistribution.

Government and Economic Efficiency

The term efficiency as used in economics has a wider connotation than in everyday speech, when it usually implies simply that production is at minimum cost. In economics, efficiency has this meaning too, but it extends also to the allocation of goods and services itself. Cases where there are too few of some goods and services or too many of others are taken as evidence of inefficient production. They can occur because of lack of competition, differences between social and private costs or benefits, or other failures of the market system.

There are many areas where the state intervenes to try to improve resource allocation – we can only illustrate them here by looking at a few.

Competition Policy

Industrial concentration in large enterprises, both overall and in some sectors, is, as we saw in Chapter 3, considerable. It is clear, too, that the power that stems from the control of a high proportion of an industry's output in a few large businesses can be a matter for public concern. Firms, or groups of firms, which attain such positions are said to have a degree of monopoly power, enabling them to fix prices and act in other ways damaging to consumers. Such behaviour can be long lasting if it prevents the entry of new firms into the industry.

Barriers to entry can take many forms. Some are man-made, such as the patenting of products. Others are technological, e.g. deriving from substantial economies of large-scale production that leave room for only one or a few firms operating efficiently.

Government may choose from a range of policies to control privately owned monopoly power. One alternative, out of vogue at present, is nationalisation. Another, currently more in favour, is regulation. As a third option, the state can set up special institutions to deal with particular aspects of competition policy. This has happened in the UK. There are three major strands of what is called competition policy, which is operated by a Director General of Fair Trading (DGFT) and the Secretary of State for Trade and Industry:

- **monopolies**
- **restrictive practices**
- **mergers**

Monopolies

The first strand began in 1948, with the creation of a Monopolies Commission, later renamed the **Monopolies and Mergers Commission** (MMC) (see below). This body can be called upon by the DGFT, or the Minister, to investigate monopoly situations (which are defined as those where an enterprise controls at least 25 per cent of the market).

Where the MMC finds a monopoly does exist, it reports on how the public interest is affected and, if adversely, makes recommendations. The Commission is given only broad guidelines on how to interpret the public interest, e.g. how the enterprise's activities affect competition, consumers, innovation and international trade.

Over the years, the Commission has made about two hundred reports – covering a wide range of industries, recently investigating, for example, razor blades, instant coffee, photocopying, beer, credit cards, cross channel ferries, London Underground, artificial limbs and advertising restrictions by doctors and civil engineers. In some cases it was felt that no action was needed. For example, the 1991 report on instant coffee found profitability to be high and the dominant firm to control almost 50 per cent of the market. Nevertheless, it was felt that 'Nestlé had achieved its high market share by successfully developing products and brands that consumers regarded as good value for money in a market characterised by a wide degree of consumer choice and competition.'[7] In many other cases, the Commission found practices operating against the public interest, especially price-fixing and measures to prevent the entry of new firms. In the case of the supply of beer, for example, the Commission found that the complex monopoly situation did operate against the public interest and made a number of recommendations, including one for a limit on the number of pubs that a brewery could own.

A further step in the government's monopoly policy was the Competition Act 1980, which gave the DGFT powers to deal with 'anti-competitive practices', without the need for a full reference to the MMC. These include such behaviour as refusal to supply, e.g. to a discount store which sells at 'cut' prices, and the tying of sales of one product to those of another. The DGFT receives about 1,500 complaints a year of anti-competitive practices, though the majority do not need action. An interesting recent example concerned Yves St Laurent and its refusal to supply perfume to Superdrug (see Box 6.1).

7 Annual Report of the Director General of Fair Trading, 1991, page 31.

Box 6.1

Adverts for Cheap Perfume Blocked

The perfume industry has used its influence to stop a chain of chemist's shops advertising cut price fragrances in British magazines, it was alleged yesterday.

Superdrug, which sells perfumes such as Chanel and Yves St Laurent, at 15 of its 670 shops in Britain at discounts of up to one third, says that the advertising ban is part of an attempt to keep prices artificially high.

Four British magazine publishers have refused to carry a £250,000 advertising campaign promoting discounted perfumes, a decision described by Superdrug as 'a clear case of pressure being applied by the perfume companies'.

The advertisements were turned down by Conde Nast, which publishes *Vogue*, IPC, the National Magazine Company and Emap. They were part of a plan to boost Superdrug's £10m annual perfume sales.... Stephen Quinn, publishing director of *Vogue*, told a Sunday newspaper that the decision to refuse the advertisements had been 'purely commercial'. He said 'Only a fool would accept cut-price advertising from Superdrug for a magazine like *Vogue*. We have a longstanding relationship with fragrance houses like Chanel and Yves St Laurent, who are constantly telling us how disturbed they are by this type of discounting.... The perfume companies are refusing to sell to Superdrug partly because they do not like its discount policy and partly because they feel that its shops do not have the right atmosphere and style for their products.'

Superdrug says that manufacturers are trying to protect excessive profit margins and cuts the price of many leading makes by up to a third.

The Independent, 5 October 1992

This news item raises many important aspects of competition policy, including refusal to supply and price maintenance. Can you identify any other issues? The case was referred to the Office of Fair Trading. At the time of writing, its decision on what action to take is still awaited.

Restrictive practices

The second strand in competition policy concerns collusion by groups of firms in restrictive practices, e.g. to fix prices. Collusive agreements (with exceptions, e.g. patents) must be registered with the DGFT, who can take proceedings against them to a Restrictive Practices Court. The presumption of the law is that such agreements are contrary to the public interest unless special circumstances exist (so-called 'gateways') and that they provide a *net* benefit to the public. Only a tiny proportion of the 4,500 registered agreements have been taken to court. About two per cent were declared void as against public interest, the majority being allowed to continue.

One pervasive practice was treated separately. The Resale Prices Act 1964 prohibited even individual manufacturers from agreeing (with retailers) to fix minimum resale prices of their goods. This piece of legislation was particularly effective, and resulted in the virtual disappearance of the previously widespread practice of fixed prices in shops in Britain. In two cases, books and pharmaceuticals, exemption was granted by the Restrictive Practices Court. The DGFT was pressed to review the case of books in 1990, but he decided against referral back to the Court for reconsideration. Nevertheless, one major bookseller (Dillons) began recently to discount selected titles in its shops.

Mergers

The third strand in competition policy focuses on mergers. As we saw in Chapter 3, merger waves have characterised recent British economic history, as they have throughout the industrialised world. The Monopolies and Mergers Commission was given extended powers in 1965, when 'Mergers' was added to its name. The Secretary of State for Trade and Industry has the power to refer any merger proposals to the Commission if they might lead to the creation of a monopoly market share (i.e. over 25 per cent) or involve the take-over of assets above a threshold (currently £30 million).

Investigating merger proposals has occupied an increasing amount of the MMC's time. The great majority of technically referable mergers have not, however, been sent to the MMC, because the public interest has not been seriously threatened. On any referred merger, the Commission is required to consider the likely effects on competition and must make recommendations within a stated time limit, now normally set at three months. The

Secretary of State then decides whether to allow the merger to proceed, with or without conditions. Recent cases referred to the Commission include Tate and Lyle and the British Sugar Corporation, Gillette and Swedish Match NV (owners of Wilkinson Sword), Elders IXL and Scottish and Newcastle Breweries, Coats Viyella and Tootal, GEC Siemens and Plessey, International Thompson Organisation and Horizon Travel. A fair proportion of referred mergers are found to contain at least some elements judged contrary to the public interest – all but the last of the mergers listed in the previous sentence, for instance.

Assessing competition policy

British competition policy represents a distinctive approach. In contrast to policy elsewhere, e.g. in the USA, the underlying philosophy, especially for monopolies and mergers, has been to adopt a case-by-case approach, with potential benefits and detriments to the public interest being weighed against each other.

This approach has been criticised because it tends to work slowly. Moreover, the findings of the MMC do not have to stand up to public enquiry as do judgments of the Restrictive Practices Court. For another thing, the government of the day has not always accepted the recommendations of the Commission, and reliance has often been placed on voluntary assurances from firms, rather than on orders by the Minister. Ways of circumventing orders have also been found, by demerger, for example.

Mergers policy has been said to be too weak, because the onus of proof is on the MMC to show that a merger is against the public interest, rather than on the parties to show that it is not so. A government review of mergers policy in 1988 stressed the length of time taken in merger reviews, and proposed the introduction of prenotification, as practised in other countries.

Policy on restrictive practices, generally regarded as successful in the 1950s and 1960s, came under strong criticism in another official review,[8] which found it no longer suited to present-day conditions. The investigative powers of the DGFT were felt to be

8 Department of Trade and Industry, Review of Restrictive Trade Practices Policy, Cm 331, 1988.

too weak, and the penalties for ignoring the law ineffective in preventing seriously anti-competitive covert agreements and practices. This view found an echo in a recent statement by the DGFT that 'A continuing priority for the Office's Competition Policy Division was to uncover secret – and therefore unlawful – price-fixing and otherwise blatantly anti-competitive agreements.'[9] Existing policy was also attacked as costly in so far as it involves processing of harmless mergers. Proposals, not yet implemented, were made for the abolition of the registration system and its replacement by a ban on all agreements with anti-competitive effects (subject to the right of appeal to the Restrictive Practices Court), stronger powers of investigation by the DGFT, and heavier fines (to a maximum of 10 per cent of the value of a firm's turnover).

Competition policy and the EC

UK competition policy must work within the context of the European Community, where policy is based on Articles 85 and 86 of the Treaty of Rome, and applies where trade between member states is concerned. The DGFT acts as a 'competent authority' to assist the EC in the application of Community rules.

Article 85 deals with restrictive practices which reduce competition and must be notified to the Commission. Article 86 concerns market dominance, the abuse of monopoly power. It also covers mergers between companies with a turnover greater than 5,000 million ECU, global, and 250 million ECU, within the EC.[10] Two recent cases illustrate the work of the EC. In the first, Peugeot was told to withdraw an instruction to French dealers not to supply Ecosystem, an intermediary which tries to buy cars for consumers where prices are lowest. In the second, a company called Tetra Pak was found to have abused its dominant position in the market for machines and cartons by practices aimed at reducing competition and maximising profits. The company was fined the record sum of 75 million ECU.

Increasingly EC rules and regulations have influenced UK policy in recent years. For example, it is the EC that we have to

9   Annual Report of the Director General of Fair Trading, 1991.
10   £1 = ECU 1.25 approximately, January 1993.

thank for declaring that the BBC and Independent Television Publications had abused their power by prohibiting others from publishing comprehensive television listings. We no longer have to buy both the *Radio Times* and *TV Times*!

Regulating natural monopolies

A different type of policy to those described above is called for in the case of (natural) monopolies, where competition can have only a limited role. The mechanism involves regulation, and the chief areas where it is used are in the newly privatised public utilities, gas, electricity, water and telephone services in particular.

New regulatory machinery has been developed to monitor and control their activities. It is operated by specialised 'Offices' – OFTEL (for telecommunications), OFGAS (for gas), OFWAT (for water) and OFFER (for electricity). One objective of the regulatory bodies is to monitor quality, e.g. the number of telephone boxes out of order. Another is to protect the consuming public from exploitation. A choice of methods is available – to regulate profits or prices. Difficulties arise with both techniques, especially since the regulator has limited information about the companies he administers. Firms have an incentive (in the interests of their shareholders) to try to overstate costs if prices are regulated, or to understate profits if controls are related to accounting profits. The UK opted for price regulation, in the hope that this would encourage efficiency and cost cutting. Maximum prices are set by reference to the average rate of inflation given by the Retail Price Index (RPI), account being taken of productivity changes and investment needs. For example, since 1984, OFTEL has set price limits varying between RPI − 3 (allowing prices to rise, on average, by 3 per cent less than the inflation rate) to RPI − $7\frac{1}{2}$. OFWAT has set limits for the area water companies, averaging a little over RPI + 5, because of the need for substantial investment in the industry. The regulatory system has not been in force long enough for its efficiency to be reliably assessed. It has, however, been observed that profits in the regulated sector have been on the high side, especially during the recession – e.g. in the case of British Telecom, which earned also a higher rate of return than comparable companies elsewhere in the world.

Regional Policy

As we saw in Chapter 3, industries are not evenly spread over the country but tend to concentrate in particular areas. Heavy dependence on one or more failing industries caused serious local pockets of unemployment in the interwar years and government action was taken to alleviate this problem. The first step was taken in 1934 when certain 'Special Areas' were scheduled as 'Depressed' and commissioners were appointed to try to attract new industry to them. Postwar Distribution of Industry Acts reinforced this policy, giving powers to the government. These included building factories for letting in the areas (renamed **Development Areas**) and making loans and grants to attract firms. At the same time, a programme was initiated for the creation of 32 'new towns' – now complete with over 2 million inhabitants – in more prosperous regions.

Government control over factory location was materially strengthened by legislation whereby new factories required planning permission from the local authority, and larger factories also required the granting of an industrial development certificate. The government was able, until 1982, to influence industrial location by granting or withholding these certificates – a powerful weapon.

Outside Northern Ireland, which is treated separately, the areas of Great Britain which qualify for assistance fall into two categories: Development Areas and Intermediate Areas (see Figure 6.11).

Development Areas are those judged to have the greatest needs. The help available is targeted at job-creation and includes (discretionary) grants for new investment under **Regional Selective Assistance** (which replaced Regional Development Grants in 1988), and **Regional Enterprise Grants**, available for firms with fewer than 25 employees. Additionally, an Urban Regeneration Programme concentrated on problems of decaying inner cities. A dozen Urban Development Corporations have been set up, in London Docklands, Merseyside and similar areas in other city centres with finance for environmental improvement as well as grants for private investment. Finally a small amount of EC aid

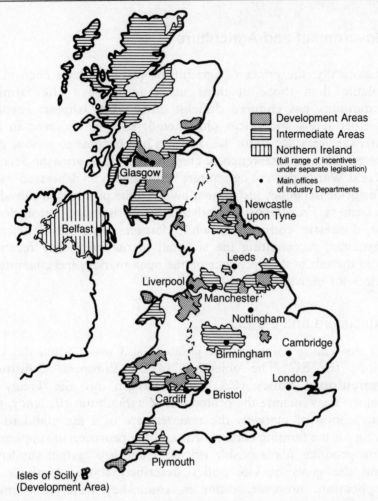

Development Areas

Intermediate Areas

Northern Ireland
(full range of incentives
under separate legislation)

• Main offices
of Industry Departments

Glasgow

Newcastle
upon Tyne

Belfast

Leeds

Liverpool

Manchester

Nottingham

Cambridge

Birmingham

London

Cardiff

Bristol

Plymouth

Isles of Scilly
(Development Area)

Figure 6.11 Location of industry policy, 1992 – areas entitled to
assistance
Source: *Britain 1992, An Official Handbook*

arrives from the **European Regional Development Fund**. It is
an open question whether EC funds were additional to, or
substitutes for, assistance from the UK government.

Unemployment rate differentials among the regions have
tended to narrow over recent years, though it is difficult to know
how much this is the result of government policy.

Government and Agriculture

Historically, the prices of agricultural products have been more volatile than those of most other industries. The farming community has endured difficult times when harvests reached bumper levels and prices plummeted, such as occurred in the interwar years. By 1930, the situation had become so serious that the government intervened. It continued to do so after the Second World War to prevent agriculture returning to its depressed state. The principal policy instrument involved the payment of subsidies to farmers. Free import of foodstuffs into Britain kept prices down for domestic consumers, while farmers received deficiency payments, representing the shortfall in the price they received from the sale of their produce on the open market, and guaranteed prices for individual products.

Agriculture and the EC

All this changed (except for potatoes and wool) when the UK joined the EC. The objectives of the European **Common Agricultural Policy** (CAP) were written into the Treaty of Rome. They include the promotion of agricultural efficiency, the stabilisation of markets, the maintenance of a fair standard of living for the farming community, and the provision of supplies of farm produce at reasonable prices. There is a certain similarity with the goals of UK policy described above. Methods of application, however, differ in some key ways. The most important is that the CAP operates an internal system of minimum prices above those in world markets.

The machinery of the CAP involves (i) the annual setting of the target prices for individual products by the Council of (agricultural) Ministers, (ii) imposition of variable import levies (VILs) on imports from outside the Community, and (iii) intervention buying by EC agencies in member countries to maintain domestic prices. Commodities bought by intervention cannot normally be sold inside the EC without upsetting the support price so, where possible, they are disposed of cheaply to Third World countries. The proceeds of the VILs are paid into the

European Agricultural Guidance and Guarantee Fund (EEAGGF, or FEOGA – the French abbreviation by which it is also known). Most of Fund income goes to pay 'export restitution payments', i.e. subsidies to the intervention agencies to help cover losses on exports.

The operation of the CAP has been widely regarded as unsatisfactory, particularly by countries such as the UK with a small agricultural sector. The scope for disagreement among member nations on the level of support for individual products and the method of financing it is tremendous. About two-thirds of the entire EC budget has been spent on agriculture, the level of support being so high at times as to generate enormous surpluses of some commodities – 'mountains' of butter and sugar, and 'lakes' of wine and milk. Moreover, as the EC has moved from being a net importer to a net exporter of agricultural products, it has been accused, not without some justification, of 'dumping' – e.g. by the USA in the Uruguay trade negotiations (see above, page 156).

The search for ways of reforming the CAP has been in train for several years. It has not been easy to find solutions acceptable to member states with varying interests, e.g. relatively poor countries with substantial agricultural sectors, such as Greece and Portugal, those such as France, which have a strong farm lobby, and those, such as the UK, which have not.

The UK has pressed hard, and with some success, for a reduction in the level of agricultural support. Since 1988, there has been a legal limit on CAP support expenditure, and 'stabilisers' have been brought in for most commodities. These ensure that CAP support is automatically cut as output passes predetermined levels.

Further reforms resulted from the MacSharry Plan (named after the EC Commissioner for Agriculture), which calls for the gradual reduction of support prices and their replacement by farm income subsidies (in 1992 it was agreed that the support prices for cereals would be cut by 29 per cent over three years). 'Set aside' reductions in acreage, with monetary compensation for farmers, have also been introduced for several products, though there is scepticism about how far they will result in reductions in output.

Housing, Education and Health

This is a long chapter and we shall cover only three more areas where intervention has been common: housing, education and health.

Housing

There is a long tradition that minimum standards of housing should be available for all, regardless of income, especially where there are children in the household. A distinctive feature of houses is that their cost is high – it is rare that anyone can buy one out of current income. It has also been argued that those living in rented accommodation should enjoy a certain security of tenure.

Subsidised housing for the 'needy' has, therefore, been accepted as a state responsibility. In 1980, about a third of houses were occupied by tenants of flats and houses owned by local authorities. The proportion living in council accommodation fell to 20 per cent by 1990, largely because of privatisation sales. The Housing Act of 1980 gave council house tenants of at least three years' standing, the right to buy the property. About a third were sold, at an average discount of 50 per cent.

Owner-occupation has been rising over a longer period – from 50 per cent to nearly 70 per cent between 1970 and 1990. Non-profit-making housing associations have become the main providers in the subsidised housing sector. They offer housing for rent (or sale) to disadvantaged groups, including the elderly, the disabled and those in low-paid employment.

The government intervenes in the housing market by allowing relief against income tax on mortgage interest payments on loans of up to £30,000 (at the standard rate of tax only). This policy has been attacked as largely responsible for the excessive house prices boom of the late 1980s. It is argued that the tax relief does not benefit *new* purchasers of houses. Removal of the concession is clearly politically difficult, though its real value has been depressed by holding the maximum eligible loan at £30,000, despite inflation (see page 179).

There are housing regulations on health, environment, and planning grounds and, for the greater part of the present century, rents have been controlled in the private sector. Rent control was introduced as an emergency wartime measure in 1915. Landlords of unfurnished flats and houses at the lower end of the market were prohibited from raising rents unless improvements had been made (or rates increased). Tenants were also given security from eviction. The measure had been intended as a temporary one but persisted, in one form or another, for over half a century. By 1939, about a third of all privately rented houses and flats were subject to restrictions. Rent controls continued after the Second World War with the effect that the supply of property for rent was severely restricted. The Housing Act of 1980 brought the first reversal, by introducing 'shorthold' lettings, reducing security of tenants against eviction from life to a shorter period of 1–5 years, by agreement. Also significant was the Housing Act of 1988, which deregulated rents in the independent rented sector, where they are now set by agreement between landlords and tenants, though housing associations are required to provide accommodation at low rents or sale prices.

Education and health

There are several reasons why the state intervenes in health and education. One is a belief that access to minimum standards should be available to everyone, regardless of income. There is an additional reason in the case of education. If the state did not provide minimum standards, some parents might decide to spend less (perhaps even more) on their children's education than the children would (later, as adults) have wished to have had spent. Furthermore, it is argued that society, as well as the individual, benefits from having its members healthy and well educated. This is obvious in the case of, say, infectious and contagious diseases, but of wider importance is the beneficial effect on economic growth and, more vaguely perhaps, social cohesion. Resources allocated to both education and health involve investment in human capital, increasing individuals' earning power, job choice and ability to work well.

Tools of intervention are both budgetary and rules and regulations. Compulsory school attendance dates back to 1876, but the school leaving age has been raised, of course, since then. Compulsory health insurance was brought in by the Lloyd George Government in 1912, well before the advent of the National Health Service (1948). Another example of the use of rules is that for the compulsory wearing of car seat belts.

Approximately £1 out of every £6 or £7 in the state budget (excluding interest on the national debt) goes on health and education respectively (see above Figure 6.3). For those who choose to opt out of state education or health there are no provisions for tax deductions in the UK as there are in some other countries, partly because the public sector is so very large (only about 600,000 out of $9\frac{1}{2}$ million children attend private schools, for example). Most expenditure on education is financed out of general taxation, though there are some user charges, e.g. for school meals and loans for university students. Recent changes in policy include the delegation to schools of the management of their budgets. The intention is to allow a role for market forces, but teachers have largely opposed the change, which makes greater demands on time spent on administration rather than teaching.

Nearly 80 per cent of the cost of running the National Health Service comes from general taxation; the rest is met from national insurance contributions and from charges for items such as drugs, spectacles and dental treatment to non-exempt users (those other than children, OAPs, students and low-income families in the main). NHS hospitals also accept private patients who pay their full costs. Despite the large public provision, the UK spends a lower proportion of its total income on health (about 6 per cent) than several other countries (e.g. the USA 11 per cent; France, Germany and Italy 8–9 per cent[11]).

A desire to improve efficiency in the NHS led the government, in 1989, to propose changes giving a greater role for market forces in resource allocation. The principle is similar to that in the case of

11   These statistics need careful interpretation. Expenditure on health will be high if doctors and other health workers are highly paid, for example. The evidence is that the British are at least as healthy as Americans, despite much higher expenditure in that country.

schools (see above), but more extensive. Both hospitals and general practitioners now operate within an 'internal market'. The former receive budgets (the size depending on numbers of patients and their health risks) from Regional Health Authorities, out of which they meet the costs of providing their own services and buy hospital treatment for patients. Hospitals are free to supply services to any doctors demanding them, at prices agreed between the parties. Organisational innovations also include an option for hospitals to acquire self-governing status, freeing them from regional health authority control.

These changes have proved highly controversial, the medical profession itself being divided on the issue. Some doctors have expressed support in principle, but others oppose it, especially resenting spending extra time on administration. Note, too, that the internal market does not operate as do markets for goods and services where buyers decide how to allocate their expenditure to maximise their satisfaction. The NHS internal market offers more choice not to patients as consumers, but to doctors and hospitals.

Miscellaneous measures

There is not space in this book even to list the manifold measures that governments have used, and still use, to influence resource allocation in the UK. Their range and diversity may be gleaned from mentioning a few – taxation may promote efficiency, e.g. to stimulate investment or savings (PEPs and TESSAs tax concessions of recent years); safety standards and misleading trade descriptions legislation can raise product quality. The Director General of Fair Trading has a responsibility for consumer protection, as does a National Consumer Council. In the area of environmental protection there are Pollution Inspectorates, a National Rivers Authority, and in that of investment protection, there are bodies set up under the Financial Services Act 1986. Multiple activities by the Departments of Trade and Industry, of Employment and other departments and ministries are too numerous to mention.

Privatisation

We end this chapter on microeconomic policy with a section on privatisation. We shall be brief because the subject has already been dealt with on several occasions above. We described asset transfers in Chapter 3, and the sale of council houses and regulatory machinery for controlling gas, water, electricity and telephone services in this chapter (see above, pages 59–62 and 213).

The term 'privatisation' means different things to different people. To some it is synonymous with denationalisation. However, by privatisation most economists mean a whole range of measures, developed by Conservative governments since 1979, aimed at the promotion of three goals. The first goal, most relevant at this point in the book, is increased use of market forces in resource allocation. The second goal is to foster 'popular capitalism' by raising the proportion of the population owning company shares. The third goal concerns use of revenues from asset sales for contra-inflation and other macroeconomic policies, which we discuss in Chapter 9.

The goals of the privatisation programme have been pursued by various means, including asset transfers, deregulation, subcontracting/franchising, and charging for state-provided services which were previously free (or subsidised).

On the policy of asset transfers, little needs to be added except that share issues in privatised companies proved immensely popular, both with employees and with the general public, since most were offered at heavily discounted prices, yielding immediate capital gains. Critics, not surprisingly, have stressed the cost to the taxpayer (called 'giving away the family silver' by former Prime Minister the late Harold Macmillan, Earl of Stockton). One of the strongest criticisms of the denationalisation measures, however, is that increasing competition was not always given sufficient priority. To an extent this may be because the privatisation programme had too many conflicting goals. For example, in order to make the share issues successful, British Telecom and British Gas were sold as single concerns complete with their monopoly powers. Had they been broken into separate competing components, they would hardly have appeared as attractive propositions for prospective purchasers.

Increased powers for market forces have been the motive for other privatisation measures, e.g. deregulation, subcontracting/ franchising, and introducing or raising charges for state services previously provided free, or at less than cost.

Deregulation means the removal of restrictions on competition. The ending of legal monopolies for qualified opticians in the sale of spectacles and of solicitors in conveyancing of house property are examples of the deregulation measures of the 1980s. Another is the repeal of the legislation limiting competition among the operators of road passenger transport, i.e. buses and coaches.

Subcontracting, or franchising, introduces competition to the provision of state-financed services by allowing outside contractors to tender for the right to do the actual supplying. It has been used with a measure of success by some local authorities, e.g. for refuse collection, and by hospitals for services such as cleaning.

A final aspect of the privatisation programme aimed at strengthening market forces concerns the introduction or raising of charges for state-provided benefits, e.g. for dental treatment under the NHS. The underlying principle is that beneficiaries from expenditure should pay for it. There have also been discussions about charging for education by the issue of vouchers which could be used only to buy schooling, but the idea has yet to be implemented.

Questions and exercises

(For key to abbreviations identifying sources, see pages xv–xvi)

1   Refer to the report on the budget in one of the 'serious' newspapers. Identify a budget change which might have the following effects: (i) redistribute income (a) more or (b) less equally, (ii) encourage business investment, (iii) promote personal saving, (iv) pursue a goal other than (i)–(iii).

2   What is the maximum sum your parents could give you without incurring (i) any possible and (ii) certain inheritance tax liability this year. How much could they leave so as to (i) avoid tax on their deaths and (ii) pay an average tax rate of 15 per cent? Do your answers tell you how progressive the tax is?

3 Draw Lorenz curves to show the distribution of household income before and after tax last year. Compare your results with Figure 6.6(ii). (ST or ET)

4 Classify all government outgoings last year and 10 years previously according to (i) exhaustive expenditure, (ii) transfers. Comment on the changes.

5 Draw a graph similar to Figure 6.8 showing the course of retail prices over the past two years in each of the following groups: (a) food, (b) leisure, (c) transport, (d) housing, (e) all items. Write two paragraphs identifying the characteristics of two people with the same incomes, one of whose standard of living had risen and the other for whom it had fallen since two years previously. (AS or MDS)

6 Find press articles about two reports by the Monopolies and Mergers Commission, one a merger, the other a monopoly case. (T has an excellent index.) How far were the recommendations in line with the outline of competition policy in the chapter?

7 Refer to Table 2.2 on page 62. Select six privatised companies and compare the share price today with that of a year ago. Do you wish you had bought all, none or some of the shares, or put an equal sum of money into the basket of shares making up the FT100 index of share prices? (Ignore dealing costs.) (FT, T)

Appendix 6

Table A6.1 UK central government current income and expenditure 1981 and 1991 (£ million)

Income	1981	1991
Taxes on income	36,134	75,105
Taxes on expenditure	32,271	82,905
Social security contributions	15,916	36,643
Gross trading surplus	−26	−457
Rent, interest, etc.	6,970	10,636
Other miscellaneous	950	1,752
Total current income	92,215	206,584

Expenditure		
Final consumption	33,879	74,442
Subsidies	5,171	5,298
Grants to persons	30,100	63,966
Grants to local authorities	15,201	47,730
Grants paid abroad (net)	1,607	1,049
Debt interest	10,122	16,340
Total current expenditure	96,080	208,825
Balance (current surplus)	−3,865	−2,241

Source: *UK National Accounts*

Table A6.2 UK general government expenditure, selected years since 1980–1 (percentage distribution by function)

	1980–1	1985–6	1990–1	1991–2 estimated
Defence	12.2	12.9	11.2	10.5
Overseas services, including overseas aid	1.5	1.3	1.4	1.4
Agriculture, fisheries, food and forestry	1.8	2.1	1.5	1.4
Trade, industry, energy and employment	5.3	6.0	3.8	3.3
of which: Employment and training	*2.1*	*2.2*	*1.5*	*1.3*
Transport	4.7	4.2	4.1	4.4
Housing	6.2	3.0	2.5	2.7
Other environmental services	3.9	3.0	3.7	3.7
Law, order and protective services	4.3	4.7	5.8	5.9
Education and science	14.9	13.1	14.5	14.2
Arts and libraries	0.6	0.6	0.7	0.7
Health and personal social services	15.4	14.9	16.9	17.1
of which: Health	*13.0*	*12.7*	*14.2*	*14.4*
Social security	26.3	31.3	30.1	31.7
Miscellaneous expenditure	3.1	2.9	3.7	3.0
Total	100.0	100.0	100.0	100.0

Source: *Autumn Statements, Statistical Supplements*

Table A6.3 Percentage shares in total income of non-retired household, 1989

	Original income (a)	Gross income (b)	Disposable income (c)	Post-tax income (d)
Bottom 20%	2.7	7.1	7.6	6.9
Second bottom 20%	7	11	12	11
Middle 20%	16	16	17	16
Second top 20%	26	23	23	23
Top 20%	49	42	41	43

Note: See Figure 6.6 for explanation of cols (a), (b), (c) and (d).

Source: *Economic Trends*, June 1992

Table A6.4 Retail prices, 1980–1992

	All items	Food	Housing
1980	70.6	76.1	59.6
1981	79.1	82.5	70.3
1982	85.8	88.9	79.2
1983	89.7	91.8	81.2
1984	94.3	97.0	88.7
1985	100.0	100.0	100.0
1986	103.4	103.3	105.8
1987	107.7	106.4	114.8
1988	113.0	110.1	125.0
1989	121.8	116.3	150.3
1990	133.3	125.7	181.9
1991	141.1	132.2	178.7
1992*	147.1	135.9	176.9

* First half of year

Source: *National Institute Economic Review*

7
National Income and Balance of Payments

At this point in the book, we pass from a consideration of the allocation of resources among industries and sectors to look at the economy as a whole. We start to concern ourselves with totals, or aggregates. This short chapter describes two of the most important of them: (1) the sum total of all outputs – what is known generally as the national income, and (2) the balance of payments – the record of transactions between residents and non-residents.

National Income

The national income is a measure of all goods and services produced in the economy during some period of time (usually a year) and valued in money terms.[1] It can be estimated in any one of three ways by summing:

- all incomes
- all outputs
- all expenditures

In principle, all three methods will give the same answer. This is because the value of output produced is equal to the value of expenditure needed to purchase it and to the income claims generated by its production.[2] One of the advantages of having three ways of estimating the national income is that they throw different lights on its composition.

1 National income accounts are discussed in Lipsey–Harbury, FP2, Chapters 26, 30 and 32.
2 Because all value produced must belong to someone.

Figure 7.1 shows the breakdown of national income estimated in each of the three ways.

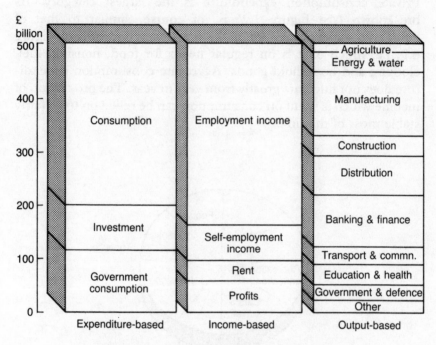

Figure 7.1 Gross domestic product, 1991
Source: *UK National Accounts*

Expenditure-Based Measure of National Income

There are three major components of national expenditure:

- consumption
- investment
- government

and a fourth of relatively small magnitude:

- net exports

Consumption

Private consumption expenditure is the largest category. Its breakdown (see Figure 7.2) is, of course, similar to that of household expenditure, which we previously observed in Figure 6.9, i.e. much of it is on regular needs for food, housing, fuel, clothing and household goods. Aggregate consumption expenditure does not fluctuate greatly from year to year. The proportion of income which is spent on consumption can be relied on to be fairly stable most of the time.

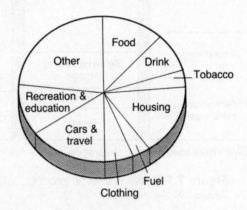

Figure 7.2 Consumer expenditure 1991
Source: *UK National Accounts*

Investment

The second component of national expenditure, investment, tends to be more volatile than consumption. Investment is of two kinds:

- **fixed capital formation** in plant, machinery, equipment and housing
- **change in holdings of stocks** of goods at various stages in the production process

Figure 7.3 shows the composition of fixed capital formation in 1987. Less than 20 per cent of the invested total is in the public sector, two-thirds of which consists of new building. The remainder is private sector capital formation. All, except dwellings, raise the productive potential of the economy and, given favourable circumstances, can lead to economic growth. The proportion of gross domestic product going to fixed investment has varied between 16 and 20 per cent in the UK over the past 20 to 30 years. Most of the time this has been notably less than other countries, such as France, Germany and Italy, where the proportion has more commonly exceeded 20 per cent (see Figure 3.7, page 77).

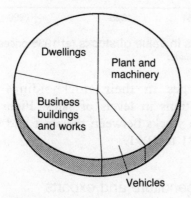

Figure 7.3 Gross domestic fixed capital formation 1991
Source: *UK National Accounts*

The relative volatility of aggregate investment expenditure mentioned earlier is traceable not so much to fixed capital formation as to the second component of investment – changes in stocks (or inventories) of goods and materials held by businesses. They are considered in economics as part of investment and play a key role in economic theory.[3] Although, to an extent, firms decide for themselves the size of stocks they wish to carry, they also find

3   See Lipsey–Harbury, FP2, pages 342–3.

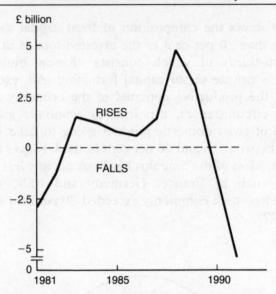

Figure 7.4 Changes in value of stocks (at 1985 prices) 1981–1991
Source: *UK National Accounts*

involuntary changes in their stockholdings as a result of unexpected alterations in levels of sales. Figure 7.4 shows the annual changes in stocks between the start and end of each year for the period 1981 to 1991.

Government expenditure and exports

The other two categories of aggregate expenditure are government and (net) exports. The former were considered in Chapter 6, where some determinants of government expenditure were discussed. Somewhat surprisingly, perhaps, public spending fluctuates remarkably little in the short-term, mainly because most of it involves long-term commitments which are procedurally difficult to alter.

Finally, net purchases of goods by foreigners (exports net of imports) are a part of national expenditure. They are discussed in the second part of this chapter. However, we should explain why net exports are not shown in the left-hand section of Figure 7.1. One reason is that in 1991 net exports were negative, because the value of imports exceeded that of exports. Another is that in most recent years the values of total imports and exports are too close for even a net positive figure to show up in the diagram.

Income-Based Measure of National Income

The second column in Figure 7.1 (on page 229) shows the main categories of national income. These were discussed in Chapter 4 when we were looking at the distribution of income among factors of production (see pages 105–7 and Figure 4.2). Only two matters need further attention. In the first place, note that the only incomes included are factor incomes, i.e. incomes earned by supplying factor services for current production. We know (from Chapter 6) that some individuals receive incomes from the state, e.g. retirement pensions, unemployment benefits, etc. These are transfer incomes. They are paid by taxing some people and using the proceeds to pay state benefits. Since we are interested in measuring the income derived from contributions to production by factors of production, we do not include transfer payments.

In the second place, note that for some purposes we want to know the amount of income people have available for spending – for an example see Figure 6.6, page 196. This is called **personal disposable income**. To calculate it, we add total factor and transfer incomes to persons, and deduct income taxes and national insurance contributions.

Savings

One of the key variables in national income analysis is savings. Persons, businesses, and even the government save when they do not spend all of their income. Personal savings are closely related to personal disposable income. They do not appear in Figure 7.1 because they are, by definition, income not spent on consumption. They can, however, be estimated and Figure 7.5 shows the course of personal savings expressed as a percentage of personal disposable income between 1981 and 1991.

The diagram shows a downward trend in the **savings ratio** (the proportion of personal income saved) during the 1980s, from a

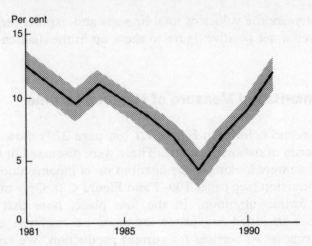

Figure 7.5 The savings ratio, 1981–1991. Savings as a percentage of personal disposable income

Source: *UK National Accounts*

Note: The ratio is shown with a thick pen because it is not known very precisely (see Box 6.1)

high of about 15 per cent at the very beginning of the decade. There was a small upturn in 1984 and a rise again at the end of the decade lasting into the 1990s.

There is no simple explanation of these trends. The ratio is the result of many complex factors. Personal savings are stimulated by high rates of interest; they tend to rise in booms and to fall in slumps; and they are affected by taxation (see above, page 221). However, recent history of the savings ratio has led many commentators to talk of the drop of the ratio to a historical low of 5 per cent in 1988 as 'The Savings Puzzle'.[4] One explanation which has been offered is that soaring house prices at the time raised the wealth of owner-occupiers and lowered their need to save. It should be appreciated that a substantial portion of personal savings are contractual and, therefore, invariable, e.g. life assurance premiums and mortgage repayments on house purchase loans. It is dangerous to read too much into the meaning of trends in the savings ratio, which is a national income statistic known with remarkably little accuracy. The shading around the ratio line

4 See *Lloyds Bank Economic Bulletin no. 165*, September 1992.

Box 7.1

Saving Key to the Future

Changes in the proportion of income saved, the savings ratio, have extremely important effects on the country's economic performance. An understanding of likely movements in the savings ratio provides the key to projection of UK economic recovery and to prospects for growth in the medium term. Yet saving is poorly measured....

The saving ratio is an extremely inaccurate statistic. It suffers from being calculated from the difference between two very large numbers, consumer spending and personal disposable income, which are themselves subject to inaccuracy. For example, if consumer spending is equal to 90% of income, but spending and income are only measured within 2% of their correct value (actual measurement error is probably in excess of this), the saving ratio could vary by +/− 35% simply as a result of this measurement error. In other words, if the correct saving ratio is 10%, its measured value could be as high as 13.5% or as low as 6.4%.

Lloyds Bank Economic Bulletin
no. 152, August 1991

This extract is intended to urge you to treat published statistics, official and other, with great caution – even though, or perhaps because, they are reported to one or more places of decimals. Of course, some data are more reliable than others. The series of total consumption expenditure, for example, is recognised as having a very much smaller degree of unreliability, while personal savings is one of the least reliable. The savings ratio is, incidentally, likely to be even more unreliable than the figure for total savings – because it is the result of dividing a very unreliable figure by another which is also not completely reliable.

on the graph in Figure 7.5 indicates that it is not known very precisely.

Output-Based Measure of National Income

This measure of national output was encountered in Chapter 3, which described the structure of British industry (see pages 68–70). There is, however, one aspect that requires further explanation. The value of the output of each of the main sectors in the economy is known as a *net* output, or **value added**. Since we want to know the value of final output, we must not count the total value of sales every time a good changes hands. If we added together the gross sales revenues of all businesses, this would involve **double counting** – because the outputs of some firms are the inputs of others. Hence, when calculating national output, we deduct the purchases of inputs by firms from other businesses from the gross output in order to arrive at the proper figure for added value. An illustration of the method of calculation used in one industry (energy and water supply) is given below.

Method of calculating value added tax

	£ million	£ million
Revenue from sales	46,275	
Plus: Rise in stocks of finished products	111	
Gross value of output		46,386
Less: Purchases of inputs, fall in stocks of materials, stores, fuels etc.		-27,980
Value added (net output)		18,406

Source: *Census of Production: Business Monitor*, PA 1002
(Figures relate to Energy and Water Supply 1989)

The National Accounts

In a complex economy such as the UK, where there is a large government sector and there are many international transactions, the national income is estimated annually and is published in the official *UK National Accounts*, often known as the 'Blue Book'.

There are several standard forms in which the accounts are used in economic analysis. The relationships between them are shown in Figure 7.6.

Foreign trade

The top row in Figure 7.6 shows **total domestic expenditure**, broken down into its main components – consumption, investment and government. However, we need to take account of exports and imports. To derive total expenditure on UK products, it is necessary to add expenditure by non-residents on UK exports to domestic expenditure. This gives **total final expenditure**

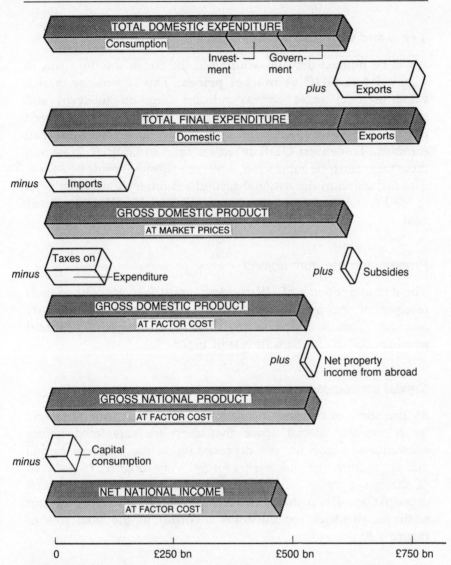

Figure 7.6 National income and product 1991 (relationship between major definitions)
Source: *UK National Accounts*

(TFE). To derive total UK output, deduct expenditure on imports. This total is known as **gross domestic product** (GDP).

Taxes and subsidies on expenditure

It will be noticed that the wording in the bar in the third row of Figure 7.6 is **GDP at market prices**. This is because market value includes taxes on expenditure (e.g. on tobacco) and subsidies (e.g. on housing). Taxes cause market values to exceed factor earnings, while subsidies allow market values to be less than earnings. To convert GDP at *market prices* to GDP at *factor cost*, these taxes must be subtracted, while the subsidies must be added. The deduction in the national accounts is often shown simply net as 'deduct net taxes on expenditure'. This yields **GDP at factor cost**.

Property income from abroad

The national income of UK residents must take account of (net) receipts of income derived from the ownership of property overseas. This is added to the GDP to yield **gross national product** (GNP) in the fifth row of Figure 7.6.

Capital consumption

All measures of national income or output dealt with so far are 'gross' in the special sense that they are calculated before allowance is made for the depreciation in the value of capital that arises from age and market forces. Very roughly, 15 per cent of the gross value of output is needed to make good such depreciation. When this is deducted from GNP it gives the **net national product** (or **national income**) in the final row of Figure 7.6.

The Reliability of National Income Statistics

Figures of national income in official publications appear to have a high degree of numerical precision. However, one should not be misled by this apparent accuracy. It is no simple task to estimate all the elements needed to compute the national income.

Of course, some of the data are more reliable than others – unfortunately not always those most important for economic analysis. We have already mentioned that personal savings is an especially questionable statistic.

Consider another illustration. When the national income is estimated by each of the three methods described at the beginning of this chapter, the answer should, as we have seen, be the same. An indication of the minimum errors involved is shown by the differences in the figure arising out of each method. To reconcile them the Blue Book gives a 'residual error' which must be included to make the income data add up to the same total as the expenditure data. The discrepancy varies between $\frac{1}{2}$ per cent and 2 per cent of the total.

Errors of 1 to 2 per cent are bothersome when calculating totals, but they can be serious when calculating growth rates, which are usually based on year-to-year changes in GDP of no more than 3 to 4 per cent per annum, i.e. the error in the estimated GDP can be up to half, or even more, of the growth rate being measured. For this reason, although trends in the growth rate over several years can be significant, not too much should be read into changes in the measured growth rate from one year to the next. Figure 7.7[5] illustrates this point. It shows the range between the highest and lowest estimates of the year-to-year growth rate of GDP for some recent years. Although the three measures of GDP should give the same answer, the range between them varies. Sometimes they can be close, e.g. in 1990 the range was 0.6 to 0.9 per cent. At other times they can be far apart, e.g. in 1984 the output-based estimate was 3.3 per cent, whereas the income-based estimate was a mere 1.1 per cent.

Living Standards and the National Income

The national income, as we now know, is a measure of a nation's output of goods and services. It would be reasonable to infer that it

5 The figure for 1990–1 is missing, because the 1992 Blue Book does not continue past practice of publishing growth rate tables based on GDP estimated in the three ways.

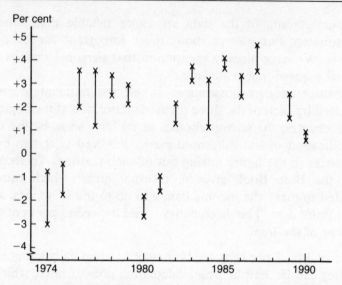

Figure 7.7 Estimated year-to-year changes in GDP, 1974–1990 (the height of the bars shows the range between the highest and lowest estimates of the growth rate for each year)
Source: *UK National Accounts*

is, therefore, a good indicator of the standard of living. If we divide the national income by the number of people living in a country we obtain a figure of income per head of the population. This is, indeed, related to living standards. However, the two are not the same.

The national income does not measure everything that contributes to living standards. There are many differences between the concepts and we can mention some of the more important ones here. Nearly all arise from the fact that the goods and services included in the national income total are limited to those that are bought and sold in the market place or provided by the state (in which case, incidentally, they are mostly valued at cost). There are some important omissions from the national accounts which contribute to living standards.

Among the exclusions are environmental beauty and cultural inheritances. A different type of omission is leisure. If people decide to produce fewer goods and services and to spend more time at home or on holiday, they may feel that their living standards have risen, though measured national income will actually show a fall.

We must also consider exclusions that are due to the nature of economic organisation. Some services, for example, are performed without money transactions taking place, while others, which may be equally important, go unrecorded. Principal among the former are services of housewives, as distinct from those of paid housekeepers; do-it-yourself jobs undertaken instead of paying for work to be done; and illegal transactions, e.g. in drugs and tax-dodging work paid in cash in the 'black economy'. The size of the black economy is, for obvious reasons, not known precisely. Estimates put it at anything up to $7\frac{1}{2}$ per cent of GDP.

A final exclusion is relevant to comparisons of national income over time. This is the inability of statistics to make full allowance for changes in the quality of products. Many modern goods, such as cars, television sets and hi-fi equipment, perform better and need less maintenance than in the past. Yet they are often cheaper than previous models. The value of output of these products in the national accounts does not therefore show a rise. Indeed, reductions in expenditure on maintenance and repairs might suggest that national income had even fallen.

We can conclude that there are substantial differences between measured national income and what goes to make up the standard of living of the population. We must treat the statistics with caution.

A last consideration deserves comment before we move on. The matters mentioned so far suggest that living standards may be higher than would be indicated by the size of the national income. There are, however, reasons why the opposite may be the case. One is that quality changes can move in two directions. We explained (two paragraphs earlier) how rising product quality may not be accompanied by a rising GDP. The reverse applies if quality deteriorates, e.g. mail is delivered less frequently than in the past and road congestion diminishes some of the pleasures of motoring.

Another reason why living standards may not have risen as much as national income statistics would indicate is the existence of what have, perhaps unfortunately, been called economic 'bads' (the use of the word 'bads' is analogous to that of the word 'goods' – both imply value judgements). These are things like pollution and spoliation of the countryside that have sometimes accompanied rapid economic growth. They can lower the standard of living even when measured national income is rising.

The distribution of national income

The previous section concerned the *average* living standards in a nation. However, we know (from Chapters 4 and 6) that national income is not evenly divided among the population. Disparity extends also to the distribution of income among regions of the UK. Figure 7.8 shows per capita income for each region of the UK relative to the average for the UK as a whole. The spread is considerable. The South East leads the field, with Northern Ireland in the rear, reflecting the fact that GDP per capita in the South East is over 50 per cent higher than in Northern Ireland. Even these figures are themselves averages, and our knowledge of regional variations in unemployment and in earnings (see pages 115 and 125) should lead us to expect further variation within regions too.

Explanations of local differences are complex, but include reasons why levels of economic activity and of wages and salaries differ around the country, reflecting, among other things, the effects of market forces. It should not be inferred, of course, that living standards necessarily vary as greatly as do incomes per head. There may well be offsetting living costs, such as expensive travel and housing in high income regions, and compensating non-monetary rewards of country living.

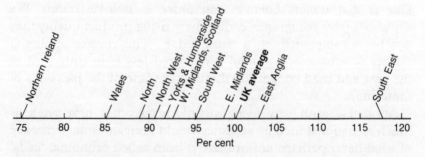

Figure 7.8 Regional income per head 1990 (each region is shown as a percentage of the UK average GDP)
Source: *Regional Trends*

Real and Nominal National Income

GDP measures the money value of final goods produced during a year. Thus, it has a price and a quantity component; a given change in GDP can be caused by many different combinations of price and quantity changes. A 10 per cent rise in GDP might, for example, be caused by a 10 per cent rise in prices, all quantities remaining unchanged; by a 10 per cent rise in quantities, all prices remaining unchanged; or by any appropriate changes in both prices and quantities. For some purposes the money value of national income is the measure required. However, sometimes we wish to know what is happening to the *quantity* of output, in which case we need to separate changes in GDP caused by variations in prices from changes caused by variations in quantities of output.

To estimate the change in the volume of GDP, output is valued in constant prices. Each year, the aggregate quantity of output is estimated. Instead of valuing these volumes at the prices current in each year, all are valued at a single set of prices that ruled at any one, called the base, year. For example, when the volume of 1991 GDP is valued in 1985 prices, we measure what the total value of output would have been if prices had not changed between 1985 and 1991. The change in the GDP valued at constant prices is a measure of the pure quantity change. Thus, the *UK National Accounts* show 1991 GDP to be £574 billion in the current prices of 1991, but only £409 billion valued at 1985 prices, in which year GDP was worth £357 billion. This implies that the volume of output has risen by 14 per cent, i.e. at constant prices 1991 GDP is 14 per cent higher than 1985. The rise in the price level between the two years (of 41 per cent) has not been allowed to affect the figures.[6]

Figure 7.9 shows trends since 1970 in **nominal** (or money) GDP (as national income measured at current prices is called), and **real** national income measured at constant prices. It can be seen that the two series have diverged very considerably. Nominal income in 1991 was over ten times its level two decades earlier,

---

6   Compare the rise in the value of output – 60 per cent, from £357 billion to £574 billion.

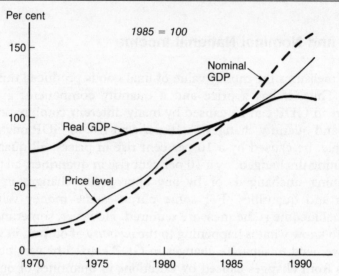

Figure 7.9 Gross domestic product 1970–1991, nominal and real GDP and the general level of prices

but real income was up by only about 20 per cent. The difference between the two series is due to inflation, the course of which is also shown in the Figure. The price level rose over the period approximately sevenfold. We consider inflation again in Chapter 9. One should add, perhaps, that the population of the UK grew by about 3 per cent over the period, so that real income *per capita* rose by rather less than 20 per cent.

The Balance of Payments

The ways in which transactions between residents and non-residents of the UK affect the calculation of the national income have been described earlier in this chapter.[7] There is, however, a separate account known as the balance of payments which records all payments and receipts between residents and non-residents over a period of time, usually a year.

7　The balance of payments is discussed in Lipsey–Harbury, FP2, Chapter 32.

Current and Capital Transactions

The balance of payments is usually divided into two sections:

- the **current account**
- the **capital account**

The current account records payments and receipts for goods and services. The capital account lists transactions in external assets and liabilities, i.e. as lending or borrowing on short or long terms. Included here are transactions made by the Bank of England on behalf of the UK government (see above pages 322–4), previously listed separately in an account called Official Financing.

Taken together the two sections of the balance of payments must balance. This is true by accounting convention. Thus, a deficit on the current account must be offset by a surplus of exactly the same amount on the capital account, and vice versa.

The current account

Two sets of items are contained in the current account:

- transactions involving goods, called **visible** trade
- transactions involving services, known as **invisibles**

Figure 7.10 shows the history of the current account balance of payments since 1980. The UK has traditionally recorded a surplus of receipts over payments on its current account as far back as the nineteenth century. This has been the result of surpluses of invisible earnings being more than enough to offset deficits on trade in visible goods.

Recent history has been a little different. In the early 1970s, the current account moved into deficit, as UK exports lost ground to competitors and the quadrupling of the price of oil by the action of the OPEC group of countries in 1973 pushed up the price of imports. Then, from the late 1970s, North Sea oil came to the rescue. Oil exports exceeded imports for the first time in 1980,

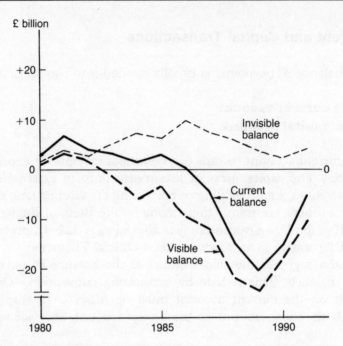

Figure 7.10 Current account balance of payments 1980–1991
Source: *Annual Abstract of Statistics*

and for three years even the visible balance went into surplus. Thereafter the traditional pattern began to reassert itself, though the visible balance deteriorated after 1986 as lower prices and output adversely affected oil exports. Additionally, an exceptionally large quantity of imports was sucked in by a consumer boom and a strong sterling exchange rate (see below), which did not help exports either. The invisible surplus also diminished and failed to cover the deficit on visibles, for reasons we shall shortly see.

An important feature of the current balance record displayed in Figure 7.10 is its volatility. This is almost entirely due to swings in the balance of visible trade, sometimes reaching crisis proportions.

In view of the importance of invisible transactions, we look at this account in more detail (see Figure 7.11). The main item responsible for the overall net credit balance in 1991 was financial and other services, including banking, insurance, financial services associated with the City of London and royalties. Historically, the

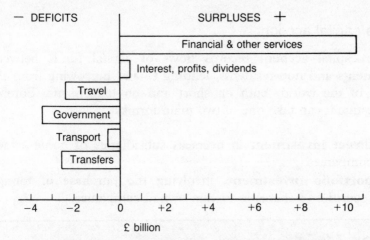

Figure 7.11 Invisible trade balances, UK, 1991
Source: *UK Balance of Payments*

item in the second row of the Figure, interest, profits and dividends on past overseas investments, has been the largest net credit item. It fell from a peak of nearly £6 billion in 1986 to less than £0.5 billion in 1991. This has been substantially because of relatively high interest rates in this country, which means high earnings on UK assets owned by non-residents.

Among other items, travel, transport, government and transfers all show net debits. Foreign travel payments and receipts cover spending by tourists and businessmen and women. This was a net credit item in the 1970s, but the upward trend in holidays abroad transformed it into a net debit in all but a single year since then. The sea transport account used also to be a substantial source of net income to the UK, but the decline in Britain's merchant fleet turned it into a net outflow from the late 1970s, though it has been close to balance since the mid-1980s. Civil aviation's story is of a similar, though more recent, move from surplus to deficit (in the second half of the 1980s). The drain among invisibles due to government includes military and diplomatic expenditure abroad, aid to developing countries and contributions to international organisations, such as the EC. Finally, the traditionally unfavourable item, called transfers, comprises mainly personal transactions involving gifts and asset transfers by migrants.

The capital account

The capital account records flows of capital funds between residents and non-residents, lending to and borrowing from the rest of the world, both on short and on long terms. Foreign investment can take one of two main forms:

- **direct investment** in overseas subsidiaries of home-owned companies
- **portfolio investment**, involving the purchase of foreign securities or shares in foreign-owned companies.

Box 7.2

Foreign Investment in UK Falls for First Time for Ten Years

Foreign investment in Britain dropped last year for the first time in almost a decade. Although Britain remained the preferred destination in Europe for American and Japanese firms to set up subsidiaries or expand, attracting investment is becoming more difficult, according to the Invest in Britain Bureau (IBB)....

Malcolm Day, a director of IBB, said a drop in the number of foreign investment projects in Britain also reflected the UK's past success. American companies were easily the biggest overseas investors in Britain during 1991. Their subsidiaries initiated 104 investment projects, creating 8,225 jobs. German companies were the next largest inward investors, starting 60 projects creating 2,125 jobs. Japanese companies were in third place by number of projects, beginning 44 investments.

According to the IBB, during the 39 years to the end of 1990, the UK attracted 37.5% of total American direct investment in countries of the EC. During the 40 years to March 1991, the UK won 39 per cent of Japanese investment in Europe.

The Times, 16 July 1992

This news item highlights the importance of foreign investment in the UK. There is an underlying theme in the article that the more the better. Do you agree? What are the

Both types of transaction appear in the capital account of the balance of payments, but it is exceedingly difficult to know, especially with portfolio investment, which are really long term. Once a person or a company has bought shares in a foreign company they may be held indefinitely, perhaps resulting in the acquisition of a controlling interest. Alternatively, they may be sold the week after they are bought. Moreover, a great deal of international investment is done by multinational corporations (see pages 95–7) which switch funds among subsidiaries in different countries, and their accounting practices sometimes make it hard to identify all the international investment that they engage in.

These difficulties do not, of course, mean that we have no idea about what is going on. Figure 7.12 traces the recent history of UK investment overseas (outflows of capital), and investment in the UK by non-residents (inflows of capital). It can be seen that the

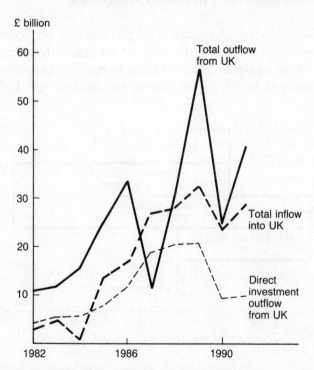

Figure 7.12 Private investment outflows and inflows 1982–1991
Source: *Annual Abstract of Statistics*

sums involved are very large. The exceptional £56 billion capital outflow in 1989, for example, is not far short of half the bill for all visible imports in that year.

The diagram distinguishes direct foreign investment by the UK from the total, which includes portfolio investment. The trend in direct investment is steadier than the total, portfolio investment being more volatile.

The gross value of the accumulated overseas assets owned by UK residents (persons, corporations and government) is around £950 billion, or roughly half the value of the nation's total domestic capital assets. However, accumulated liabilities are almost as large. Hence, the net asset position of the UK on overseas account is now positive only by about £15 billion.

How the Balance of Payments Balances

As previously stated, the balance of payments is an accounting device and must balance – the sum of all credit items must be matched by an equivalent sum of debit items. For example, if the current account is, say, £10 billion, in surplus, this could be

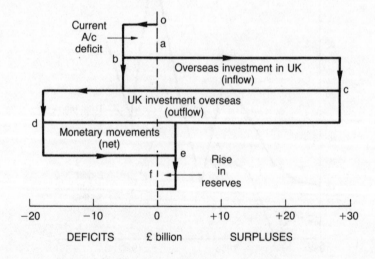

Figure 7.13 Balance of payments, UK 1991
Source: *Annual Abstract of Statistics*

financed by lending £10 billion to foreigners, or by accumulating reserves of foreign exchange of £10 billion. To see how this works, for the UK, examine Figure 7.13, which is based on the balance of payments for 1991.

Start at the top of the diagram, at point a, on the vertical zero line 0–0. Flows that move the account to the right of this line are surpluses; flows that move it to the left are deficits.

First, consider the current account deficit (£5.2 billion). This takes you in the direction of the arrows to the deficit point b.

Next, consider the inflow of funds from overseas into the UK (£28.7 billion). This moves you along the arrows to point c, which represents a net credit of £23.5 billion (a credit inflow of £28.7 billion less a debit outflow on current account of £5.2 billion).

Third, consider the outflow of investment from the UK (£41.2 billion). This moves you along the arrows to point d, back into deficit of £17.7 billion (£41.2 billion minus £23.5 billion).

Fourth, consider the net inflow of short-term monetary movements (£20.4 billion), which takes you along the arrow to point e, representing a net deficit of £2.7 billion (£17.7 billion minus £20.4 billion).

We have now considered all monetary flows, ending up with a surplus of £2.7 billion. This is not quite the end of the story. The surplus yields an increase in the reserves of foreign exchange held by the UK. In the account it takes you to point f in the diagram – f is on the zero line, as was a where we started.

Exchange Rates

Balance of payments flows are affected by rates of exchange because non-residents and residents use different currencies. For example, UK residents importing goods from Canada need to exchange their sterling for Canadian dollars to pay for imports. The lower the price of dollars (Can.) the fewer pounds have to be given up for them, and the stronger the demand for Canadian exports tends to be.

Exchange rates can be fixed or flexible in the sense of being allowed to fluctuate with market forces. The pound sterling has

Box 7.3

How Mr Soros Made a Billion by Betting Against Sterling

Anatole Kaletsky talks to the billion dollar brain behind much of the Black Wednesday speculation that sterling would quit the ERM

George Soros is an intensely intellectual man who spends much of his time in Eastern Europe. He is also the world's biggest currency speculator. In the two weeks leading to Black Wednesday, Mr Soros engaged the British government in the highest-stakes game of poker in history.

He bet $10 billion that Mr Major would fail in his irrevocable and 'over-riding objective' – to keep sterling in the ERM. Everyone now knows that Mr Major lost his side of the gamble. On Saturday in a long interview at his house in London, Mr Soros decided to describe his side of this poker game.

'We did short a lot of sterling and we did make a lot of money, because our funds are so large'.... Unlike academic economists, Mr Soros does not think currency speculation is needed to pull market prices to realistic levels.... 'Speculation can be very harmful, especially in currency markets. But measures to stop it, such as exchange controls, usually do even more harm. Fixed exchange rate systems are also flawed, because they eventually fall apart. In fact any exchange rate system is flawed, and the longer it exists the greater the flaws become. The only escape is to have no exchange rate system at all, but a single currency in Europe, as in the US. It would put speculators like me out of business....'

The Times, 26 October 1992

This news item tells you something about the mechanisms of floating and fixed exchange rate systems. It will make more sense after you have read Chapter 9.

Do not take the idea of Mr Soros 'betting' literally. He did not go to Ladbrokes or Coral, he 'bet' by selling the sterling currency because he expected it to fall in price – i.e. be devalued. He did not have sterling to sell, as a matter of fact, so he sold what he had not got hoping that he would be able to buy it when the price fell. This is what is meant by 'selling short'. He bought $15 billion's worth of pounds for $14 billion (when sterling had fallen about $7\frac{1}{2}$ per cent in price) and sold it for $15. The only unusual feature of the transaction, to the man or woman in the street, is that he sold *before* he bought.

Mr Koros was on a one-way bet. There was intense speculation in the media that sterling would devalue. It might not have happened, but the exchange rate certainly was not about to go UP! Even if he had guessed wrongly his loss would have been limited. He could still have bought back the sterling at the same price as he sold it. That is one of the disadvantages of fixed exchange rates. There are advantages, which we shall discuss in Chapter 9, e.g. that importers and exporters trade with confidence if they know the prices they will receive or pay for goods.

belonged to both fixed and fluctuating regimes in recent history. Until the First World War, most exchange rates were fixed in what was known as the gold standard. After a period of relatively flexible rates, the system of fixed exchange rates returned after the Second World War. In 1971, the government let sterling float more or less freely on world currency markets (subject to intervention by the Bank of England to avoid excessive short-run volatility in the exchange rate, see below, pages 323–4). This has been the position since that time with the exception of the years between 1990 and 1992, when the UK belonged to the **Exchange Rate Mechanism** (ERM) of the European Community. During this period the rate at which sterling exchanged for the currencies of other ERM members was fixed within close limits. Exchange rates between sterling and other currencies, such as the US dollar, remained flexible. (The dollar is not, of course, in the ERM.)

Figure 7.14 traces the course of the sterling – D-Mark exchange rate since 1980. It shows, therefore, the history of the currency in both floating and fixed rate regimes. Sterling fell fairly steadily in value against the D-Mark through the 1980s until the government entered the ERM in October 1990, when the central value of sterling was set at DM2.95 to £1. It was allowed to fluctuate

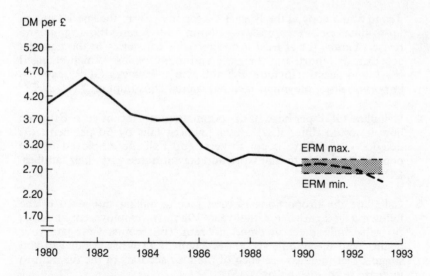

Figure 7.14 Sterling – D-Mark exchange rate 1980–1992
Source: *Economic Trends*

within limits of 6 per cent either side – i.e. there was a 'floor' rate of D-Mark 2.78 to £1, below which sterling could not fall and remain in the ERM. As a result of serious pressures, the rate dropped below the floor in September 1990 and sterling membership of the ERM was suspended. At the time of writing (January 1993), the exchange value of sterling had fallen to D-Mark 2.45 to the pound – a devaluation of roughly 20 per cent. It is uncertain whether the pound will re-enter the ERM. We discuss these matters further in Chapter 9, when ERM regulations and issues of international economic policy will be considered.

Questions and exercises

(For key to abbreviations identifying sources, see pages xv–xvi)

1   Copy (or trace) Figure 7.6 and write in the values (in £ billion) in 1991 and a more recent or earlier year for all segments of the diagram. Which segment has changed the most? (*AS* or *UKNA*)

2   Draw a graph similar to Figure 7.9 showing year-to-year changes in each of the series. Compare your graph with Figure 7.9. What different lessons do you learn from each? (*UKNA*)

3   Try to find a copy of the Blue Book for any year in the last 10 and an up-to-date one. Prepare a two-column table setting the original and revised figures for at least a dozen major categories in the national accounts as reported in the early and late versions. Which changed most and least? (Include the following: savings, GDP, exports, imports, self-employment income, capital consumption.) (*UKNA*)

4   Calculate GDP per head of the population in a recent year. Estimate how it would differ if (i) unemployment falls by 50 per cent, (ii) defence expenditure is cut to zero, (iii) half the employed female population decide to quit work and stay at home with their families. (*AS*)

5   Calculate the proportions of total income falling into each of the following categories for the year 1985: (i) employment income, (ii) self-employment income, (iii) rent, (iv) profits. Compare your results with the middle section of Figure 7.1? What events can you suggest that might cause each of the four sections of the diagram to increase in relative terms? (*AS*)

6   Prepare a table for the past 5–10 years showing (i) total outflow of investment overseas, (ii) a rate of interest in the UK, (iii) a rate of interest in a foreign country and (iv) the pound–dollar exchange rate. Do any of the series appear to be correlated? (*NIER, AS*)

7   Construct graphs to show the relationships between (i) volume of UK exports and relative UK unit labour costs, (ii) volume of UK imports and real GDP in the UK. Use index numbers where possible. Are there lessons to learn from any of the graphs ? (*NIER, UKNA*)

Appendix 7

Table A7.1   UK National Product, 1981 and 1991 (£ million)

	1981	*1991*
At market prices:		
Consumers' expenditure	155,412	367,853
General government final consumption	55,374	121,899
of which: Central government	33,879	74,442
Local authorities	21,495	47,457
Gross domestic fixed capital formation	41,304	95,442
Value of physical increase in stocks and work		
in progress	−2,768	−5,303
Total domestic expenditure	249,322	579,811
Exports of goods and services	67,432	135,115
Total final expenditure	316,754	715,006
less imports of goods and services	−60,388	−140,415
Gross domestic product at market prices	254,851	574,146
Net property income from abroad	1,251	328
Gross national product at market prices	256,102	574,474
Factor cost adjustment:		
Taxes on expenditure	42,465	83,023
Subsidies	6,369	5,878
Taxes *less* subsidies	36,096	77,145
Gross national product at factor cost	220,006	497,329
less Capital consumption	−31,641	−63,968
Net national product at factor cost	188,365	433,361

Source: *UK National Accounts*

Table A7.2 UK National Accounts, values and volumes, 1971, 1981 and 1991

	1985 = 100		
	1971	*1981*	*1991*
Nominal series			
GDP at factor cost	14.5	71.3	160.7
GDP at market prices	14.4	71.0	161.4
Real series			
GDP at factor cost	75.4	89.3	114.4
GDP at market prices	74.7	89.3	113.8
Consumers' expenditure	71.5	89.5	122.9
Gross fixed capital formation	85.4	80.0	120.1
Exports	55.9	86.2	120.7
Imports	57.3	79.4	136.0

Source: *UK National Accounts*

Table A7.3 UK balance of payments on current account, selected years since 1946 (£ million)

	Exports	*Imports*	*Balance (visibles)*	*Invisible credits*	*Invisible debits*	*Balance (invisibles)*	*Balance (current account)*
1946	960	1,063	−103	885	1,012	−127	−230
1950	2,261	2,312	−51	1,383	1,025	+358	+307
1960	3,737	4,138	−401	2,207	2,034	+173	−228
1970	8,150	8,184	−34	5,126	4,269	+857	+823
1980	47,422	45,909	+1,513	25,934	23,818	+2,116	+3,629
1985	77,988	80,334	−2,346	80,662	74,979	+5,683	+3,337
1990	101,718	120,527	−18,809	115,150	113,370	+1,780	−17,029
1991	103,413	113,703	−10,290	116,164	112,195	+3,969	−6,321

Sources: *Economic Trends* and *Monthly Digest of Statistics*

Table A7.4 UK balance of payments on capital account, 1986, 1988 and 1991 (£ million)

	1986	1988	1991
Lending by UK			
UK investment overseas			
Direct	−11,678	−20,944	−10,261
Portfolio	−22,277	−11,239	−30,908
Lending by UK banks	−53,747	−19,690	32,231
Other lending	−1,959	−3,842	−9,281
Borrowing by UK			
Overseas investment in UK			
Direct	5,837	12,006	12,045
Portfolio	12,181	15,564	16,627
Borrowing by UK banks	66,868	34,088	−24,024
Other borrowing	4,531	6,214	19,069
UK Government			
Reserves (increase)	−2,891	−2,761	−2,262

Source: *Monthly Digest of Statistics*

8
Money and Banking

Aside from a brief reference in Chapter 1 to money, this book has been written as if the 'filthy lucre', as the New Testament called it, did not exist.[1] A visitor from space, reading the previous chapters, might be excused for thinking that money, per se, was of insufficient importance to merit much attention.

This would, of course, be wrong. Money matters in some important ways that we learn about in economic theory. Moreover, even in this book where we have concentrated almost exclusively on the real side of the economy – on the supply of real resources, goods and services – we have valued them always in money terms. In Chapter 7 on the national income we used money values to add together production of various kinds, this being the only economically relevant way to add such diverse things as aerospace equipment, bread, cinema tickets and dwellings. It is time to look at the nature of money and at financial institutions in the UK

Functions of Money

The money function described above is acting as a **unit of account**. Money does more than this. It is a **medium of exchange** and a **store of value**. Its existence is of immense help

1 The subject matter of this chapter is covered in Lipsey–Harbury, FP2, Chapters 33–7.

260 An Introduction to the UK Economy

in lubricating the complex economic system of a country like the UK, although it can cause problems too – especially those arising from inflation, when the value of money falls.

Forms of Money

People have employed a variety of objects to perform the functions of money, from seashells and cattle in primitive societies to cigarettes in prisoner-of-war camps. Although we rarely use primitive currencies nowadays, there are more types of money in use than we might at first imagine.

Currency

The kinds of money most commonly employed to make small payments are notes and coins, together called currency. Gold and silver used to circulate in Britain before the First World War. Today coins are made of bronze or of alloys of copper and nickel. They cannot be refused for the settlement of debts up to certain amounts, for which they are 'legal tender'. Pound coins have unlimited validity, 50p and 20p coins are legal tender up to £10, 10p and 5p coins up to £5 and bronze pennies up to 20p.

For larger payments, where coins would be unsuitable, debts may be settled in notes. Bank notes, or paper money as it is sometimes called, have an interesting origin. In the seventeenth century the most general form of money was the gold coin. Rather than keep a large quantity of gold at home, people used to take it for safe keeping to local goldsmiths, who were early bankers. In return for the gold the goldsmith issued a receipt, on which was stated his promise to pay on demand to the holder of the receipt the amount of gold mentioned. Following upon this, the custom grew for individuals to accept such receipts, or notes, in payment for debts since, with the signature of a reputable goldsmith, later a banker, they were 'as good as gold'.

Today, bank notes are the principal form of paper currency, although it is no longer open to any banker or goldsmith to issue them. In England and Wales this right is now exclusive to the Bank of England (see below). Bank notes, however, still retain their original form. If you look at a £10 note you will find printed there a statement signed by the Chief Cashier of the Bank of England which reads 'I promise to pay the bearer on demand the sum of ten pounds'. This no longer has a real meaning. Gold is no longer obtainable on demand in exchange for notes. So what do you get if you take a £10 note and ask the Bank to keep its promise? Another £10 note. Bank notes are legal tender without limit.

Finally, we should point out that currencies other than sterling are capable of performing the functions of money. Of particular importance in this respect is the ECU, the use of which has been increasing lately. ECU stands for European Currency Unit. It is a 'basket' of the currencies of member nations. The value of the ECU at any time is calculated by reference to the values of the currencies of the EC member states which make it up. The ECU performs a specific function for the European Monetary System (EMS) (see pages 327–9), but is also used as a unit of account in the Community's budget and, for example, for price-setting within the Common Agricultural Policy. The SDR, the currency unit of the International Monetary Fund (see page 326), can play similar roles.

Bank deposits

By far the most important means of settling debts in modern Britain is carried out through banks, and usually involves the drawing of cheques. Cheques originated at roughly the same time as bank notes. After depositing gold with a local bank or goldsmith, people commonly wrote letters to their bankers instructing them to pay monies to named persons. The letters were given to the creditors, who passed them to their bankers to collect the cash for them. Soon this form of settling debts became so important that it was unnecessary to write a special letter every time one wanted to make a payment, as the banks themselves began to print letter forms, known as cheques. These need only the insertion of the amount, the date, the name of the payee and the signature of the person making the payment. Today banks issue chequebooks to their customers, although there are other means of transferring money to and from bank accounts – e.g. direct debits and standing orders. Note, credit cards reduce the number of cheques that need writing. They have become common in the last 20 years or so. Since 1970, the number of credit cards in use has risen from 2 million to 30 million. At the same time, the number of autoteller machines has risen from zero to 17,000. The unsurprising consequence was that people held many fewer notes and coin for every pound of expenditure in 1990 than in 1970. This has important implications for monetary policy, as we shall see in the next chapter.[2]

The advantages of making payments through banks are simplicity and safety, especially when the sum involved is large. All businesses use banks, as do many private individuals. The importance of bank deposits in comparison with the volume of notes and coin in circulation is shown in Figure 8.1. Note that the Figure is a simplification of the stock of money in existence. There is no single statistic that can be regarded as the measure of the supply of money. Several are available, based on different definitions, and all have their uses.

Sight and time deposits

As Figure 8.1 shows, there are two kinds of bank deposits:

- **sight deposits**, sometimes kept in current accounts
- **time deposits**, sometimes kept in deposit accounts

Sight deposits are withdrawable on demand and without notice, merely by presenting a cheque. Traditionally they used not to earn interest but, mainly to counter competition from building societies (see pages 276–7), banks began recently to pay interest on some money held in current accounts. The cost to banks of running such accounts is charged to customers, though not always directly.

2 Consumer expenditure rose nearly ninefold between 1970 and 1990; notes and coin in circulation rose only four and a half-fold.

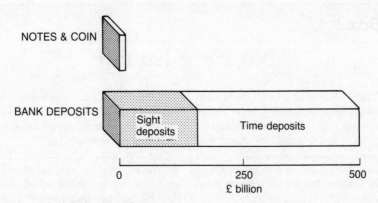

Figure 8.1 Currency and bank deposits, 1992
Source: *Financial Statistics*

Most businesses need to keep as sight deposits only the amounts they expect to need quickly. They, therefore, hold some as time deposits, where they earn interest. Notice is formally required for their withdrawal. In practice, however, banks seldom object if customers make transfers of reasonable amounts for immediate payments. Indeed, the distinction between time and sight deposits is breaking down.

Non-sterling deposits

Figure 8.1 is restricted to bank deposits held in sterling. Businesses and individuals may choose to hold some of their cash balances in foreign currencies, either for making purchases overseas or for conversion into sterling when circumstances are favourable. The size of non-sterling deposits can vary enormously, reflecting balance of payments inflows and outflows of capital in search of high interest rates (see page 248–50).

Deposits of non-banking financial institutions. Banks are one of a range of financial institutions, performing overlapping functions. People choose to keep credit accounts with institutions such as building societies rather than, or as well as, with banks. These

Box 8.1

No Free Lunch

What the British tabloid press likes best is savaging royalty. Next comes bashing banks. Last year the clearing banks were blamed for squeezing small businesses during the recession. Now their sin is to be considering routine charges for retail banking services....

Free current accounts emerged in Britain in the mid-1980s, mainly in response to competition from building societies. Until Midland Bank broke rank in 1984, banks had charged for basic services such as cheque processing and other sorts of money transmission. Midland made banking 'free' for customers who stayed in credit. By the time rivals reacted a year later, it had attracted 500,000 new customers....

Not everyone has gained. The foolish or unlucky who allow their accounts to be overdrawn suffer punitive charges and interest rates. NatWest charges £20 to send a letter telling customers of unauthorised overdrafts. Less than a third of the average bank's customers bear all the costs of basic services, while the flush majority have a free ride. For how much longer?

The Economist, 5 September 1992

This press comment provides a little background to changes in the structure of financial institutions that have been taking place in recent years. This comment in *The Economist* illustrates some of the detail and shows that the process is not yet ended (if it ever will be).

There seems to be a logic in the principle that the costs of banking should be borne by those who incur them. However, banks are not simply retail outlets that sell the services of transmitting money. If you recall that the prime source of banks' income comes from lending at a profit, you might think a little differently perhaps.

deposits can be drawn on to settle debts and should, therefore, be included in the money supply, for some purposes. The total deposits of building societies are in fact substantial – over £200 billion in 1992, bearing comparison with those of banks. However, the bulk are regarded as long-term investments and only a relatively small proportion are used for current transactions.

Definitions of the Money Supply

Economic theorists define an abstraction called money that is distinct from all other financial assets. In the real world, however, there is a spectrum of assets which have some of the characteristics of money. Thus, there is no obvious dividing line between what is and is not money. The line can be drawn finely to exclude everything but currency, which performs money's function of being a medium of exchange. A wider definition of the money supply fulfilling that function would include sight deposits with banks.

If we want to define the money supply as financial assets held as a store of value as well as a medium of exchange, we should include time deposits and those in building societies, which are speedily convertible at a fixed rate of one for one. For example, you cannot pay your bills with a time deposit but in practice you can easily transfer it into a sight deposit on a pound-for-pound basis. This makes a time deposit almost as good as money.

The government publishes statistics of several definitions of the money supply, or '**monetary aggregates**', which are used in connection with monetary policy (see Chapter 9). The spectrum of financial assets which make up one or other of the official statistics of the money supply includes currency, sight and time deposits with banks, and deposits with building societies.

Each measure of the money supply focuses on a particular point in the spectrum and includes, as a group to measure, everything up to that point. When the Bank of England decides to change the measures of the money supply, this leaves the spectrum of assets unaltered, but changes the specific groupings that are included. The three monetary aggregates currently in use in the UK – M0, M2 and M4 – are listed below and in Figure 8.2, together with a new aggregate, M3H, brought in for comparisons with other EC countries.

Several other measures of the money supply have been used in the past. They are not easy to keep track of. Definitions are changed, old measures are replaced by new ones, sometimes only slightly different and, even more confusing, some just have their names changed. To avoid complications we have put details of all obsolete measures in a footnote.[3] (We dare not omit them, lest they be resurrected!)

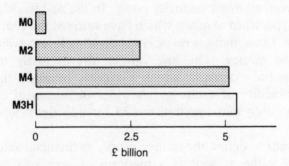

Figure 8.2 Measures of the money supply, 1992
Source: *Monthly Digest of Statistics*

It is useful to consider the aggregates as extending from a definition called narrow money to another called broad money, with an intermediate aggregate between them. Narrow money is associated with a high degree of **liquidity**, which means that it is readily available to finance spending. Broad money, in contrast, includes assets which are not quite so readily available for the settlement of debts. A common reason for relative illiquidity is that assets comprise deposits earning (higher) interest in return for being withdrawn only after notice is given, or a penalty paid.

3	For full details, refer to the *Bank of England Quarterly Bulletin*.
Note, the following monetary aggregates are no longer in use:
M1	comprised notes and coin plus the sterling sight deposits of the private sector with the banks.
M3	comprised M0 plus private sector sterling bank sight and time deposits. This measure was known as Sterling M3 until 1987.
M3c	consisted of M3 plus private sector holdings of foreign currency bank deposits. This measure was known as M3 until 1987.
M5	consisted of M4 plus private sector holdings of certain other financial assets, including bills of exchange and Treasury bills and some national savings. This measure was known as PSL2 until 1987.

Measures of the Money Supply

M0 is the definition we call narrow money. It most nearly corresponds to the concept of 'high-powered money' used in economic theory. M0 is almost entirely notes and coin held by the public and in banks. The small residue consists of working balances held by the banks at the Bank of England (see below).

M2 consists of notes and coin *plus* sterling retail deposits of banks and building societies. The term 'retail' was redefined with effect from December 1992, to better measure deposits that are easily withdrawable for current expenditures. For building societies this broadly means all deposits held by persons *plus* those by businesses of less than £50,000. For banks, retail deposits are those 'typically' taken in the bank's branches.[4]

M4 is the broad money definition. It consists of M0 plus retail and wholesale (i.e. non-retail time deposits of banks and building societies).

M3H is a new 'harmonised' monetary aggregate introduced in 1992, by agreement with the central banks in the EC, designed to aid comparisons among member states. M3H is defined as M4 with two additional items – foreign currency deposits held by UK residents with banks and building societies in the UK, and sterling and foreign currency deposits held by UK public corporations in the UK.[5]

---

4 See *Bank of England Quarterly Bulletin*, August 1992, for full details (which could have been changed by the time this book is published!).

5 M4 accounts for about 95 per cent of M3H, but the additional components of M3H tend to behave rather erratically.

The magnitudes of the monetary aggregates in Figure 8.2 are stated at current values. Changes in the money supply can be adjusted, allowing for inflation, to yield 'real' money supply figures (comparable to real income as distinct from nominal income – see pages 243–4). Note, the measures are of the *stock* of money and should not be confused with a measure of *changes* in the stock called DCE, standing for Domestic Credit Expansion, once used in the UK.

The Banking and Financial System

The importance of banks has already been mentioned in connection with the supply of money. Now we examine them in more detail. This can be done under four heads:

* **commercial (or deposit) banks**
* **investment banks**
* **non-banking financial institutions**
* **central bank** (the Bank of England)

Commercial/Deposit Banks

For well over 100 years the principal type of banking institution has been a commercial enterprise, formed as a joint stock company. Previously, the joint stock form of organisation had been prohibited to banks, leaving business in the hands of a multitude of small private partnerships and the Bank of England, the latter being founded by Royal Charter (see pages 281–5). It took a year of financial crises in 1825 to bring about a change in the law.

Bank mergers in the nineteenth century, during the First World War and in the 1970s brought the number of banks down to the present level.[6] Four large banks – Barclays, National Westminster

6 There was an attempt at another merger in 1992, between Lloyds and Midland. However, it was pre-empted by a take-over bid for Midland from Hong Kong and Shanghai Banking Corporation. It is thought unlikely that the Monopolies and Mergers Commission would have approved of a Lloyds–Midland merger anyway.

(NatWest), Midland and Lloyds (in size order in 1991) account for the bulk of banking business; others include Royal Bank of Scotland, Bank of Scotland, Trustee Savings Bank and Abbey National (also in size order 1991).

Bank clearing

The major commercial banks in Britain are sometimes known as clearing banks. Here is why.

Every time someone draws a cheque in favour of another person it is necessary to transfer a sum of money. If both accounts are at the same bank it is a simple matter; the bank makes entries in the two accounts, debiting one and crediting another. If the accounts are at different banks, this procedure is not possible. One solution would be for the bank of the person making the payment to transfer cash to the other bank, which is what happened in the past. However, the bank clerks who used to carry cash around the City of London realised that their work could be cut if they met to sort out the payments that were due, particularly when it happened that a clerk from bank A was collecting from bank B, while his counterpart from bank B was collecting from bank A. Even if the amounts were not equal the smaller could be offset against the larger and the clerk from the latter bank could collect the difference, thus halving the work.

The essential requirement for the successful working of this system of offsetting claims against one another, known as clearing, was that the clerks should meet. In the eighteenth century they organised themselves to do so. Now, clearing is done by computer, with differences among banks settled by cheques drawn on the banks' accounts at the Bank of England.

Assets and liabilities of commercial/deposit banks

Commercial banks are in business to make a profit. They are essentially borrowing and lending institutions, i.e. they borrow from one set of people and lend to others at a profit. How is it possible for a bank to 'lend other people's money' which it is supposed to be keeping in safe custody? What happens if the people who have deposited their money with a bank demand payment and the bank is unable to satisfy them?

These questions cannot be answered in full here. However, a clue to the answer comes from appreciating the experience of early goldsmith-bankers that it is rare for a significant fraction of their customers (let alone all of them) to wish to withdraw money at the same time. A banker needs to hold only enough cash in reserve to meet the needs of those who do make demands.

Bankers can keep their cash reserves low by holding some liquid assets which are, so to speak, 'near money', in the sense of being speedily and easily exchangeable into cash. So protected, bankers can make loans which earn interest. The best proportions of liquid assets, including cash, to deposits evolved in the light of experience. Traditionally, a figure of about 8 per cent was preferred. In modern times, the freedom of banks to decide how to allocate their assets is limited by the government, acting through the Bank of England. We consider this matter later in this and the next chapter.

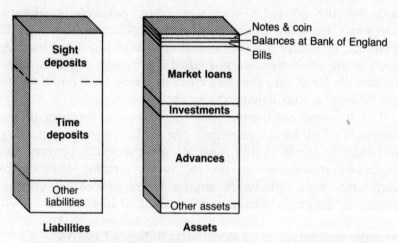

Figure 8.3 Sterling liabilities and assets of UK banks, 1992
Source: *Financial Statistics*

Figure 8.3 shows the two sides of the banks' business as shown by the assets and liabilities in their balance sheets.

Liabilities

The liabilities, which we have already mentioned, consist almost wholly of sight and time deposits standing to the credit of the banks' customers.

Two sets of liabilities are included in the 'other' category of Figure 8.3. One consists of liabilities to the banks' shareholders. The other is certificates of deposit – notes (receipts) issued by the banks which are in circulation in the money market; they have to be paid when presented by a holder at the maturity date.

Assets

The asset side of the banks' balance sheet may be examined using the concepts of profitability and liquidity. The latter, you will remember, refers to the speed and ease with which an asset may be turned into cash.

Notes and coin held in the vaults are the banks' first line of reserve. They are perfectly liquid and earn no interest.

Balances at the Bank of England are credits belonging to the banks at the Bank which, among other things, acts as the 'bankers' bank'. Commercial banks hold such balances, called **operational deposits,** on which they can draw at their convenience. They are also required to hold some balances at the Bank, on which no interest is earned. The latter are known as '**cash ratio deposits**' to distinguish them from 'operational deposits', because their amount is related to their total deposits. Freezing liquid assets in this way can be used as an instrument of monetary policy. Cash ratio deposits are also the chief source of revenue for the Bank of England.

Bills comprise two types of fairly liquid asset – **bills of exchange** and **Treasury bills.** Both are, in effect, short-term loans with an average duration of about six weeks. Bills of exchange come into existence when an individual or institution has an immediate need for cash.

Suppose, for example, an exporter of goods has outgoings to make between the time merchandise leaves the factory and arrives overseas, when a foreign importer will pay for them. The exporter can draw a bill of exchange to cover the expected revenue. The importer then accepts the obligation to pay the sum involved in, say, three months' time, thereby enabling the drawer to sell (or **discount**) the bill in the City and receive cash immediately. The price of the bill depends on the discount rate, which determines the rate of interest paid on the bill. If it is, for example, 12 per cent per annum, a three-month £100 bill will yield £97. (The discount rate is almost, but not quite, the rate of interest. Thus a £100 three-month bill sold for £97 carries a 3 per cent quarterly discount rate, although the borrower pays £3 interest and gets £97 which implies an interest rate of $\frac{3}{97}$, i.e. approximately 3.09 per cent).

Treasury bills are similar to bills of exchange; they are promises by the government to pay sums of money in the future. The Treasury sells batches of bills weekly, to finance government expenditure. The price of a Treasury bill is less than the sum it will fetch when redeemed. The difference between them depends partly on how long one has to wait to maturity. The discount between the price and maturity value determines the interest rate earned by holding them.

Market loans are assets with a high liquidity comprising short-term loans to city financial institutions, including discount houses (see below).

Investments are longer-term securities, mainly those issued by the government. The liquidity of the banks' portfolio of securities depends on how long before they reach maturity. Those which are almost due for redemption are highly liquid, whilst those with longer to run are less so. Securities can, of course, be sold at any time at the prevailing market price, but this varies from day to day as market interest rates change, the liquidity of the securities being related to the certainty of the sum realisable on sale.

Advances to customers are the largest group of assets held by the banks. They are both the least liquid assets and the most profitable. Advances may be made on overdraft, with permission for borrowers to overdraw their accounts up to stated limits, or as straightforward loans. The overdraft system is convenient for borrowers whose needs fluctuate, as interest is paid only on the amount actually borrowed. Sometimes the banks require collateral security, e.g. businesses may be required to deposit share

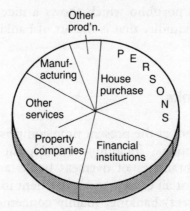

Figure 8.4 Loans and advances to UK residents (amounts outstanding end May 1992)
Source: *Bank of England Quarterly Bulletin*

certificates, but loans are often made to businesses on the strength of trade prospects. The rates of interest charged vary from time to time, with the riskiness of the project for which the loan is to be used, and with the credit standing of the borrower. Banks publish their **base lending rates,** to which charges to borrowers are linked.

The distribution of loans and advances among the main classes of UK borrowers is shown in Figure 8.4. It is a very different distribution from that of 10 to 20 years ago. In the mid-1970s the production industries accounted for over half of all bank advances, with loans to persons and financial institutions taking only around a fifth. The expansion of the personal sector, to become the largest single category, is partly the result of banks competing with building societies in the provision of loans. Now, loans to persons and financial institutions together absorb more than half of the banks' total lending.

We conclude this section on the clearing banks with a general comment. All the ways in which banks choose to use their resources (except only holding cash) involve the sacrifice of ready money for some asset which will bring in a larger sum at a future date. In general, the longer the wait and the greater the risk, the more profitable the loan will be. To sacrifice all for the chance of large profits could soon lead to the collapse of a bank. It is the maintenance of a portfolio which shows a nice balance between profitability and liquidity that is the art of banking.

Investment Banks

The banking system at the present time comprises more than 500 authorised institutions, including the deposit banks described above, and 250 branches of overseas banks and other banking institutions. Almost all engage to some extent in what is known as retail (or high street) banking, mainly concerned with cash and withdrawal facilities and the transfer of funds by cheque and other means for personal and business customers. Another type of business is wholesale banking, involving holding large deposit accounts and the management of financial funds in short- and long-term loans and investments, where many dealings are among the banks themselves.

Once, one could identify two fairly distinct sets of banking institution. On the one hand, there were deposit banks while, on the other hand, there were **merchant banks**, or accepting houses. The distinction has become blurred as banks of each type have diversified to areas of business previously served mainly by the other.

The term **accepting house** sprang originally from the role played by financial houses, with well-known names such as Baring, Hambros, Lazard and Rothschild, in accepting (i.e. guaranteeing) commercial bills of exchange (see above pages 271–2). By maintaining agents in the major trading centres of the world, they were able to check on the financial standing of traders. In return for a commission, they would add their names to that of the original acceptors (or accept the bill themselves), thereby assuring British exporters that they would be paid in full for their goods, when the bill of exchange matured.

Merchant banks have continued to perform this accepting function, though it has become a small part of their business. They diversified in several directions, taking a particular interest in advising companies on mergers, take-overs and financial recon-structions. Another growing activity has been underwriting new capital issues of shares, i.e. guaranteeing to buy any stock remaining unsold, in return for a commission.

The developments described in the preceding paragraphs have involved the virtual end of separate deposit and, what is now called, investment banking, i.e. the functions performed previously by merchant bankers. The integration occurred because all large UK and overseas deposit banks acquired an existing merchant bank, or entered the field independently.

Non-Banking Financial Institutions

Outside the banking sector as defined in the previous section are certain other distinctive financial institutions, including discount houses, building societies, insurance companies and pension funds.

Discount houses

As their name implies, these institutions discount bills of exchange and Treasury bills in what is sometimes called the money market. To do so, either for the government or for private traders, they must, of course, have a supply of cash. They acquire cash by short-term borrowing from the banks, who lend at relatively low rates of interest. The discount houses can usually show a profit by charging a rate for discounting slightly above the rate which they have to pay for this accommodation.

Although the bills which they discount usually become due for payment only after anything from two to six months, and the money which they borrow is repayable at shorter notice, the discount houses are not normally left short of funds. This is because it generally happens that when one bank is calling in its loans another is offering more to the discount market. Even if this is not the case, the discount houses can always turn to the Bank of England which acts as a 'lender of last resort'. If they are forced to borrow from the Bank, it is likely to be on unfavourable terms. Hence, they will probably show a loss on such transactions, which they try to avoid. The frequency with which the discount houses are forced 'into the Bank' depends upon the general financial state of the country and the monetary policy of the government.

The discount houses hold on to many of the bills which they discount, but they also rediscount some with the banks which, as we have seen, like to keep a proportion of their assets in this form. When bills are rediscounted, they are sold by the discount houses at a price which represents the rediscount rate. In fairly recent times discount houses have also become dealers in other government securities as they approach maturity. The freedom of action of the discount houses became constrained in 1981, when they became subject to controls similar to those imposed on banks in the government's monetary policy (see page 286).

Building societies

In terms of sheer size the largest category of non-banking financial institutions is building societies. Their total accumulated funds in 1992 amounted to over £200 billion – a figure comparable with the sterling deposits of the banks (see Figure 8.1).

Building societies originated in the eighteenthth century, when many were founded by small groups of people to finance the building of their own homes. There were about 1,000 societies 50 years ago. Today, only just over 100 remain, the number having been reduced by amalgamations. Three of the largest, Halifax, Nationwide Anglia and Woolwich, hold half of the total deposits of all societies.

The prime function of building societies is not the building of houses but the lending of money for house purchase. This accounts for about 80 per cent of the societies' funds. The remainder is held in a range of more or less liquid financial assets. The method of borrowing money from a building society is known as obtaining a **mortgage**. Someone wanting to buy a house, or flat, obtains a loan and pays interest on it, surrendering to the society the title to the property. Some income tax relief is available on interest payments (see page 179). For suitable houses in first-class condition societies are, normally, prepared to lend about 90 per cent of the value of the property. The borrower then has to find the balance elsewhere and to pay off the mortgage over a period of 15 to 20 years, or even longer.

In case of default, societies can repossess the property and sell it to reimburse themselves. Repossessions are not in the interests of building societies, because their business thrives on healthy borrowing and lending. In the depressed economic conditions of the early 1990s, however, building societies were involved in repossessions on an unprecedented scale. The problem was particularly serious for people who had bought their houses at earlier high prices. If they were thrown out of work and unable to meet their mortgage payments, they found that, in the depressed state of the housing market, the sale of their property would not yield sufficient funds to discharge their debt. They are said then to have 'negative equity' in their houses. The numbers with negative equity were estimated to be nearly 800,000 in 1992.

Building societies borrow from the public in order to lend to house buyers. They offer a range of accounts carrying rates of interest which vary with the amount deposited and ease of access for withdrawal. In many ways, deposits in building society accounts nowadays closely resemble those of the bank.

The Building Societies Act 1986 freed societies from many restrictions on their activities and opened the way for them to engage in a wider range of activities, including life assurance, estate agency and stockbroking. They were able also to offer new financial services to customers. Many such services, e.g. money transmission, investment, insurance and pension fund management, had been operated only by banks. Building societies are now competing with banks at the same time as banks are competing with building societies in their traditional speciality – house purchase loans. Increasingly building societies are offering chequing accounts, credit cards, cash tills and other banking facilities. The distinction between the two types of institution is breaking down, as witness the change of status of the second largest building society (Abbey National), which became a bank in 1989.

Insurance companies

Insurance companies take over from individuals specific risks in return for a payment known as a premium. They can do so because a risk may be uncertain for an individual but predictable for a company which specialises in risks of a particular type. A business can have no idea whether its factory will be damaged by fire next year, nor can individual motorists know whether they will meet with an accident. However, an insurance company, dealing with thousands of similar risks, is in a different position, as the law of averages works with large numbers.

On the basis of claims experience and detailed statistical analyses, insurers can predict the probability of certain events taking place; the essential principle of insurance being the pooling of risks and their proper classification into groups. For example, the premium payable to insure family cars used for social and domestic purposes is very different from that to insure high-performance cars for youthful drivers.

There are several types of insurance. Marine insurance covers ships and cargoes for maritime perils. Much of this insurance is done through the institution known as Lloyd's, where single large risks are spread among a number of **underwriters**. Fire insurance covers material loss to buildings and contents from fire and kindred perils. Accident insurance means what it says, the principal class being motor vehicle cover.

By far the most important insurance category from the viewpoint of sources of finance is life assurance, which has a unique characteristic. Whereas in the case of fire or accident there is uncertainty as to whether or not an incident will take place, in the case of life assurance there is no doubt as to whether a person will die. The uncertainty is when the unfortunate event will take place. Life assurance enables individuals to provide for their relatives on their death, or for a lump sum at a fixed future date, such as when they expect to retire. Life assurance companies have data on the risk of death for various classes of individual. For example, they know that the risk varies with age and premiums rise accordingly – the older a person is when he or she takes out a life assurance policy, the higher the rate of premium.

Insurance funds are large because they accumulate over long periods. They are invested in ways which allow for claims to be met and profits to be earned. The Life Offices have the largest sums to invest but the total accumulated funds of all insurance companies stood at about £250 billion at the end of 1991. The relative importance of the different classes of asset held is shown in

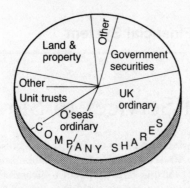

Figure 8.5 Insurance companies' assets, end 1990
Source: *Financial Statistics*

Figure 8.5. Government securities used to be the largest category but, increasingly, insurance companies have turned to investing in shares (mainly ordinary shares) in home and overseas companies. This is how their role in controlling companies came about (see page 52). These days, over half of the assets of insurance companies are invested in companies, including unit trusts.

Pension funds

Employers in the public sector and many privately owned companies provide employees with pensions on retirement, as do some trade unions. In certain pension schemes employees make contributions as well as employers. Pension (or super-annuation) funds accumulate from the contributions made during the working life of employees. They are used to purchase securities and shares which earn interest and dividends that are exempt from income and capital gains taxes. Pension funds may be self-administered or handled by insurance companies or banks.

Pension funds began to take off in the 1960s. By the end of 1987 the accumulated funds were approaching £200 billion. Moreover, nearly two-thirds of the assets held by pension funds consist of ordinary shares in joint stock companies. The managers of pension funds, therefore, play a role in the ownership of British industry similar to that of their counterparts in insurance companies.

The Changing Financial System

Box 8.2

Financial Services to Slow Down

Financial and business services have been the most successful sector of the UK economy in the 1980s, in terms of employment creation and output growth.... The expansion of financial services has been due to three main trends. First, ... as consumers become wealthier, they want to both save and borrow more at different stages in their life cycle. Second, both business and government are becoming more sophisticated in their operations. They require more expert services from outside.... Third, it has been a major objective of government policy to liberalise financial services.

Financial and business services play a key part in the growth rate of the whole UK economy. In the 1980s, the rest of the economy grew at 1.8 per cent in real terms. The 6.7 per cent growth of financial services raised the growth rate of the whole economy to 2.3 per cent.

Lloyds Bank Economic Bulletin,
January 1991

The extracts we chose from this article do not explain its title so much as the recent history of the financial sector. The prediction may not prove to have been right anyway. It is largely based on a belief that the main cause of the growth in the 1980s was a series of once-for-all acts of deregulation. Since the article is likely to be at least two years old by the time you read this book, you have an opportunity to test it. See Question 1 at the end of the chapter.

Our description of the UK financial system has shown that it does not comprise distinct types of institution, each with its own function. Such was not too far from the case in the past. However, the last 25 years or so have seen certain important changes in the nature of the financial system. Concentration in fewer and fewer firms has been accompanied by diversification and the extension of international links, so that the dividing lines between the different types of institution have become blurred.

We explained how banks and building societies are growing more alike; how previously separate deposit and merchant banks have become linked within single institutions, competing over a wide range of activities; how concentration in fewer and fewer firms has resulted from mergers of building societies and other institutions. It needs only to be added that all these tendencies are widespread, as the entire financial system is in the process of profound structural change. This is occurring within a framework that is increasingly international, as overseas banks, stockbrokers, insurance companies, etc., move into the UK to join the development of a new structure, which is well characterised by the term 'despecialisation'.

The Bank of England

The last major financial institution to be discussed here is the Bank of England.[7] Whilst all the important institutions mentioned so far are privately owned commercial bodies, the Bank of England is not. It is a central bank operated on behalf of the UK government.

The history of the Bank of England goes back to 1694 when it was founded by Royal Charter. Originally a private concern, its shares were taken over by the government when it was nationalised in 1946, though the Bank had for many years before then been an instrument of public policy. A few relics of ordinary banking business remain, but today the Bank is on an entirely different footing from the commercial banks, over which it exercises a profound influence. The Bank of England acts as banker for the commercial banks and carries out a number of functions for the government.

The Bank manages the currency, issuing or supervising the issue of notes and coin.

The Bank acts as the government's bank. Tax and other revenues are held in accounts at the Bank, known as Public Accounts, on which the government draws to pay for its expenditure.

7   The Bank of England is dealt with in Lipsey–Harbury, FP2, Chapter 27.

The Bank manages the national debt, issuing securities when required to replace others reaching maturity, and paying interest to holders.

The Bank has a general responsibility for the efficiency and competitiveness of the banking system. It licenses and supervises '**authorised deposit takers**'. If mismanagement, or fraud, is suspected, the Bank can order the suspension of activities, as was done in 1991 in the case of BCCI (Bank of Credit and Commerce International).[8]

The Bank manages the nation's official foreign exchange reserves, held in the **Exchange Equalisation Account**. It has the right to intervene in foreign exchange markets to support the exchange value of sterling or to reduce fluctuations in the exchange rate. This activity is discussed in Chapter 9.

The Bank plays a key role in the government's monetary policy. We shall return to this function shortly. First, it will be helpful to inspect the balance sheets of the two main departments into which the Bank of England was divided by the Bank Charter Act of 1844.

The Issue Department

The Bank of England has a monopoly of the note issue in England and Wales, though certain banks in Scotland and Northern Ireland have limited issuing rights. The balance sheet of the Bank's Issue Department, shown below, lists its assets and liabilities.

Bank of England, Issue Department
Balance sheets, 24 June 1992 (£ millions)

Liabilities		Assets	
Notes in circulation	15,990	Government securities	10,589
Notes in Banking Dept	10	Other securities	5,411
	16,000		16,000

Source: *Financial Statistics*

8 This does not mean there is nothing to worry about. The BCCI case involved fraud on so massive a scale that Lord Justice Bingham was asked to investigate. His report, published in 1992, was heavily critical of the Bank in discharging its statutory duty.

At one time the Bank's notes had to be backed by gold. Today, they are covered by government and other securities in the **fiduciary issue** (from the Latin *fiducia* meaning trust).

The Banking Department

The more important, as well as the more interesting, of the Bank of England's activities concern the Banking Department. It is here that the Bank functions as the government's bank and the bankers' bank.

The chief classes of assets and liabilities of this department are shown in Figure 8.6, which bears a similarity to Figure 8.3, which displayed the balance sheet of the commercial banks. The similarity is more apparent than real because of the totally different functions of the institutions.

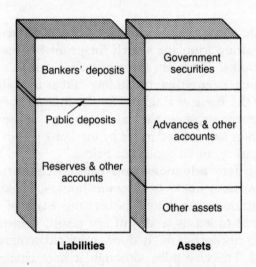

Figure 8.6 Bank of England (Banking Department) liabilities and assets, 24 June 1992
Source: *Financial Statistics*

Liabilities

Bankers' accounts relate to the Bank of England's function as the bankers' bank. These are credits standing on deposit in favour of the clearing banks and discount houses, i.e. assets to them, but liabilities to the Bank of England. They include operational and cash ratio deposits (see above, page 271).

Public accounts relate to the Bank's function as banker to the government. It is under the title of public accounts that the government banks its money. The size of the public accounts reflects the current state of official finances – the flow of tax receipts and public expenditure.

Reserves and other accounts include the small amount of ordinary banking business in which the Bank of England still engages. The private customers used to be overseas banks and other City institutions but nowadays they are mainly employees and ex-employees of the Bank itself.

Assets

The assets side of the Bank's activities shows a marked difference from that resulting from the search for profitable lending of the commercial banks. There are three principal groups of assets.

Government securities (including Treasury bills) are not purchased by the Bank of England for the interest they carry, nor for liquidity purposes, as is the case with the commercial banks. Purchases and/or sales of securities by the Bank are an instrument of monetary policy, to be explained below.

Among the item **advances and other accounts**, the most significant are those made to discount houses, banks and other financial institutions. As stated earlier, the Bank of England is always prepared to act as lender of last resort, if institutions are temporarily in need of cash. It does so by rediscounting bills of exchange and Treasury bills, although it may charge a rate of interest which is penal, i.e. in excess of the current market rate. Such loans are regarded by borrowers as temporary expedients, to be avoided if possible.

Other assets include premises and equipment, other securities and notes and coin. The last of these are the carry-over of the note issue from the Issue Department, available for release at any time required.

Monetary policy

We return finally to consider the role of the Bank of England in operating the monetary policy of the country.[9] We have already made passing reference to techniques used in this policy. We shall return to it again in the next chapter, when we shall look also at the goals of policy. It will, however, help that later discussion to have a summary of the main instruments here.

Note, first, that the Bank of England, unlike central banks in some other countries, is not independent of the government. It has a degree of autonomy in its day-to-day operations in carrying out policy, but the policy itself is determined by the Chancellor of the Exchequer on behalf of the government of the day.

All the techniques of monetary policy are ultimately intended to influence the amount of lending by banks and other financial institutions. This objective can be seen from two viewpoints. Banks can be encouraged to make, or discouraged from making, loans. Alternatively, since every successful lender implies a successful borrower, the incentive can be aimed at borrowers, who may be encouraged to borrow, or discouraged from borrowing. These supply and demand aspects roughly correspond to the two main types of techniques available to the Bank. The standard method of influencing banks' willingness to lend puts pressure on, or removes pressure from, their cash and other liquid assets. The traditional way of influencing borrowers is by raising, or lowering, interest rates to encourage or discourage them.

The technicalities of monetary policy are complex and have changed substantially over the years. No attempt can be made here to offer a comprehensive description of all of them. There have, however, been two landmarks in recent years which are notable for signifying changes in the emphasis of monetary control techniques. They occurred in 1971 and 1981 when the Bank of England

9 The theory and practice of monetary policy are discussed in Lipsey–Harbury, FP2, Chapter 37.

published two papers, *Competition and Credit Control* and *Monetary Control – Provisions*, respectively.

Bank liquidity

The first paper focused on bank liquidity in a wide sense. Certain liquid assets (mainly cash, market loans, bills and short-term government securities) were designated '**eligible reserve assets**' and the banks were required to hold $12\frac{1}{2}$ per cent of their liabilities in one or other of them. The system weakened the control of the Bank of England because many of the reserve assets were also held by the non-banking private sector. The banks could replenish their reserves by buying assets from other sources. Indeed, the introduction of the system was accompanied by an unparalleled increase in the UK money supply.

The reserve asset system operated until 1981, when *Monetary Control – Provisions* shifted the emphasis to control of the cash base. Banks were required to hold a small percentage of their '**eligible liabilities**' (originally 5 per cent reduced now to 4 per cent) in a non-operational account at the Bank of England. These are the cash ratio deposits mentioned earlier (see above, page 271).[10] The provisions were not limited to the banks, but applied to a wider range of institutions, including the discount houses.

Interest rate policy

The previous section deals with Bank control over lending. Monetary policy to influence borrowers has taken several forms, including hire purchase restrictions (now defunct, minimum cash deposits and/or maximum time for repayments). The main

---

10   There is a family resemblance between cash ratio deposits and two earlier instruments, 'Supplementary Deposits' introduced in 1960, and penal, non-interest-bearing Supplementary Special Deposits (SSD, known as the 'corset') in 1973. Both were balances frozen in the banks' accounts at the Bank of England. SSDs were abandoned in 1980. Special Deposits have not been called for since 1980, but are still shown in the Bank's balance sheet – at zero. Note, too, the method of open market operations to influence bank liquidity belongs in a theoretical text and is not discussed here.

technique of changing interest rates was demoted in the 1981 paper.

Traditionally, the Bank's power to change interest rates arose from its function as **'lender of last resort'**. In times of cash shortage, for example, the Bank could charge a rate of interest above the market rate, and this higher rate would filter through to the rest of the financial system. For over 200 years the weekly announcement of **Bank Rate**, the rate of interest at which the Bank of England was prepared to rediscount eligible bills of exchange (including Treasury bills), was watched closely by financial institutions all over the world. After 1972 Bank Rate was renamed **Minimum Lending Rate** (MLR), but changes continued to be watched for evidence of the government's intentions. In 1981, the use of MLR was abandoned, other than in exceptional circumstances. It was restored briefly in 1985 and again in 1992 to support the sterling exchange rate. The Bank continues to provide funds to the discount houses when they are in need, but does not formally publicise the rate at which it is prepared to do so, though this may often be inferred from its activities.

The Bank of England and the European Community

An issue of significance is the extent to which the Bank of England can make independent decisions. We mentioned earlier that the Bank operates monetary policy, but the government of the day makes the key decisions within which the Bank must operate. Such has generally been the case for many years, certainly since nationalisation in 1946. In some other countries the central bank has a greater degree of autonomy in decision-taking, and the whole question of the powers of national central banks takes on a new dimension in the European Community, if the **Maastricht Treaty** of 1992 goes ahead.

The Treaty has extremely wide implications and we shall return to it in the next chapter, when we shall discuss its implications for the balance of payments. At this point, we confine ourselves to proposals within the narrow issue of monetary policy – in particular the proposal to set up a **European Central Bank** (ECB) to operate a single monetary policy for the whole of the EC.

By that time, national central banks are to be independent of their national governments.

The full monetary union envisaged in the Maastricht Treaty is far from realisation. It comes into effect only after ratification by the parliaments of all EC members. At the time of writing, one member, Denmark, has rejected the Treaty, and the UK is still debating it. The timetable towards full monetary union (including the replacement of the currencies of member states by a single currency for the EC) proceeds by Stages. The creation of the European Central Bank is due only in the final Stage 3. In Stage 2, the proposal is for other new institutions: a **Council of Economic and Finance Ministers** (ECOFIN) and a **European Monetary Institute** (EMI). EMI is to consist of the governors of the central banks in each EC member state. The role of EMI will be advisory only in Stage 2.

Thereafter, as soon as a date is set for Stage 3 (after 1996), a **European System of Central Banks** (ESCB) is to be created to strengthen co-ordination of monetary policies and to run the EMS. In Stage 3, an independent European Central Bank (ECB) is to be established and given the prime function of maintaining price stability in the Community as a whole. However, before this can happen the economies of EC members will need to have moved closer together. Certain '**convergence criteria**' will be applied to test readiness to move into Stage 3. It is, moreover, envisaged that all members may not wish to enter Stage 3, UK and Denmark being especially doubtful, unless the Maastricht Treaty is amended.

Questions and exercises

(For key to abbreviations identifying sources, see pages xv–xvi)

1   Refer to Box 8.2 on page 280. Try to test the prediction in the box about the future growth in the size of the financial sector. Compare (i) output, (ii) employment in the financial services sector between 1989 and last year. Do not forget to make your estimates about relative growth (i.e compare the financial sector with the whole economy). (Use *UKNA* for (i) and *MDS* for (ii))

2   Use the data in Table A8.2 (in the Appendix) which gives foreign currency as well as sterling assets and liabilities of the banks, to draw

as much as you can of a diagram similar to Figure 8.3, which is limited to sterling deposits. How do the two diagrams differ?

3 Draw a graph showing trends in the total liabilities over the past 10 years of banks, building societies, insurance companies and pension funds. What does the information tell you about changes that have taken place in the financial system in the UK? (*AS*)

4 Compare the rates of interest that you would pay to (i) discount a two-month £10,000 Treasury bill issued today, (ii) discount a six-month £10,000 trade bill issued six months ago, (iii) borrow £10,000 overnight and (iv) borrow £10,000 on mortgage from a building society. How do you think the different rates can be justified? (*T, FT,* and ask a local building society branch for (iv).)

5 Prepare a graph showing the course of the following over the past 10 years: (i) M0, (ii) M2, (iii) M4, (iv) M3H, and (v) total consumer expenditure. Which measure of the money supply is best correlated with (v)? (*AAS, FS, MDS*)

6 Construct a table and a diagram similar to the balance sheet on page 282 and Figure 8.6 showing the balance sheets of both departments of the Bank of England for a recent date. Compare your table and the Figure with those in the book. Which of them differ more? (*FS* or *Bank of England Quarterly Bulletin*)

Appendix 8

Table A8.1 Monetary aggregates, UK. Amounts outstanding at end-years (£ billion), 1982–91

Money supply measure	1982	1983	1984	1985	1986	1987	1988	1989	1990	1991
M0	12	13	14	14	15	16	17	18	18	19
M2	107	119	133	146	167	185	215	236	255	278
M4	155	175	199	225	262	303	355	422	473	502

Note: for definitions see page 267.

Source: *Annual Abstract of Statistics* and *Financial Statistics*

Table A8.2   Banks: liabilities and assets of reporting institutions, end May 1992 (£ million)

Liabilities		Assets	
Notes outstanding	1,815	*Sterling assets*	
		Notes and coin	3,456
Sterling deposits: total	526,812		
Sight deposits		Balances with Bank of England:	
UK banks	15,759	Special & cash ratio deposits	1,382
UK Public sector	2,426	Other	63
UK Private sector	147,102	Market loans	
Overseas	14,647	Discount houses	8,373
Time deposits		Other banks	86,795
UK banks	77,218	Certificates of deposit	19,024
UK Public sector	2,644	Overseas	26,794
UK Private sector	155,017	Other	4,592
Overseas	59,708	Bills	
Certificates of deposit	52,291	Treasury bills	3,196
		Other	8,880
Other currency deposits: total	598,152	Advances	
Sight and time deposits		UK private sector	363,642
UK banks	76,422	UK public sector	3,335
Other UK	37,321	Overseas	13,855
Overseas	428,526	Investments	
Certificates of deposit,		British government stocks	5,091
etc.	55,883	Other	28,374
		Other currency assets	
		Market loans	547,331
		Bills	10,264
		Acceptances	21,561
		Investments	59,520

Source: *Financial Statistics*

Table A8.3 Bank of England, balance sheet, 24 June 1992 (£ million)

Issue Department

Liabilities		Assets	
Notes in circulation	15,990	Government securities	10,589
Notes in Banking Department	10	Other securities	5,411
	16,000		16,000

Banking Department

Liabilities		Assets	
Public deposits	84	Government securities	1,234
Bankers' deposits	1,518	Advances and other accounts	2,317
Reserves and other accounts	3,602	Premises, equipment and other securities	1,657
Other	12	Notes and coin	10
Total	5,216	Total	5,216

9
Growth and Stabilisation Policy

Chapter 6 dealt with microeconomic policies related to efficiency and equity in the allocation of resources. This chapter considers **macroeconomic** policies concerned with growth and stabilisation of the economy as a whole.[1]

Economic Fluctuations

The long-term rate of growth of real output in the UK since the beginning of the present century has averaged about 2 per cent per annum. If you examine year-to-year changes, you will find that economic activity – ouput and the general level of employment – proceeds on an irregular path. There are forward sprints interrupted by pauses and even relapses. These short-term fluctuations are known as the **trade cycle**, or business cycle.

Trade cycles are characterised by four phases, and two turning points:

- **boom** when output and employment are at high levels
- **recession**, when output and employment are falling

1 This chapter deals with material discussed in Lipsey–Harbury, FP2, Chapters 37–45.

(a recession is now recognised in the UK when output declines continuously for three quarters)

- **slump,** when output and employment are at low levels.

  (A severe slump is called a **depression**)

- **recovery,** or expansion, when output and employment are rising
- **peak** or upper turning point, from which the economy moves into recession
- **trough** or lower turning point, from which the economy moves into expansion

Trade cycles have been observed well back into the nineteenth century, when their duration was reasonably regular, lasting 8 to 10 years, and with no prolonged booms or slumps (see Figure 9.1). The experience in the present century has been rather different. For Britain, the period between the two World Wars was one of almost continuous slump. The Great Depression of the 1930s was unparalleled in its severity and was international in that few countries escaped it. The 1920s were, however, a period of boom for most of the rest of the world other than UK.

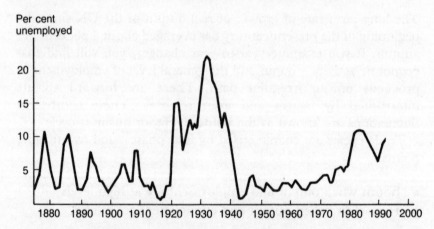

Figure 9.1 Percentage unemployment since 1875

Sources: *Abstract of British Historical Statistics*, B R Mitchell and P Deane (Cambridge University Press, 1962), *Annual Abstract of Statistics* and *Monthly Digest of Statistics*

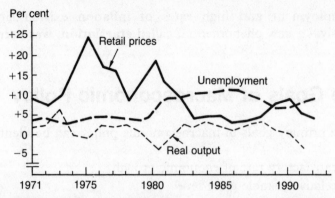

Figure 9.2 Unemployment (percent) and year-to-year changes in real output and retail prices since 1971
Sources: *Annual Abstract of Statistics* and *Monthly Digest of Statistics*

During the Second World War, unemployment fell to an extremely low level. For the first 25 years following the war, unemployment still fluctuated, but the fluctuations were over a much narrower range than in any comparable period. Even with all possible allowances for changes in the definitions of the unemployment statistics, that period was one where the average level of unemployment was exceptionally low.

In the early 1970s, the pattern changed yet again. Figure 9.2 shows that an upswing was in progress at the start of the decade. Then, in 1974, the UK and the rest of the world slipped into a recession, which bottomed out in 1975. The following recovery was short-lived and, in 1979, the economy was in the midst of a new recession, the worst since the 1930s.

Note, the decade of the 1970s was different in an extremely significant way from previous experience. In the typical cycle of earlier years, the tendency had been for inflation to be associated only with booms, while slumps were periods of relatively stable, or even falling, prices. Between 1971 and 1982, in contrast, the price level rose continuously and substantially even in years of falling output. The lowest inflation rate was 7 per cent and the highest 24 per cent (1974–5), while the average rate was over 12 per cent per annum. For the first time, the rate of increase in the general level of prices no longer followed its traditional pattern. High unemployment and high rates of inflation existed simultaneously – a new phenomenon, called **stagflation**, was born.

The Goals of Macroeconomic Policy

Three primary goals of macroeconomic policy can be identified:

- a satisfactory rate of economic growth
- a relatively stable price level
- a low and stable level of unemployment

In addition, a fourth goal related to the balance of payments and the exchange rate may be distinguished. It is secondary, in the sense that there is neither immediate nor lasting advantage to a country from having a satisfactory balance of payments, *per se*. However, an unsatisfactory balance of payments and/or a volatile exchange rate, may inhibit attainment of one or more primary goals. We now discuss the primary goals, turning later to deal with balance of payments problems and policies.

Economic Growth

There is no need to rehearse the reasons why economic growth is a desirable objective of policy – it is the major cause of rising living standards. Moreover, as we explained earlier (see page 21), even small differences in growth rates can lead to large differences in income per head because of the power of compound interest. This is exactly what happened after the Second World War.

As can be seen in Figure 9.3, during the 1960s and 1970s the UK's growth rate lagged far behind that of other major developed countries. During the 1980s, economic growth slowed down on a world scale. Apart from Japan, which was still the leader, the average growth rate in industrialised countries had dropped to just over 2 per cent per annum. The UK's performance over the decade was around the average, a relatively better performance than earlier.

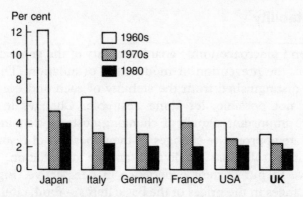

Figure 9.3 Comparative rates of growth of GDP, selected countries, 1960s, 1970s and 1980s
Source: *International Financial Statistics*, and *NatWest Bank Economic and Financial Outlook*

Despite this late rally, the long-term result was that income per head in the UK, which had been significantly above the average of EC countries in 1960, had fallen by 1990 to well below Germany and France, and approximately the same as Italy, a country which 25 years earlier had a per capita income only half that of the UK (see Figure 5.11).

The reasons for international differences in growth rates are complex. Growth depends, ultimately, on the quantity and quality of the factors of production available and on the efficiency with which they are combined.

Some observers laid the blame for the UK's poor performance on its relatively low proportion of national income devoted to investment (see Figure 3.7). It is certainly the case that the country at the top of the economic growth 'league table', Japan, has consistently maintained a ratio of investment to GDP well above that of other major industrialised countries. The differences between the UK, on the one hand, and countries such as France, Germany and the USA on the other, have been smaller. Furthermore, the correlation between high investment and high growth rates is not perfect; it is clear that other forces are also at work. It is important to remember, too, that high growth is only one of several policy objectives. When others, such as quality of life and reduction of pollution, come into conflict with the goal of high growth, compromises have to be reached.

Price Stability

The second macroeconomic goal is stability of the general level of prices, i.e. the prevention or moderation of inflation. This target must be distinguished from the stability of each and every price, which is not possible, let alone desirable. Changes in relative prices are important signals of changing costs or demand. They can activate appropriate changes in the allocation of resources.

It is often said that we live in an age of inflation, so it is instructive to put current experience in perspective. Figure 9.4 shows changes in the prices of the basic items – food, clothing and fuel – in a worker's budget in southern England since 1275, based on calculations made by Professor Henry Phelps Brown for the period ending in 1959 and extended to 1990.

The average rate of increase of prices over the whole period was about 0.5 per cent per year. The data also show that our inflationary era is not unique. Although there have always been

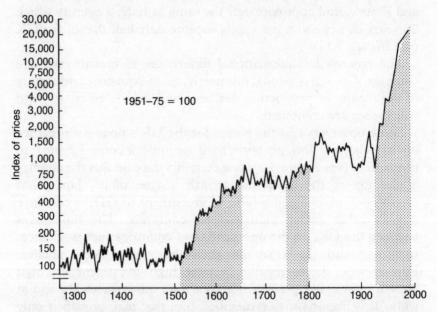

Figure 9.4 Price index of consumables in southern England 1275–1990 (the cost of living index has been used to extend the series beyond 1959; the shaded areas indicate periods of unreversed inflation)
Source: *Lloyds Bank Review* and *Annual Abstract of Statistics*

short-term year-to-year ups and downs, 700 years of price level history is divided between periods of a stable price level, on average, and periods when the trend has been sharply rising. The long-term drift has, however, been upwards, and only in the nineteenth century was there any appreciable trend of (slightly) falling prices.

Experience in more recent years is better known. In the 1950s, the price level rose relatively moderately, by 3 to 5 per cent per annum. In the 1960s, the inflation rate crept a little higher, prices having risen by about 50 per cent by the end of the decade. The 1970s witnessed a significant upsurge in the rate of inflation, especially after the oil price rise of 1973–4 (see page 245), though certainly not because of it alone. So-called double digit inflation, i.e. 10+ per cent per annum, first occurred in 1974, when the rate accelerated, reaching 24 per cent the following year. Over the decade of the 1970s, prices rose on average by 250 per cent. From 1982, the inflation rate fell back to the single digit level, dropping to 4 per cent in mid-decade, before accelerating again to almost 10 per cent in 1989. Between the years 1970 and 1992, the price level had jumped more than sevenfold. A pound in 1992 had the purchasing power of about 13p in 1970.

In an international context, the UK's record has been variable, but rather middling in the last two or three decades, usually just on the wrong side of the average of EC member countries. Figure 9.5,

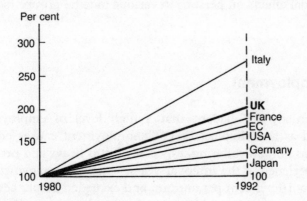

Figure 9.5 Inflation rates, selected countries (consumer prices in 1992 as a percentage of 1980)
Source: *National Institute Economic Review*

covering 1980 to 1992, shows prices rose in the UK less than in Italy, but significantly more than in Japan and Germany.

The effects of inflation

Inflation has many consequences. It distorts the allocation of resources, for example by making 'investment' in 'collectables', e.g. works of art and postage stamps, more attractive than real investment in productive activities, as individuals seek 'hedges' for their savings which at least keep pace with the general level of prices. Inflation, especially at an unpredictable and variable rate, makes it difficult for businesses and private individuals to plan with confidence for the future and it may affect the balance of payments (see below).

One notable effect of inflation is on the distribution of income, penalising those with incomes fixed in money terms, e.g. holders of annuities, while favouring others with incomes rising faster than the rate of inflation itself. In Chapter 4, we showed something of the way in which different groups of workers manage to increase their relative earnings (see pages 120 ff), and it may be that the relative strength of trade unions in various occupations and industries may partly determine the extent to which inflation affects their members. We saw also, in Chapter 6, that inflation can fall unevenly on different categories of expenditure, with differential effects on persons in various income groups (see pages 202–3).

Full Employment

It is virtually self-evident that a high level of employment is regarded as a desirable target. Unemployment causes economic waste and human suffering, especially if it is heavy and prolonged. The experience of the interwar years, when unemployment never fell below 10 per cent per annum, and exceeded 20 per cent in the Great Depression, was dramatic. During the Second World War the coalition government of the day declared 'as one of their primary aims and responsibilities the maintenance of a high and stable level of employment after the war'.[2] This principle remains today, though other objectives, at times conflicting, have interfered with its achievement.

Short-run and long-run trends in unemployment have been charted earlier in this book (see Figures 1.15, 9.1 and 9.2). We now add Figure 9.6, which sets Britain in an international context.[3] The UK record has been variable. In the period up to 1980, unemployment rates in this country were often below those of other major industrial countries, including the USA. In the early 1980s the UK record tended to be of relatively high unemployment rates, but in the latest year, 1992, on which Figure 9.6 is based, the UK is in a middle position.

Statistics of the numbers unemployed expressed as a percentage of the labour force can be misleading because:

- they ignore the distribution of unemployment
- they need to be considered in the light of jobs available

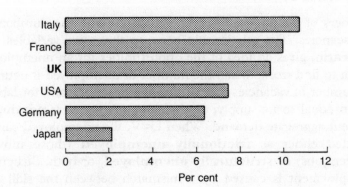

Figure 9.6 Unemployment rates (standardised), selected countries, 1992

Source: *Employment Gazette*

2 Employment Policy, Cmd 6527, 1944.

3 As explained in Chapter 4, measured unemployment rates are sensitive to definitions of who to count as unemployed and who to include in the totals on which percentage rates are calculated. The text here is based on international definitions.

The distribution of unemployment

When unemployment strikes, its impact does not fall evenly among the population as a whole, but bears much more heavily on some groups than on others, as we saw in Chapter 4. You may wish to refer back to pages 115–18 on this matter, but we remind you of the main conclusions, which were that unemployment varies regionally, with race, age and qualifications. Characteristics favouring low unemployment are living in East Anglia, the East Midlands and the South East, being white, age group 45+, and being relatively highly qualified. Characteristics favouring high unemployment are living in Northern Ireland, North and North West England, being Pakistani or Bangladeshi, age group 16–24 and having poor qualifications. An additional social matter of relevance is that about a third of unemployed men and a quarter of unemployed women were out of work for more than a year.

Job vacancies

Numbers of unemployed can be compared with the numbers of job vacancies. The relationship between these two variables, the **U–V ratio,** gives an idea of the opportunities for an unemployed person to find work. When the number of unemployed is equal to the number of vacancies (U=V), the aggregate demand for labour is then equal to its supply, so that unemployment is not due to deficient aggregate demand. When U=V, the unemployed can be regarded either as **frictionally unemployed** (those moving between jobs) or **structurally unemployed,** or both. Structural unemployment is caused by a mismatch between the skill and regional components of labour demand and supply, e.g. a vacancy for a plasterer in Perth when a carpenter is unemployed in Cardiff. A boom is associated with V>U,[4] i.e. the demand for labour exceeds the supply of people seeking jobs. In contrast, a slump is associated with U>V, i.e. there are more people seeking jobs than jobs available.

4   Symbols > and < mean 'greater than' and 'less than'.

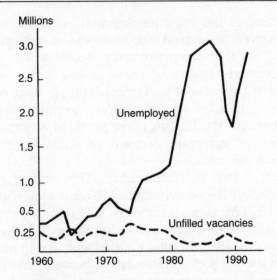

Figure 9.7 Unemployment and job vacancies since 1960, UK
Sources: *Annual Abstract of Statistics* and *Monthly Digest of Statistics*

Figure 9.7 shows the relationship between U and V since 1960. It can be seen that in the 1960s there was a fairly close correspondence between these two variables (as there was in the 1950s), implying some kind of job available for every unemployed person looking for one. Since the early 1970s, however, U has exceeded V, often by substantial numbers.

The Phillips Curve

Thirty-five years ago Professor A. W. Phillips published a paper showing a relationship between unemployment and the rate of change of money wages in the UK over the preceding century. This paper became famous and the relationship subsequently came to be known as the **Phillips curve**.

The curve showed a clear statistical association between percentage unemployment rates and the rate of change of money wages. It was interpreted as revealing the effect of aggregate demand on inflation. This is legitimate on two assumptions. First, that changes in aggregate demand *cause* changes in the level of unemployment in the opposite direction. In other words, the higher the aggregate demand, the lower the unemployment (and vice versa), so that unemployment becomes a measure of aggregate demand. The second assumption is that wage costs are an important element of final prices. Thus, as wage costs go up (give or take quite a bit for other forces), so must prices. Under these assumptions. the Phillips curve provided an explanation of the influence of aggregate demand on inflation, through its influence on wage costs.

Figure 9.8 shows this relationship. The original curve that Phillips plotted for the century up to 1957 is drawn, together with a series of points for subsequent years. The latter are marked with dates, except for 1958–66, for which the proximity of the cluster of points makes their identification both difficult and unnecessary. It is clear that the fairly close relationship between unemployment and increases in money wages continued for the decade after Phillips wrote his article.

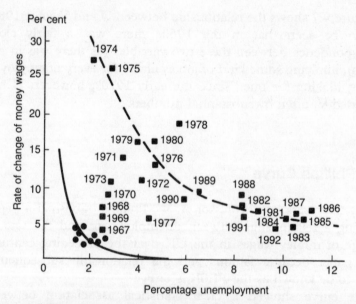

Figure 9.8 The relationship between wage inflation and unemployment since 1862 (the curve is fitted to the period 1862–1957; the unlabelled dots cover the period 1958–66; the labelled squares cover the period 1967–1992)
Sources: *A W Phillips Economica* 1958; *Annual Abstract of Statistics and Monthly Digest of Statistics*

The relationship was shattered at the end of the 1960s by an explosion in money wages when, for no obvious reason, wages rose faster and faster. The stable Phillips curve relationship that had lasted for a century appeared to have broken down.

By 1974, with unemployment not significantly different from the 1967 level, wage inflation had jumped from 4 per cent to nearly 30 per cent. The observations over that period are consistent with a major upward shift in the Phillips curve. Since that time the observations suggest that the pressure of aggregate demand, as measured by unemployment, still affects money wages but at a much higher level. The data for 1974 to 1992 trace a different Phillips curve (shown as a broken line in Figure 9.8), where the rate of increase of money wages is still associated with the level of unemployment, but at much higher average levels of wage increases than before.

The Tools of Macroeconomic Policy

Effective government policies for growth, price stability and full employment require:

- priority ranking of goals, especially when conflicting,
- understanding of the *causes* of unsatisfactory behaviour in the economy,
- availability of up-to-date information upon which to base policy.

Two main sets of instruments can be distinguished for the pursuit of the goals:

- **fiscal policy**
- **monetary policy**

We consider them, initially, as if no complications arose from the balance of payments. For the UK, which has a large overseas sector in its economy, this is allowable only as a starting point. We discuss balance of payments policy at the end of the chapter.

Fiscal Policy

Fiscal policy is the use of the government's budget to influence total spending and, therefore, the level of economic activity. Such policy acts through the level of aggregate demand and is often referred to as **demand management**.

Fiscal policy can be used in a variety of ways. In the first place, taxes and subsidies can be varied to discourage spending on consumption and/or investment in times of excessive boom and, conversely, to encourage spending when the level of activity is low. The government can make changes in the budget and it has the power to vary tax rates on customs and excise duties by up to 10 per cent without the prior approval of Parliament. This provision, known as the 'Regulator', has not been used for many years.

The second means of influencing total spending relates not to the private sector but to the government itself. There is no reason why the state has to balance its own budget, i.e. raising in taxation exactly the same amount as it spends. In times of boom it can run a budget surplus, while in periods of recession it can run a budget deficit. Deficits tend to stimulate the economy because the government puts more in by way of spending than it takes out in taxes. Surpluses tend to depress the economy (which might be a good thing if there is an overly strong boom) because they do the reverse. The extent to which the government and the nationalised industries borrow to finance an excess of expenditure over receipts is known as the public sector borrowing requirement (PSBR, or PSDR when negative).

A third method by which the state can affect total spending is relevant when the government is trying to reduce total demand. 'Cash limits' for particular categories of expenditure by government departments and local authorities were introduced in 1976.[5]

The overall impact of the government's fiscal policy is sometimes referred to as its **'fiscal stance'**. (This has at times been measured by changes in the PSBR. This is not adequate, because changes in the PSBR are partly the result of changes in the

5 External financing limits (EFLs) had a similar function to cash limits for the nationalised industries (see page 59).

level of activity itself.) Fiscal policy is affected by the relationship between government expenditure and tax rates. Changes in either alter the PSBR, but so does a change in the level of economic activity. A slump tends to lower tax revenues, because incomes fall, and to raise expenditure, especially on welfare payments. The combination of the two can raise the PSBR with no change in fiscal stance.

The ideal fiscal objective is to stabilise aggregate demand at a level just sufficient to produce full employment, without causing excess demand to create inflationary pressures. Since private sector expenditure is constantly changing, this type of stabilising fiscal policy requires that the government's fiscal stance be continually adjusted in an offsetting manner. Such **'fine tuning'** was tried by many governments in the 1950s and 1960s, but the record suggests that aggregate demand was often destabilised rather than stabilised. Why was this so?

One reason is that fiscal policy is difficult in practice because the available data on which it must be based may be unreliable and out of date. We saw something of the unreliability of some national income data in Chapter 7 (pages 238-9). If the government alters its fiscal stance, this will affect the economy's behaviour over the coming months. To adjust its stance in a stabilising way the government must know what private expenditure will be over the forthcoming months, not what it was over past months. What the government needs is information on planned (*ex ante*) expenditures, whereas, apart from surveys by the Confederation of British Industry on investment intentions, almost all such information is of the realised (*ex post*) kind.

Cyclical indicators

Successful economic forecasting depends on the availability of advance signs of changes in the major components of economic activity. This is because it is much more difficult to identify cyclical turning points than to project steady trends, whether upwards or downwards.

A great deal of research has been carried out to establish reliable leading indicators of cyclical activity, i.e. statistical series which lead rather than lag behind movements in the general level of

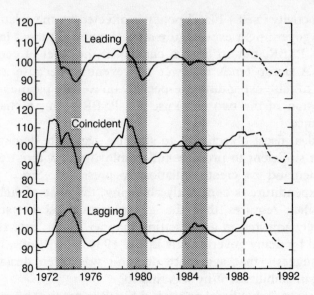

Figure 9.9 Cyclical indicators for the UK economy 1972–1992
Source: *Economic Trends*

economic activity. Some of them, e.g. the rate of interest on three-month bills of exchange and the number of dwellings started, have an average lead of a year or more, while others, such as sums advanced on hire purchase and new car registrations, have a lead of only a few months. None is entirely reliable and the government uses composite index numbers of 'shorter' and 'longer' leading indicators, whose behaviour during the period 1972 to 1992 is charted in Figure 9.9.

Automatic stabilisers

Fortunately, much of the job of stabilising the economy against short-term fluctuations can be done without having to rely on policy-makers' discretion, by using **automatic stabilisers**. These automatically raise government receipts, or lower government expenditure, during the upswing of a trade cycle, and have the opposite effects in the downswing. For example, social security benefits rise when increasing numbers of people become unemployed, and fall when they are re-employed. Similarly, progressive taxes tend to take smaller bites during periods of recession and low incomes than during booms and periods of high incomes. Hence these help automatically to stabilise incomes and expenditures.

Monetary Policy

The second set of instruments for controlling the level of activity is known as monetary policy. It is operated by the Bank of England and was described in the previous chapter (see pages 285–7). To refresh your memory, monetary policy seeks to influence the amount of lending by banks and other financial institutions, which depends on the willingness of banks to lend and their customers to borrow. The main techniques available are (i) acting on the liquidity of the banks, and (ii) changing interest rates. The former has often been related to specific targets for one or more of the monetary aggregates described in the previous chapter (see pages 265–8).

Monetary policy in practice

Monetary policy since 1980 has passed through two phases. In the first, which lasted until 1986, policy was based on a strong belief that the prime cause of inflation was monetary expansion. The leading exponent of this view, Professor Milton Friedman of Chicago, advocated controlling the money supply as *the* key variable. That a clear correlation exists between the rate of inflation and the money supply is not in dispute, as Figure 9.10 shows by plotting the Retail Price Index alongside the money supply aggregate M0. It is less clear whether the statistical association is causal. Indeed, economists of widely differing persuasions accept the correlation between monetary aggregates and inflation, but interpret the causal forces that give rise to it very differently. (We should point out that the statistics used for Figure 9.10 are in crude, or nominal, form, whereas adjustments, e.g. for inflation, may improve analysis.)

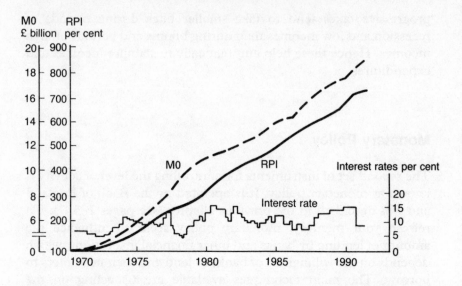

Figure 9.10 Money supply (M0), retail price index (RPI) and interest rates since 1970
Sources: *Annual Abstract of Statistics, Financial Statistics* and *Monthly Digest of Statistics*

Monetary policy in the early phase of the Thatcher governments was associated with specific monetary targets. From 1980, the annual budget address by the Chancellor of the Exchequer set targets for the money supply (and for the PSBR) in what was referred to as the **Medium Term Financial Strategy** (MTFS). Several measures were targeted at different times. New ones were introduced and old ones dropped. For instance, a favourite early target, M1, gave way to £M3 (neither of which is still published) as interest-bearing sight deposits grew in popularity.

As the Bank of England switched targets among the various monetary aggregates, substitution took place, giving rise to **'Goodhart's Law'** (after Professor Charles Goodhart). The 'Law' says that, if the government aims to restrict growth of a particular monetary asset, other monetary assets will take the strain and grow instead. The validity of Goodhart's Law may be judged by the fact that, in 1987, the government dropped the idea of specific targets for any broad monetary aggregates. This date marks the beginning of the second post-1980 phase of monetary policy, since when the MTFS has received little attention. Only narrow money, M0 (largely currency, sometimes called the **cash base**), introduced in 1983, has been specifically targeted, and not all that closely (within the range 0–4 per cent in the 1992 budget speech, for example) though other monetary aggregates have been 'monitored'.

The main problem of trying to implement the strict kind of policy of the early years turned out to be identifying *the* monetary target. Confirmation of Goodhart's Law led to gradual acceptance that there is a spectrum of closely substitutable monetary assets and no unique 'money supply'. Moreover, many changes in the structure of monetary markets and financial arrangements were taking place.

You will, perhaps, remember from Chapter 8 (see page 262) that there was a massive growth in the use of credit cards and autoteller machines between 1970 and 1990 . At the same time, the number of current bank accounts grew from 17 to 43 million. The, unsurprising, consequence was that people held many fewer notes and coin (the main component of M0) for every pound of expenditure in 1990 than in 1970 – approximately half as many, in fact.[6]

These changes were part of profound reorganisations that were taking place, not only in the UK but worldwide (see Chapter 8). Among relevant innovations were the gradual disappearance of the distinction between banks and building societies and between sight and time deposits. Furthermore, a whole new set of highly liquid credit instruments was being developed, such as certificates of deposit. Possibly most important of all, the revolution in communications brought about by satellites and computers led to the globalisation of the financial system. Funds move effortlessly now around the world in response to small changes in the credit terms. Would-be borrowers who fail to raise funds at home can easily turn to foreign money markets. Simple rules for controlling the money supply broke down, as the whole concept of the relevance of national credit conditions came under question.

As a result of all these changes, the naïve monetarist position is no longer held by the major monetary authorities throughout the world. Today, central banks realise that to prevent the outbreak of

6 Consumer expenditure rose nearly ninefold between 1970 and 1990; notes and coin in circulation rose only four and a half-fold.

inflationary pressures they must watch an array of supplies of monetary assets and of real interest rates. If these, collectively, indicate that monetary conditions are too slack, the central bank tightens its monetary policy. In the UK, the Bank of England does this by raising the rate at which it is prepared to lend, and by purchases and sales of short-term securities in its open market operations.

Fiscal Versus Monetary Policy

Fiscal policy developed out of ideas of John Maynard Keynes writing in the 1930s, while monetary policy returned to prominence later with the support, in particular, of Milton Friedman of the University of Chicago.

The view of many early Keynesian economists was that monetary policy was powerless to influence the economy, while fiscal policy was highly effective. Early monetarist economists were much influenced by the evidence of the failure of fine tuning, but felt that monetary policy could exert a powerful influence – if it were directed to manipulating 'the' money supply.

The Keynesian and monetarist positions were based on different views about how the economy works, e.g. of the responsiveness of investment by businesses and of the demand for money to changes in the rate of interest. As a result of experience over more than four decades, most economists now agree that fiscal and monetary policies have important parts to play in whatever short- or long-term policies governments wish to pursue. The conclusions seem to be as follows. (1) Successful central banking cannot be reduced to blind rule-following. It remains an art, in which many economic indicators need to be studied and an array of fiscal as well as monetary policy instruments used. (2) Given sufficient determination, a central bank can pursue a monetary policy that is sufficiently restrictive to hold inflation to low levels – although the short-term cost may be a recession with accompanying high unemployment.

In the recent past, the UK government has moved away from a position of over-reliance on monetary policy, especially of the extreme kind built into the MTFS with closely targeted money supply aggregates. Fiscal stance, aided substantially by the proceeds of privatisation sales on the PSBR, played a part in the reduction of the inflation rate until the end of the 1980s.

In 1987 and 1988 income tax rates were lowered and the PSBR became negative – i.e. the government had a surplus and began to pay off the national debt. Similar fiscal policies were followed in the 1980s by many EC countries, with a view to controlling budget deficits and encouraging long-term growth. By the end of the decade supporters of these policies could point to some fall in the level of unemployment, some increase in the rate of economic growth, and a fall in the size of the national debt.

The success was short-lived. The tax cuts of the Lawson era and a less restrictive monetary policy set the economy on to an upward growth path, with a strong boom in consumer expenditure. By 1989, inflationary pressures began to reappear. The policy chosen to deal with them was determined raising, and holding, of interest rates at a high level(see Figure 9.10). The inflation rate eventually responded, but the ensuing recession persisted for longer than any since the Second World War, dragging the unemployment rate steadily upwards.

Moreover, another problem appeared – the state of the balance of payments – as the UK decided to join the Exchange Rate Mechanism of the European Community. We shall consider this matter in greater detail in the final section of this chapter, on international economic policy. There is, however, an aspect of UK membership of the EC which must be dealt with now.

The European Community and Monetary and Fiscal Policies

At the conclusion of our discussion of the role of the Bank of England in the previous chapter, we mentioned the serious implications of the Maastricht Treaty for the ability of national authorities in the UK and other member states to act autonomously and conduct independent monetary policies.

You may wish to reread the details of the proposals, e.g. for the establishment of the European Central Bank (ECB) due to be set up in Stage 3 of the process towards full monetary union. The ECB is to be independent and to be given a statutory duty to pursue the goal of price stability. (See pages 287–8 above.)

We repeat that the Maastricht Treaty is not, at the time of writing, certain to go ahead unamended. We should, however, advise you that loss of national sovereignty is not confined to monetary policy. Fiscal policy is likewise affected. Apart from tax harmonisation, the Treaty gives the EC power to limit the size of national debts and budget deficits in member nations. The intention is to prevent the build-up of inflationary pressures in any one country which are seriously out of line with the rest of the Community. The Council of Ministers is to be empowered to advise in Stage 2, but to issue directives in Stage 3, if a budget deficit is regarded as excessive, and due to gross errors of judgement.

Supply-Side Policies

Fiscal and monetary policies are not the only instruments that can be employed for macroeconomic reasons. There are others which we examine under the heading of **supply-side policies**. This term is used to cover a range of policies aimed at growth, stabilisation and full employment. These are macroeconomic goals, but the thread that runs through the set of policies called supply-side is microeconomic, that is to say, they are related to resource allocation. In contrast to fiscal and monetary policies targeted at controlling aggregate demand, the focus of this policy set is aggregate supply. If the quantity of goods and services can be increased, it should promote economic growth directly, with positive implications for reducing unemployment. At the same time, increasing output should help keep prices down, even in the face of rising aggregate demand.

Supply-side policies are of two main sorts, market-oriented and interventionist.

Market-oriented supply-side policies

This set of policies is based on the argument that impediments to the free working of market forces inhibit efficiency. The idea is as old as Adam Smith, but it received a new burst of support in the 1980s and 1990s, after the election of four Conservative governments (the first three led by Margaret Thatcher).

Greater freedom for market forces implies more powerful incentives. Hence policies in this category include those which might lead (1) people to work harder and (2) businesses to operate more efficiently, cutting costs and increasing productivity. There are many such policies, several of which have been mentioned earlier in the book. Examples of policies with the aim of increasing work effort are: lowering levels of social security benefits, cutting rates of income tax (see page 180), and the removing of minimum wage legislation (e.g. by the abolition of Wages Councils, see page 199). Examples of policies with the aim of increasing business efficiency are the promoting of competition (see pages 207–13), deregulation (e.g. by ending rent controls, see page 221), and the internal market in the NHS (see page 219).

Note, we have described and illustrated market-oriented supply-side policies. We have not suggested that they are necessarily more recommendable than alternatives. Each needs consideration on its merits, both as to whether it is likely to achieve its stated objectives and as to whether there may be any downside effects, e.g. on equity. To illustrate, it is a controversial matter whether the income tax cuts of recent years were, on balance, successful. It is not at all certain that they had a net positive effect on work effort, and the greater income inequality they caused may not be judged desirable or worthwhile.

Labour market intervention

There is one area which, in the view of some economists, strongly inhibits the achievement of macroeconomic policy goals. It is said that labour markets do not function very well. The argument suggests that much of the high unemployment in recent years can be explained by the fact that the general level of wages was too high. On this view, wages absorbed so high a proportion of total business income that less efficient firms were forced to close down, raising unemployment levels. Some of these economists lay the blame on trade unions. As we saw in Chapter 4 (see pages 132–8), the incidence of strikes in support of wage claims from the beginning of the 1970s until the mid-1980s was well above that of the 1950s and 1960s.

With the object of improving the working of labour markets, a number a changes in the law affecting trade unions have been introduced, mostly since 1980. They were designed to curtail union power by substantially reducing unions' ability to call strikes or take other industrial action. Provisions of the new laws include requirements for secret ballots, limitations on secondary picketing, the closed shop and other measures described in Chapter 4. These measures are additional to machinery introduced in the previous decade, when an independent **Advisory Conciliation and Arbitration Service** (ACAS) was set up, together with a permanent Central Arbitration Committee, to which disputes may be referred by agreement. In the most serious cases the Secretary of State for Employment can appoint a special court of inquiry, or committee of investigation. Their recommendations are not legally binding, but often lead to settlements.

Interventionist supply-side policies

The second set of supply-side policies is that we described as interventionist. Such policies attempt to influence prices, wages and output directly. The prime example is what is called a prices/incomes policy.

Prices/incomes policies

The prime reason for having prices/incomes policies is to control inflation. The idea is to set targets limiting price and wage increases. Such policies were in most favour when the Labour Party was in office, and a number of official bodies were established in the 1950s, 1960s and 1970s (all now defunct) to negotiate wage and price increases between employers' organisations and trade unions. They have also occasionally been used by

Conservative governments, most recently in 1992, when a 1 per cent ceiling for public sector employees was announced.

A wide range of measures is available. First, the government can simply set voluntary guidelines for wage and/or price increases, and hope they will be followed by enough people to be effective. Second, the norms can be set by consultation among trade unions, management and government and monitored by more or less independent bodies, such as the Price Commission and the Pay Board. Third, legal maximum prices and wages can be set by law. This last method has not been used in Britain, though, for a short time in the 1970s, the Price Commission was given some statutory powers.

Incomes policies appear to have been most effective in the short term and to have broken down when under pressure for too long. It seems improbable that they could ever be completely effective in the UK's complex economy. The pay of some groups of workers is relatively easy to control, e.g. those in the public sector, while that of others may be virtually uncontrollable, e.g. the self-employed. Tight incomes policies are difficult to enforce and the same can be said of price controls. The black economy (see page 241) and black markets for goods tend to flourish when pressures are applied with great rigour. Finally, it may be said that trade union support is likely to be critical for the success of prices/incomes policies, but the faith of that movement in free collective bargaining is traditionally strong and may be difficult to change.

Indicative planning

A final example of an interventionist supply-side policy, thoroughly out of favour at the present time, is called indicative planning. This may be advocated if a growth-oriented policy of expanding aggregate demand is expected to flounder because of unforeseen supply-side bottlenecks. A centrally planned economy might, at least in theory, avoid such problems, but for a mixed economy such as the UK this is certainly not the case. However, because of the complexity of the economic network and interdependence among its constituent parts, UK governments have tried to introduce machinery which, by co-ordinating plans for several industries, might assist firms to formulate more realistic plans for themselves.

Indicative planning is the term used to describe combinations of consultative machinery and sectoral projections, e.g. for labour supply, productivity and import requirements, which might help the setting of attainable targets for economic growth and other macroeconomic variables. The single, most ambitious attempt at planning in the UK was made in 1965. The Labour Government of the day set up a Department of Economic Affairs (DEA) and published a detailed National Plan, with a 4 per cent growth rate for the economy for the remainder of the decade. The plan was abandoned a year later and the DEA abolished. Moreover, even countries such as France, which used indicative planning in earlier years, have not returned to it. A weaker version of indicative planning with a longer life was the National Economic Development ment Council (NEDC, also known as Neddy). NEDC was set up in 1962 and abolished in 1992. Membership of the Council included senior industrialists and trade unionists. It met regularly under the chairmanship of the Chancellor of the Exchequer to promote co-operation and discussion of matters such as investment, productivity, training and growth.

International Economic Policy

Balance of payments problems exist whenever governments judge that they do. There are no simple rules for making such judgements. Sometimes a large deficit on the current account will be regarded as unsatisfactory. This may be so when it results from heavy foreign borrowing to finance current consumption, or when there is a rapid deterioration in the current account which causes a speculative outflow of short-term capital. At other times, a large current account deficit will be regarded as satisfactory. This may be so when it is accompanied by an inflow of foreign capital attracted by a strong and growing domestic economy. Many observers felt that this was the case in the UK in the later 1980s, though some revised their view when the deficit grew rather large.

In making judgements, it is important to remember that the balance on capital account must be matched by an equal and opposite balance on current account. Thus a large increase in net capital imports implies a corresponding large reduction in the surplus (or increase in the deficit) of visible and invisible trade.

Remember too that when we were discussing the goals of macroeconomic policy at the beginning of this chapter we described the balance of payments as a secondary goal in contrast to the primary goals of growth, price stability and full employment. It is secondary because the balance of payments may act as a constraint on the achievement of the primary goals, rather than being in itself desirable.

Exchange Rates

The influence of exchange rates on the balance of payments was first discussed in Chapter 7 (see page 251). In our present context of international economic policy, we may add that it is of crucial importance to the nature, and even the existence, of balance of payments problems, whether the exchange rate between domestic and foreign currencies is fixed or floating. When the **exchange rate is floating**, its external value is determined by the forces of supply and demand, which may keep the balance of payments in equilibrium.

Unfortunately, market-determined exchange rates can fluctuate considerably. The authorities of many countries worry that short-term fluctuations in import and export prices create uncertainty among traders, so exerting a depressing effect on the volume of trade. As a result many governments (through their central banks) adopt policies of moderate intervention to reduce short-term fluctuations in the exchange rate due mainly to movements of short-term capital, but do not try to resist long-term pressures due to factors such as differential rates of inflation and productivity growth among nations.

In **fixed exchange rate systems**, which will be discussed shortly, an overriding object of policy has to be to maintain a 'satisfactory' balance of payments position, so as to avoid heavy pressures on the exchange rate, making it difficult to hold to the fixed rate. This constraint can seriously interfere with domestic policy goals, as has happened to the UK quite frequently in the past. Expansionary policies aimed at the promotion of economic growth led to pressures on the balance of payments as imports were sucked in by rising incomes, exports declined in the face of rising prices and high domestic demand, and capital flowed out of the country because of adverse expectations among investors.

Balance of payments problems then forced UK governments of the day to slam their expansionary policies into reverse in what came to be called 'stop-go'. A recent example of this problem was described in Chapter 8. Monetary policy in the late 1980s focused on strengthening the exchange rate between sterling and the currencies of other members of the European Community to ease entry to the fixed EC Exchange Rate Mechanism (see page 253 above and below, pages 326–9).

In free market conditions the rate of exchange between currencies provides a barometer of the health of the balance of payments. Figure 9.11 shows the course of the sterling–US dollar rate since 1972. The diagram charts phases of the recent history of sterling:

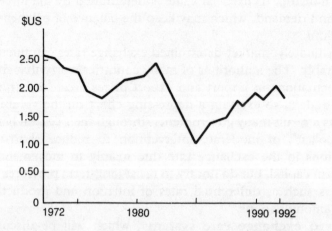

Figure 9.11 Sterling–dollar exchange rate 1972–1992, $US per £1
Sources: *Annual Abstract of Statistics* and *Financial Statistics*

- its depreciation in the years to 1977, when the current account of the balance of payments was in deficit;
- its strength in the following years to 1981, due to a combination of internal and external influences, especially North Sea oil, weakness overseas and high domestic interest rates;
- its renewed depreciation from 1981 to 1985, largely because of relatively high interest rates in the booming US economy;
- its strength from 1985 to 1992. In this period, relatively high interest rates and higher economic growth led to capital inflows, helped by huge US deficits;
- its renewed weakness, at the time of writing (January 1993), with strengthening internal pressures to adopt expansionist policies to combat high unemployment and low output.

The history of the sterling–US dollar exchange rate does not tell the story of the relationship between the value of our currency and the full range of currencies of our trading partners. One such measure, called the sterling **Exchange Rate Index** (ERI), measures changes in the sterling equivalent of a 'basket' of such currencies. ERI tends to mirror the sterling–dollar exchange rate but, because all other currencies in the basket may not move in the same direction, upward and downward swings in ERI are inclined to be moderate. Thus, in the decade of the 1980s when the pound fell against the dollar by about a third, ERI moved down by only about a quarter.

The Instruments of Balance of Payments Policy

There are two types of balance of payments policies: expenditure-changing,[7] and expenditure-switching. The former make use of fiscal and monetary policies, mentioned earlier.

There are two sets of instruments of expenditure-changing policy. One set involves the use of tariffs, import quotas and other tools of commercial policy designed to reduce imports or increase

7   See Lipsey–Harbury, FP2, pages 546–8.

exports. They were described in Chapter 5. We now consider the second set of policies to influence the balance of payments or the exchange rate. They may be directed at either the current account or the capital account, or both.

Exchange rate policies

Changing the exchange rate is a policy instrument which can only be used in a regime of fixed exchange rates. Sterling is said to be devalued (or revalued) when its fixed rate is changed downwards (or upwards). Devaluation means that foreign importers can buy more sterling with their currencies, helping to stimulate UK exports. At the same time, the sterling price of imports to UK residents rises, inhibiting the quantity bought. Whether or not such devaluation raises the value of exports or lowers the value of imports depends, among other things, on how responsive demand and supply are to price changes, and whether the inflationary pressures that tend to follow devaluation can be contained by fiscal and monetary means. When sterling was devalued as a deliberate act in 1967 (by 15 per cent), some benefit to the balance of payments followed, but not immediately.

While publicly announced exchange rate changes can only take place in a fixed exchange rate system, there is a subtler way in which the government can manipulate the exchange rate. This is by intervention in the foreign exchange market, buying and selling foreign currencies in exchange for sterling. This function is performed by the Bank of England, when it uses the official reserves kept in the Exchange Equalisation Account (see page 282). When the Bank intervenes in this way to influence the value of sterling, but not to support a pre-announced pegged rate, this is referred to as a managed or **'dirty' float.**

Capital account policies

The choice here lies between two instruments:

- exchange controls
- monetary policy

Exchange controls

Exchange controls aim to restrict the purchase and sale of foreign exchange for all purposes, including both visible and invisible transactions and capital movements. Exchange controls may be general, applying to all foreign currencies, or discriminatory, affecting only currencies in particularly short supply ('hard' rather than 'soft' currencies, in the jargon).

In the UK, exchange controls were imposed on the outbreak of war in 1939 to limit the use of currencies to essential purposes. They were progressively relaxed after the war, though more quickly for non-residents than for residents. Complete abolition of exchange controls came in 1980, since when it has no longer been necessary to obtain permission from the Bank of England to buy foreign exchange for any purpose.

Monetary policy

The mechanism through which monetary policy can influence the capital account balance of payments is by changing interest rates. Raising them encourages capital inflows and discourages outflows, and vice versa. Note, it is the level of UK interest rates *relative* to those ruling elsewhere that matters. Since there is a large volume of short-term capital in world markets seeking the highest return, interest rate manipulation can be an extremely effective device. Domestic policy implications may be inconvenient, or worse. In 1988–90, for example, when the balance of payments was under pressure, the UK government's policy of high interest rates slowed down the economy. It also had marked redistributive effects, adversely affecting, for example, borrowers locked into mortgages taken out during the preceding house price boom.

Reserves

Reserves of foreign currencies are held by the Bank of England to enable it to intervene in the foreign exchange market. In 1992 the UK's official reserves stood at about £25 billion, representing the cost of about two months' imports. Such a sum may appear small by that standard, although in comparison with potential deficits on the current account it seems much larger. Even in the worst years, the reserves have almost always been more than enough to cover current account deficits. Nevertheless, investors tend to be sensitive to any substantial depletion of the reserves and their actions may depress the exchange rate and aggravate the balance of payments position. The use of substantial amounts of foreign currency reserves by the Bank of England in September 1992, when it was trying to hold the exchange rate and keep sterling in the Exchange Rate Mechanism, is a case in point (see below).

International Co-operation

This section has so far been written from a nationalistic viewpoint. We need also to consider international action to deal with balance of payments problems. This occurs at two levels – global and local. For the UK, the latter is, of course, dominated by relations with the rest of Europe. We shall discuss action on a global scale first.

Global arrangements

During the nineteenth century and early twentieth century exchange rates between the major currencies in the world were fixed through a system known as the gold standard. Each country's currency was freely convertible into a fixed amount of gold, which effectively fixed the exchange values of the currencies in relation to each other.

The gold standard broke down during the interwar years, and in the depression of the 1930s nations resorted to competitive devaluations and exchange controls to protect themselves from balance of payments deficits. Such 'beggar-my-neighbour' actions benefited no-one in the long run, but accelerated a downward spiral in world trade. During the Second World War, the representatives of the majority of countries on the 'allied' side held a conference at Bretton Woods, New Hampshire, USA, out of which grew a system, akin in some ways to the gold standard, which operated during the following 20 years.

Bretton Woods

The Bretton Woods Agreement of 1944 set up two institutions, the **World Bank** (discussed in Chapter 5,) and the **International Monetary Fund** (IMF). The main aim of the IMF was to manage a system of fixed exchange rates, which could be adjusted in the light of long-term changes in economic conditions (i.e. of the adjustable peg type described earlier). It was hoped that the system would eliminate short-term instability and competitive devaluations, while accommodating structural changes in the relative strengths of different currencies brought about by differential rates of inflation, economic growth, or any other cause.

The Bretton Woods system had to cope with three main problems. First, reserves did not grow as fast as trade. By the late 1960s, international reserves were distinctly inadequate. Second, large speculative movements of capital occurred whenever people believed that a realignment of exchange rates was needed. Capital fled from currencies expected to be devalued into currencies expected to be revalued (see Box 7.3 above). Third, and to the surprise of the architects of the system, countries tended, mostly for domestic political considerations, to cling to their existing exchange rates. They accepted devaluations and revaluations only when literally forced into them by an irresistible flood of capital – away from currencies that were overvalued and into currencies that were undervalued.

At first, the Bretton Woods system had the ample gold reserves of the USA to fall back on, but by the late 1960s the US balance of payments position had deteriorated so substantially that it suspended the convertibility of dollars into gold. Confidence in the dollar (as well as in sterling and other leading currencies) lapsed. The dollar was twice devalued, in 1971 and 1973. These events signalled the virtual collapse of the IMF rules. An agreement signed at the Smithsonian Institute in Washington in 1971, established new, temporary, parities. Within a couple of years most countries had allowed their currencies to float (UK in

1972), while trying to 'manage' to achieve short-term exchange stability.

The International Monetary Fund did not itself collapse. It adapted its rules to the situation, and in 1974 issued three new principles for countries managing their exchange rates:

- the avoidance of sudden large changes in currency values
- a call for medium-term target exchange rates
- a recognition that exchange rate management involves joint responsibilities

Special drawing rights. One response by IMF members to the shortage of international reserves was to seek ways of increasing them. A step in this direction was the introduction of **special drawing rights** (SDRs) in 1970.

Special drawing rights were fixed initially in terms of gold. Quotas of SDRs were allocated to member states for use in supporting exchange rates. The SDR system was later extended in several ways, including valuing SDRs in terms of a 'basket' of currencies, reducing restrictions on the purposes for which they could be used, and raising the rate of interest payable on them to levels comparable to those in world markets. Members' quotas were increased, to aid countries affected by the oil price rises in 1974 and 1981. These measures eased world liquidity problems, though only modestly. SDRs currently account for only a small portion of total world reserves.

European Monetary Co-operation

Since the floating of sterling in 1972 and the entry of the UK into the European Community in 1973, the prime area of international monetary co-operation of concern to Britain has been with the EC. An important early development occurred in 1979 with the launch of the **European Monetary System** (EMS). Major changes are, however, written into the Maastricht Treaty of 1992. If and when the provisions of the treaty are implemented, the final outcome is intended to be full monetary union with a single common currency to replace the currencies of member nations.

European Monetary System

The EMS set up three institutions designed to provide a degree of exchange rate stability for the currencies of participating member states:

- A European Currency Unit (ECU, see page 261) comprising basket of currencies of participating member states
- An Exchange Rate Mechanism (ERM, see page 253), to keep exchange rates between currencies within fairly narrow limits
- A European Monetary Co-operation Fund (EMCF), financed from the foreign exchange reserves of participating nations, to support individual currencies

Particular significance attaches to the **Exchange Rate Mechanism,** to which nine EC members belong. The UK did not join until 1990 (leaving in 1992, see below).[8] Under the ERM, exchange rates for the currencies of fully participating members in the EMS are prohibited from deviating by more than $2\frac{1}{4}$ per cent either side of the agreed parities. (These are called the 'narrow' limits. Wider limits, 6 per cent either way, can be applied temporarily for new members, as they were for the UK and Spain.) If the limits are reached, central banks must intervene to prevent the rate for a currency outstepping them. Thus if, say, the Italian lira falls to its limit against, say, the D-Mark, the Bundesbank (the central bank of Germany) buys lire, and the Italian central bank sells D-Marks.

It may happen that the economy of a member state gets seriously out of line, perhaps because its inflation rate is more rapid than others. The value of the currency may then diverge from parity to reach a threshold of 75 per cent of its maximum spread in relation to the ECU. A mechanism then comes into play, operating through what are called **'divergence indicators'**, when there is a presumption that the governments concerned will take

8   Greece and Portugal being the others.

appropriate remedial action: for example, to contain inflationary pressure, if that has caused its exchange rate to fall; or to accelerate economic growth, if slow expansion has caused its exchange rate to rise. In the case where the required domestic adjustments are ineffective, exchange rates may be realigned.

Given that it has been operating in a world of relatively low inflation rates, experience with the ERM has been of modest success. Realignment of currencies to new parities (which have to be agreed among all participants) occurred on a fair number of occasions in the early years of the system (for example, the D-Mark was revalued upwards seven times, and the Italian lira devalued five times between 1979 and 1987). Thereafter, realignments were rare until 1992, when the Italian lira, the Spanish peseta and the Portuguese escuda were devalued, and sterling was taken right outside the ERM (see below).

The UK participated in the ECU and EMCF, but the question of whether or not to join the ERM became a hotly contested political issue cutting across party political lines (with dramatic public disagreement between the Chancellor of the Exchequer and the Prime Minister's Personal Economic Adviser).[9] The arguments on either side involve complex economic and political issues. They include questions of national sovereignty, of the balance of power within the Community, and of the relative merits of fixed and floating exchange rates. Opponents of Britain's entry into the ERM stressed reduced freedom for the UK to conduct independent fiscal and monetary policies if these had to be used to maintain a fixed exchange rate. Proponents of UK entry argued that membership would help keep inflation down.

What happened was that it was deferred until such time as the government felt confident that it would not cause serious conflicts of the kinds we have mentioned. Unfortunately, events proved otherwise. Less than two years after entry, the UK economy was in deep recession with rising unemployment. Loud calls were heard for expansionist monetary and fiscal policies. At the same time, the pound was under pressure in the ERM, not least because German interest rates were kept high to control the inflationary pressures

9 Chancellor of the Exchequer Nigel Lawson and Prime Minister Margaret Thatcher's adviser, Professor Alan Walters.

that followed reunification of West and East Germany. Sterling slipped to its lower limit against the D-Mark. Despite heavy buying of sterling by the Bank of England and dramatic raising of interest rates, UK membership of the ERM was suspended in September 1992.

Whether, and when, the UK will apply to rejoin the ERM are important questions, though it is highly unlikely to be before 1994. A far more crucial question, however, is whether the proposals for full monetary union envisaged by the Maastricht Treaty will come to pass and, if they do, the extent to which the UK will participate in them.

European Monetary Union

We described some of the Maastricht proposals in the area of monetary and fiscal policy earlier in the book (see pages 287-8). We now amplify them, taking special account of international implications, including those for exchange rates. In one respect this is a straightforward matter in the long run. The Maastricht Treaty looks forward to the time when the EC becomes a full economic and monetary union, when the existing currencies of member states are replaced by the ECU. If and when that happens, exchange rates will be fixed in a permanent and irrevocable way – exactly the same way as they are fixed within the UK itself, because only sterling circulates in Lanark, Liverpool, London and Llandrindod Wells. If and when the ECU is the only currency in the EC, no question of exchange rates between that currency and itself will arise.

The Treaty recognises that full monetary union is realistically attainable only if the economies of member states converge in a number of significant respects. The Maastricht advance towards monetary union is scheduled to proceed by Stages. At the time of writing, we do not know how fast or far that advance will be (but see the final paragraph in this section). Ratification by EC members' national parliaments signals the start of Stage 1, during which the drive for convergence accelerates and obstacles to the free movement of capital within the Community are removed.

According to plan, Stage 2 comes into operation for all ratifying member nations on 1 January 1994. A European Monetary Institute (taking over from the EMCF) and a European System of Central Banks are set up. The Community moves into Stage 3 when convergence of national economies has moved far enough. The decision on readiness for Stage 3 is made by the Council of Ministers. In addition to taking account of general developments towards integration of markets, four criteria are laid down to test for convergence. A member nation is ready to move to Stage 3, when its

- inflation rate is within $1\frac{1}{2}$ percentage points of that of the lowest EC states.
- exchange rate against the ECU has been within the narrow band of the ERM for two years without realignment
- budget deficit and national debt are not excessive (limits set of 3 per cent and 60 per cent of GDP, respectively)
- long-term interest rates are within 2 percentage points of those of the lowest EC states

The Council of Foreign Ministers is required, by 31 December 1996, to assess which states satisfy the criteria. If a majority do so, Council may then set a date for the commencement of Stage 3, at which point the new independent European Central Bank is established, with its primary objective of maintaining price stability in the Community. (National central banks will, by then, also be independent of national parliaments.) At the start of Stage 3, qualifying member nations will fix, finally and irrevocably, the exchange rates between their currencies and the ECU, which becomes effectively the currency of all participating members. (The ECB will then take charge of the running of ERM for EC members not in the full monetary union.) Moreover, if ECOFIN does not fix the start of Stage 3 by 31 December 1997, then that stage will automatically begin on 1 January 1999.

Phased progress of Maastricht is conditional upon ratification by all member states. That does not mean that failure of all to ratify spells the end of the Maastricht proposals. It could mean revision of some clauses in the treaty, or that the proposals will be

Box 9.1

European Community – Pressing On

The Maastricht treaty is still ailing. The spectre of a two-speed Europe hovers at the door.... Under the Maastricht rules, all members sign up for the goal of economic and monetary union (EMU), but those with weaker economies would not take part. A two-speed Europe would be different: a group of members would work towards a goal, such as EMU, outside the framework of the EC....

Jacques Delors, the president of the European Commission, gave warning this week that if countries tried to delay implementing the treaty, and in particular its plans for EMU, he would not 'exclude the possibility that certain members would take initiatives'.... Such stern remarks are made in the hope that Britain will be encouraged to ratify Maastricht if it sees that its partners are pressing on regardless. But the British should not assume that the talk is mere bluff. The French and German governments are keen for everyone to ratify the treaty. But they would, as a last resort, prefer two-speed integration to none.

The Economist, 3 October 1992

This press comment appeared less than a month before the debate on the second reading of the Maastricht bill in Parliament. The bill was passed by the slender majority of three, with substantial cross-party voting. Several MPs who declared themselves anti-Maastricht refrained from voting against the bill because they were assured that the third reading would not be taken until a second referendum had been put before the Danish electorate. At the time of writing, this seems unlikely to be before May 1993, and the French are showing renewed signs of impatience.

implemented by only some EC members. The second alternative is sometimes described as a 'two-speed Europe' (see Box 9.1). The prime candidates for opting out of the fast route are Denmark and the UK. Denmark, in a referundum, decided against ratification of the treaty. In the UK, the two sides are locked in conflict at the time of writing.[10] Moreover, some commentators claim to detect, even now, a feeling of nationalism in some other countries which may retard the pace of change. (The result of a referendum in France was of only a very slim majority in favour of ratification.) As far as the UK is concerned, a clause is written into

10   The UK decided not to have a referendum (see Box 9.1).

the Treaty, to allow the UK to opt out of the move to Stage 3 without a separate decision being taken by the government and parliament of the day.

As you read these lines many months after we have written them, you should have a better idea of prospects than we have now. While we do not know how fast or far Europe will move towards full economic union, we know even less about how to judge the desirability of full integration. The issues are extremely complex and highly controversial. Many arguments hang on political issues, such as unification of foreign and social policies. One area where feelings run high relates to transfers of power from national governments to supernational authorities. How much power will be lost is uncertain. A new word, '**subsidiarity**', in the Treaty tries to cover this. Subsidiarity is neither clearly defined in the Treaty, nor does it appear in any of the dictionaries used by either of the authors of this book. It was said, by Sir Leon Britton (a UK member of the European Commission), to mean 'the principle that decisions should be taken at the lowest appropriate level: as close as possible, that is, to the people that are affected by them'.[11] Who knows how subsidiarity will be interpreted by EC authorities in the twenty-first century?

We conclude with two comments. First, the Maastricht proposals should not be judged in isolation, nor against some utopian politico-economic system that has no relevance today. Everybody has to live with governments which make mistakes and adopt policies which some people dislike. The first question is how different the outcomes would be if the UK was, or was not, a fully participating member of the EC.

The second point is that complete independence for domestic economic policy is not a serious option for nations such as the UK. It is out of the question to imagine that the government can choose goals and instruments without regard to policies and their outcomes in our trading partners. This is true whether or not the EC proceeds along the lines of the Maastricht Treaty, with the UK a full member or not. No one will ever know what is the 'right' decision for the UK to make on Europe, because we can never know what would have happened if we decided differently.

11 'Europe, Our Sort of Community', Granada Lecture, London 1989.

The World Debt Problem

The foregoing discussion of international agencies which deal with the balance of payments problems of individual countries must be seen in the context of a major problem of international indebtedness, which reached a massive scale by the early 1980s.

The origins of the problem are usually traced to the **'oil price shock'** of 1973–4, when the OPEC countries quadrupled the price of oil (see page 245), which severely hit non-oil-producing developing countries by raising their import prices and reducing their export markets. Anxious to maintain their growth rates, these developing countries borrowed to finance the deficits in their current account balances of payments. Private commercial banks were glad to oblige, partly because they had large credit balances of the oil exporters available for lending, and partly because investment prospects in the industrialised countries had taken a turn for the worse.

The situation soon became dangerous. It became disastrous after 1980. There were three main reasons for this. The first was a second oil price shock. The price of oil more than doubled between 1979 and 1980. In the second place, the slowdown of growth rates in most industrialised countries in the 1980s severely curtailed the debtor countries' ability to repay their debts through export earnings. The burden of debt was worsened by the rise in real interest rates which occurred in the early 1980s. Furthermore, every time a debtor was unable to meet even the service interest charges on the debt, these charges were added to the outstanding principal. Then, when the oil-importing countries were already mired in debt, the price of oil fell, putting developing countries which were oil producers into difficulties.

The scale of the problem continued to escalate to horrendous proportions. The total of developing countries' external debt is estimated to have risen from $US 200 billion in 1973, before the first oil price shock, to $US 1,200 billion by the end of the 1980s.

The debtor countries fall into two groups. One group, the 'middle-income' debtors, includes Argentina, Brazil, Mexico, Morocco and the Philippines. Their debt is largely owed to private banks in developed countries. The second group consists of a much poorer set of countries in sub-Saharan Africa, comprising all African states south of the Sahara, except for Nigeria and South Africa. Their debt is largely owed to governments and international organisations.

The IMF and the World Bank have sought to relieve the situation in two ways. First, they instituted policies of loan write-offs and, second, they became more aggressive in their lending policies, intervening more in the domestic economic policies of the debtor nations.

It was not until the threat of default by Mexico, in 1982, that the magnitude of the crisis facing the world's financial system was realised. Debt payments were **rescheduled** and new loans made available for Mexico and other debtor nations. The hope that they would raise debtors' growth rates and increase their ability to pay proved mistaken. Their debt-to-export ratios soared in the 1980s (i.e. their ability to service their debts by exporting plummeted).

In order to reduce the risk of total default, the US Treasury proposed that the outstanding loans be reduced. A deal was agreed for Mexico, for example, which had its $107 billion debt reduced by $15 billion. There is a continuing debate on whether to institutionalise these arrangements or deal with each case on its merits, granting debt reductions only after bold economic reforms are in place.

Increasingly, it was appreciated that the larger debtor nations in sub-Saharan Africa need an extended time horizon for debt repayment. The IMF and the World Bank, accordingly, granted credit to Africa through the 'extended fund facility' (EFF), which allowed repayment over 5 to 10 years instead of 3 to 5. At the same time the IMF and the World Bank started to subject potential borrowers to strict performance tests and attached more stringent conditions for reorganising the economic structure to promote growth and ability to repay. A debate rages on whether the policy of forgiving debt in return for greater intervention in the internal affairs of debtor nations is healthy.

A potentially even larger problem looms for the future, as the need for funds by former communist countries is expected to strain the existing resources of the world credit markets and put further pressure on the IMF and the World Bank, which may need to merge in a new institution better capable of handling the increasingly complex nature of world debt.

Concluding Remarks: Macroeconomic Policy – a Perspective

This chapter has touched upon some of the most interesting, complex and controversial issues in modern economics. We expect you found it difficult. It is. The best brains in the world have not been able to solve all the problems we have considered and to come up with policy combinations for the simultaneous achievement of the multiple aims of full employment, price stability and satisfactory economic growth – especially for a country with a large overseas sector. Nor are there clear, simple recommendations that can be made on economic grounds for many issues of the day, such as whether or not full membership for the UK in economic union with the rest of the EC is, on balance, desirable.

It must, moreover, be understood that the division of economic policy into separate micro- and macroeconomic compartments (corresponding to Chapters 6 and 9 in this book) is artificial. We described earlier the goals of micro-policy as efficiency and equity. Yet, it takes no great intellectual effort to realise that growth and efficiency are inextricably entwined and that all macro-policies have distributive implications, and therefore involve considerations of equity.

Economic policy decisions about how to solve current problems inevitably require the making of value judgements – ranking goals and judging how best to achieve them. If we understood better how the economy worked, more issues could be faster settled by recourse to facts. However, we are still learning (as we always shall be). That may not be much comfort to any who hope for final solutions to all the economy's problems, but at least it makes economics a fascinating subject, for us anyway and, we hope, for you.

Questions and exercises

(For key to abbreviations identifying sources, see pages xv–xvi)

1   Prepare graphs using axes which measure the annual percentage change in GDP and the inflation rate. Plot the data for the countries listed in Tables A9.1 and A9.2, columns (i) and (ii). What patterns, if any, do you observe in the graph? Repeat the exercise for columns (iii) in these tables.

2   Assemble data in a table setting out the trends over the last 10 years in (i) unemployment rates, (ii) interest rates (on Treasury bills), and (iii) current account balance of payments, for the following countries: the UK, the USA, Japan, Germany. What correspondences do you find among the three series for each country? (*NIER*)

3   Calculate index numbers of (i) notes and coin in circulation, (ii) M2 and (iii) bank base rates for the past 5 years (*AS*). Compare your results with the index of real consumer expenditure. (*UKNA*)

4   Construct a graph similar to Figure 9.8 except that the vertical axis is the rate of change of retail prices instead of that of money wages. Plot data for the last 10 years. Then copy the original data from Figure 9.8 for the same years. How do the two sets of data compare? (*AS*)

5   The text on page 332 warns of difficulties in predicting future progress towards full economic and monetary union along the lines of the 1992 Maastricht Treaty. Write a page updating the text. (Use what sources you can think of. *The Times* carries a monthly index [kept in public libraries] and should, therefore, be helpful.)

6   Make a list of unemployment rates for (i) each region of the UK, (ii) each nation in the EC. Express the rates of the two highest and two lowest as percentages of the averages for all (i) and all (ii). Do the measures suggest greater diversity within the UK or the EC? If you now had the same data for the year 2000, what differences, if any, would you expect? (*EG*)

7   (a)   Estimate how your family expenditure is allocated among the major categories of goods and services which are used for the collection of data for the Retail Price Index. Compare your family's allocation with that for the whole country, which is given as the 'weights' in the appropriate table in *AS* (to convert the weights to percentages, simply divide by 10).
    (b)   Refer to Figure 6.8 on p. 203 and try to estimate whether the cost of living changed more unfavourably for your family than for the

average family. Do this by looking, one by one, at each commodity group – noting whether its price change was above, or below, the change in the RPI and whether the item was a more important, or a less important, component of your expenditure than it was for the average family.

(c) Repeat (b) for the most recent annual change. (*AS*)

Appendix 9

Table A9.1 Growth of output, 1960–1991 (annual average growth of GDP), selected countries

	1960–79 (i)	1980–89 (ii)	1991 (iii)
Australia	4.3	3.3	−1.9
Belgium	4.2	2.0	1.5
Canada	5.0	3.0	−1.7
Denmark	3.7	1.9	1.0
France	4.9	2.3	1.2
Germany	4.0	1.8	3.1
Ireland	4.2	1.8	2.3
Italy	4.8	2.4	1.4
Japan	8.0	4.1	4.4
Netherlands	4.5	1.6	2.0
Spain	5.5	2.7	2.4
Sweden	3.3	2.0	−1.2
Switzerland	3.2	2.3	−0.5
UK	2.8	2.3	−2.4
USA	3.4	2.5	−1.2
EC	4.3	2.2	1.3

Source: NatWest, *Economic and Financial Outlook*

Table A9.2 Inflation rates, 1960–1991 (annual averages), selected countries

	1960–79 (i)	1980–89 (ii)	1991 (iii)
Australia	6.0	8.4	3.3
Belgium	4.9	4.9	3.2
Canada	4.9	6.5	5.6
Denmark	7.3	6.9	2.4
France	6.3	7.3	3.1
Germany	3.7	2.9	3.5
Ireland	8.2	9.2	3.2
Italy	7.9	11.1	6.4
Japan	7.2	2.5	3.3
Netherlands	5.5	2.8	3.9
Spain	9.9	10.2	5.9
Sweden	6.1	7.9	9.4
Switzerland	4.0	3.3	5.8
UK	7.9	7.4	5.9
USA	4.7	5.5	4.2
EC	6.5	7.1	4.8

Source: NatWest, *Economic and Financial Outlook*

Table A9.3 Unemployment rates, 1980–1991, selected countries

	USA	Canada	Japan	France	Germany	Italy	UK
1980	7.0	7.4	2.0	6.3	3.0	7.5	6.4
1981	7.5	7.5	2.2	7.4	4.4	8.3	9.8
1982	9.5	10.9	2.4	8.1	6.1	9.0	11.3
1983	9.5	11.8	2.6	8.3	8.0	9.8	12.5
1984	7.4	11.2	2.7	9.7	7.0	10.2	11.7
1985	7.1	10.4	2.6	10.2	7.2	10.1	11.2
1986	6.9	9.5	2.8	10.4	6.5	11.0	11.2
1987	6.1	8.8	2.8	10.6	6.5	12.1	10.3
1988	5.4	7.7	2.5	10.0	6.1	11.0	8.4
1989	5.2	7.5	2.2	9.4	5.6	10.9	6.9
1990	5.4	8.0	2.1	8.9	5.0	9.8	6.9
1991	6.7	10.2	2.1	9.3	4.3	9.8	8.9

Source: *National Institute Economic Review*

Table A9.4 Growth rates, unemployment, inflation, money stock and interest rates, UK, 1978–1991

Year	Growth rate (% change in GDP real)	Unemployment (%)	Retail Price Index (% change on previous year)	Money stock M0 (£ bn)	Interest Rates* (%)
1978	+3.0	4.4	7.4	9.8	12.5
1979	+2.7	4.0	11.4	11.0	17.0
1980	−2.2	5.0	21.0	11.6	14.0
1981	−1.1	8.3	11.3	11.8	14.5
1982	+1.8	9.6	9.2	12.3	10.25
1983	+3.7	10.6	3.7	13.1	9.0
1984	+1.7	10.7	5.0	13.5	9.62
1985	+3.8	10.9	6.1	14.1	11.5
1986	+3.0	11.2	3.4	14.6	11.0
1987	+4.2	10.0	4.2	15.7	8.5
1988	+4.5	8.4	5.2	16.9	13.0
1989	+2.1	6.3	7.8	17.8	15.0
1990	+0.6	5.8	9.4	18.3	14.0
1991	−2.4	8.1	5.9	18.9	10.5

* Minimum Lending Rate to 1981, then Bank Base Rate.

Sources: *Annual Abstract of Statistics, Financial Statistics, National Institute Economic Review, UK National Accounts*

Index

Entries are in word-by-word alphabetical order, in which spaces between words are taken into account; 'Bank Rate' therefore comes before 'bankers' accounts'.

Page references to statistical tables are in italics: *33*.

Where there are several page references for a topic, bold type indicates the most significant: **327–9**.

Initialisms, e.g. CTT, are filed as words.

References to notes are indicated by 'n': 306n.

Index by Pat Booth